REWRITING THE LANGUAGE OF POLITICS

KISANS IN COLONIAL BIHAR

Rewriting the Language of Politics

KISANS IN COLONIAL BIHAR

ARUN KUMAR

MANOHAR
2001

First published 2001

ISBN 81-7304-378-7

Published by
Ajay Kumar Jain for
Manohar Publishers & Distributors
4753/23 Ansari Road, Daryaganj
New Delhi 110 002

Typeset by
Kohli Print
107 Radhey Shyam Park
Delhi 110 051

Printed at
Rajkamal Electric Press
B 35/9 G T Karnal Road Indl Area
Delhi 110 033

To
Sahil, Palash and Maninder

Contents

Acknowledgements

This book has grown out of a Ph.D. thesis I submitted to the Department of Sociology, State University of New York, Binghamton. I acknowledge my debt to the faculty, particularly of World Historical Systems, for encouraging me to break free from disciplinary confines. Without their support, it would have been impossible for me to conceive, let alone complete, a project which constantly moves from social history to historical sociology and to social anthropology.

Kelvin Santiago-Valles, the Chairperson of my Dissertation Committee, taught me, among other things, about 'the limits of doing history' and to doubt the finalities of one's intellectual pursuits. His seminars made me realize how disciplinary boundaries are, by definition, disciplining. He convinced me of the need to transgress them. Many of his insights persist here, and, I anxiously hope, some trace of his clarity too. Giovanni Arrighi always provoked me to 'think globally' despite my concern with the local. I am grateful to Anthony King for his sharp reading of the text and some useful suggestions on Chapters 3 and 4. With deep gratitude, I remember the late Terrence K. Hopkins who encouraged us to take the 'absurd' seriously. I am also indebted to Immanuel Wallerstein, whose stimulating lectures will stay with me for a long time to come. With Mark Selden I formulated some of the initial thoughts on this work. Thanks are due to Catherine Coquery-Vidrovich who introduced me to rumours of African peasants.

Let me also acknowledge my 'first gurus' at Delhi University, especially Shahid Amin, Gyanendra Pandey and Sumit Sarkar, who initiated me into the complex world of historical enquiry. Shahid was generous with his time and helpful with his comments.

Friends in Binghamton have contributed to this project in many ways. I specially remember David Baronove, Anna Beckwith, P. K. Hui, Fouad Makki, Krishnendu Ray, Thomas Reifer, Eric Slater, and Deniz and Zafer Yenal.

During my research and writing, I incurred many debts. I thank my 'village informants' who, by generously sharing with me the ways in which they remembered their pasts, encouraged me to search for the invisible roads that connect the archives to the field. I could not have framed a single argument with confidence but for the knowledge and information shared by Shri Ram Talika Singh, Shri G.P. Singh, Shri Indrajit Singh and Manoj Kumar, among others.

Some friends read a single draft of the manuscript while others have been with it through to its final form. It is impossible to acknowledge them all, nor do I pretend to have incorporated all their criticisms and suggestions. Bibhu Mohapatra was the first audience of almost every single thought laid out here. Along with him, Ravikant Sharma emboldened and enriched my arguments with numerous critical suggestions. I take this opportunity to express my gratitude to Smita Tewari Jassal. She painstakingly combed through each draft to lend the manuscript coherence and readability. Her critical readings, especially of the second chapter, forced me to rethink many of my arguments. Thank you, Smita. Basudeb Chatterjee, Indrani Chatterjee, Nilanjan Sarkar, Ram Narayan Singh Rawat and Lata Singh read parts of the first draft as useful critics. Vinod Kumar helped me draw the maps. Monika Mehta promptly supplied me with whatever references I needed while writing.

With a sense of grief and gratitude, I would like to remember Arvind N. Das who not only shared his excitement about the manuscript, but also enriched it with his comments.

A slightly different version of the third chapter appeared in the *Journal of Peasant Studies* (vol. 28, no. 1, 2000). I acknowledge my gratitude to the Frank Cass Publishers.

I do not know if all the extra hours Maninder had to put in to run the household were worthwhile; but I do know that without her support and perseverance this work could never have been completed. Words cannot express this debt. Sahil and Palash continue to rescue me from the blues.

The usual disclaimer holds.

Map I. Bihar in 1921

Map II. Linguistic Divisions of the Plains of Bihar

Introduction

Crossing the Rubicon

I present in this volume an attempt to comprehend the political languages of the kisans in colonial Bihar. When kisans perceived shifts in focus of existing power relations in everyday life, they tried to articulate their responses and reactions, their hopes and frustrations, apathy and interventions in accordance with the cultural/moral/religious/intellectual resources available. Since perceptions varied, their actions, as expressions of desires and choices, produced many languages. Yet it is possible to identify, at any given point of time, the dominant language kisans chose to speak or the historical choices they made in the process of ordering their lives. More often than not, their articulations appeared to be couched in the vocabulary of survival strategies and/or the perpetuation of time-honoured traditions and customs, but deliberate and selective memorization and constructions cannot be ruled out. The rhetoric of revolution, which has been the most dominant grid of Marxist analyses of peasant political consciousness, in general, remained considerably alien to them. This, however, did not make them less revolutionary than any other social class, since we know that almost all revolutions have occurred in predominantly agrarian societies.

To comprehend the political consciousness of peasants in colonial Bihar, it is more important to focus enquiry on the 'normal', the 'dormant' moment that constitutes their quotidian world than to engage solely with the moment when the socio-cultural codes of power relations are openly ruptured. Secondly, to understand the history of dissent, an examination is necessary of the language in which dissent is articulated. A language evolves through taking cognizance of various factors or social grammars and in this sense the kisans of colonial Bihar also evolved an idiom to express the inexpressible and speak the unspeakable. Language, per se, has this unique characteristic of mirroring the sub/conscious of its user—to bring out the nuances of frustration and hope, desire and dilemma, confusion and trepidation, to the fore. Thus, it could appropriately be said that language informs and is informed by the way of life of its speakers. This is the decisive factor in the selection and privileging of the 'language of politics', to comprehend the lives, thoughts and actions of kisans. The trope of 'language of politics' saves one from traversing through the quagmire of ill-conceived hair-splitting debates on 'spontaneity *v.* organization', 'full-consciousness *v.* semi-consciousness', 'pre-political *v.* political', or 'reactionary *v.* revolutionary'. In this narrative, I hope, the kisans of colonial Bihar appear as subjects in their own right.

Another related and equally significant advantage of this entry point is the fact that language, in its literal and total sense, is a sum total of the cultural, moral and philosophical cosmologies of those who evolve and speak it. Unlike terms with wide-spread currency like 'peasant politics', which is more often than not contrasted with 'working class politics' and understood in terms of 'causes', 'organization', 'leadership', 'mobilization', 'politicization', 'revolutionary consciousness', etc., the political language of kisans invites us to look directly into the cultural/religious/social/moral matrix of their lives, which together fill it with a meaning. 'Language of politics' is inclusive of many moments, many emotions, and cannot evolve as a viable medium of articulation and communication except in the totality of human experience. In other words, to grasp the political language of a people at any given moment, it is necessary to probe into as many of its 'referents' as possible.

Finally, 'language of politics' as an entry point to the problematic of political culture and 'peasant consciousness', inescapably concerns itself with the issue of generalizing the political and thereby democratizing it. The emergence of a particular political language as a dominant discourse of its time, entails active popular participation. It offers a vantage point from which one may view the historicization of human agency not only during the moments of ruptures in the socio-political fabric, but also during the 'dormant interregnum' that, by definition, lies between the two points of rupture. In other words, peasant consciousness and its political culture can be studied only through the script of a political language, for consciousness is not only the subject-matter of 'political change in history' but is itself the social and cultural history of a society in which the kisan constitutes the dominant element. 'Political change' as a subject-matter would require an altogether different enquiry. My concern with the everyday life of the kisan (as opposed to, the latter in tumultuous moments), justifies the privileging of migration, crime, rumour, dharma and caste over other expressions of political desire, action and frustration (not always in this order, of course).

A brief genealogical overview of the historiography of 'peasant consciousness' helps elaborate my suggestions and assertions better.[1]

HISTORIOGRAPHY

Marx, and Marxist historians, invariably viewed peasant political behaviour in the light of a need to seize state power in order to establish the Socialist revolutionary regime led by the proletariat. In a near stage-ist scheme of things, Marx's celebration of the bourgeoisie's victory over feudal forces in general and of the French Revolution as a bourgeois revolution in particular, set the tone and parameters of Marxist enquiries into the subject all over the world. Marx reaffirmed the claims of the Enlightenment, couched in the language of Progress and Modernization and so embraced the temporal ruptures propagated by liberal historians of the age.[2] Much of Marxism's psychic energy was drawn from the way liberal historians chose to analyse the world in general and the French Revolution in particular. It is interesting to note that Marx theorized the peasantry as a political class while reflecting on the nature and outcome of the French Revolution. By describing peasants as 'clumsily cunning, knavishly naive . . . an undecipherable hieroglyphic for the understanding of the civilized', Marx expressed his feelings for the 'class that [he thought] represents barbarism within civilization'.[3]

[1] In the following paragraphs, I touch upon only the landmarks in Marxist and Marxian literature on peasantry and peasant consciousness. In no way, do they constitute an exhaustive survey of literature on the subject.

[2] See George C. Comninel (1987) and F. Furet (1981 and 1988).

[3] For Marx's views on peasantry see Marx (1940, 1963, 1976, 1993) and Marx and Fredric Engels (1992).

Nineteenth-century Western Europe constructed an ideological prism through which it could view, and determine the features of slaves, the colonized, and its own labouring folk: men, women, and children alike. It frequently needed to construct non-European traditions, religions and societies in its own image (Asad 1993) to impose the superiority of its own time (modernity), its own religion (science), and its own nature (profit). Reason, science, progress, etc., became euphemisms for the perpetuation of West European domination over the rest of the world. Marx set his scholarly project against this exploitative nature of the Western domination, yet failed to recast the prevailing Liberal episteme. He accepted the Enlightenment epistemology and told his story in the language of people in contrast to non-people, science in contrast to magic, religion, and archaic practices. He could speak of advanced people in Western Europe in opposition to the barbaric, backward, despotic savages of the rest of the world because he thought that the former were engaged in interaction with society unlike the latter whose interaction was confined to nature. The larger context in which he ended up with these questionable 'asides' was not to reproduce the racist scheme of things already prevalent in the metropolis, but to critique capital, which he rightly thought was the *raison d'être* of most of these evils.

The presumed simplicity of peasant life provided Marx with a means to contrast village with city, feudal with bourgeois, backward with progressive, tradition with modernity, emotion with reason, nature with society, and so on. It was in this sense that Marx concluded that peasants 'cannot represent themselves, they must be represented' (Marx 1963, p. 124) because, after all, they were merely 'a sack of potatoes', the 'homologous magnitudes'.

In the hands of Lenin and Lukacs, the need for an Enlightened leadership and organized party to 'arouse the inert peasantry' and take them beyond their 'natural', 'instinctive' predilection for economistic outlook, acquired further orthodoxy.[4] The reasons for Lenin's popularity are not hard to find. Those opposed to capitalism and the miseries that follow in its wake, saw in the USSR and its leadership, hope for a better future for humankind. The charismatic image of Lenin, the Bolshevik Revolution, the astronomical economic growth, 'moderni-

[4] For an insightful discussion on the importance of the Party to Lenin and Leninism, see Marcel Liebman (1975). Also useful is G. Lukacs (1971).

zation', and the overall rise of the USSR in world affairs in an amazingly short span of time—were all too fresh in the minds of intellectuals of the Third World. The victory of the USSR against Nazi Germany and the way it held its ground during the 'hot' years of the Cold War, further consolidated the ideas spreading out from the Kremlin.

The first major blow to the Leninist perspective in history writing appeared after 1956. This was the year when Hungary was invaded by the USSR and de-Stalinization was officially announced. The events brought forth a range of questions, including the role of a vanguard party, leadership, the nature of the Bolshevik revolution and the USSR as a viable state apparatus for emancipation, the formation of class and consciousness, and so on. These questions divided Marxist intellectuals and communist parties all over the world. E.P. Thompson, Rodney Hilton, Raphael Samuel (among others) parted company with E.J. Hobsbawm, Maurice Dobb, and the British Communist Party (CPGB). Their work reveals differences in the nature and significance of class, party, organization, leadership, culture, ideology, human agency, tradition, and custom. Those who remained in the Communist Party (Hobsbawm, Dobb) continued to downplay the peasant political actions as 'pre-political'. And those who left the party, re-asserted the need to do social history with the common 'man' at the centre of the enquiry.

Despite the fact that Hobsbawm decided to study rioters, mobs, bandits, and millenarians,[5] he did so in a way adhering to Marxist dogmas. He continued to think in the Leninist framework where class consciousness ('in the full sense', Hobsbawm 1971, pp. 6–7) remained a modern industrial phenomenon of which all previous struggles become a pre-history. As he acknowledged, the purpose behind studying 'primitive rebels' was 'to see whether we were right in believing in a strongly organized party. . . . And 'the answer is yes' (see Kaye 1984, p. 147). In 'Class Consciousness in History', Hobsbawm (1971) reiterated his Leninist perspective:

> Each class has two levels of aspirations, at least until it becomes victorious: the immediate, day by day specific demands, and the more general demand for the kind of society which suits it. . . . [W]orking-class consciousness at both levels implies formal organization; and organization *which*

[5] See E.J. Hobsbawm (1959, 1969, 1971, 1973, 1978).

is itself the carrier of class ideology, which without it would be little more than *a complex of informal habits and practices*. (Hobsbawm 1971, pp. 14–15, emphasis added)

Hobsbawm proceeded to remind us that these two levels of consciousness also correspond to an intellectual hierarchy, where the former concerns is itself with immediate issues and is 'spontaneous', and 'economic' in nature, while the latter is driven by long-term issues and exists by virtue of being 'political' and 'organized' on socialist principles.

George Rudé (1959, 1970) highlighted the concerns of the common people of England and France. In his writings we hear the voices of 'criminals' and the 'condemned', we see 'faces' in the 'mob' and the 'crowd'. He followed a less orthodox path than Hobsbawm and that could be due to the fact that he was never a member of any Communist party, and/or, because he had the opportunity to work with the social historians of the French Revolution (Kaye 1984, 1988).

However, on issues of 'motivation' and 'leadership', Rudé failed to go beyond Marxist dogma. Explaining the 'crowd' actions, he, too, took recourse to economic hardship, price and wage fluctuations and food shortages. Regarding the issue of leadership, Rudé frequently talked about the spread of ideas from enlightened bourgeoisie to toiling masses; the influence of 'the advanced political' groups over the lower strata; the latter's 'systematic' 'indoctrination' and so on. Kaye correctly remarks:

such words . . . clearly evidence a Leninist conception of political education: the *sans-cullotes* were on their own incapable of anything more than *economic* motivation ('trade union consciousness'), movement beyond that required the leadership and political ideas developed by bourgeois intellectuals. (Kaye 1988, p. 20)

One also finds Rudé operating within a unilinear notion of time and history in which 'inherent' ideology is (essentially) 'backward-looking' (the born sinner?) and 'derived' ideology is 'forward-looking'. With the former, masses could only 'strike' or 'riot', their struggles could only become like peasant rebellions and bring about some reforms; for revolution it is the 'derived' ideology that will play the crucial part (ibid., p. 26). He acknowledged his intellectual debt in 'The Changing Face of the Crowd':

> What I learned from Marx was not only that history tends to progress through a conflict of social classes . . . but that it has a discoverable pattern and moves forward (not backwards, in circles, or in inexplicable jerks) broadly from a lower to a higher phase of development. (ibid., p. 30)

It is in E.P. Thompson (1966 [1963], 1975, 1975a, 1977, 1978, 1991) that we see the first major break from economic determinism and find an ardent advocacy of human agency, experience, culture, and custom in exploration of social relationships. Insisting on reading Marxism as a theory of history and not as the laws of history, Thompson in the first issue of *The New Reasoner* (a journal he inaugurated with John Saville after leaving the party in 1956) rejected the base-superstructure model as static, 'bad and dangerous' (Kaye 1984, p. 172). Instead he proposed to get rid of metaphors such as 'systems' and 'elements', and suggested a reconsideration of concepts like 'mode of production', since the latter could 'provide a kernel of human relationship from which all else grows' (ibid.).

With the publication of *The Making of the English Working Class* [1966 (1963)], a departure was made possible from the ways Marxist scholars had studied class consciousness, class and its traditions, customs, and cultures. Noted Thompson:

> [T]he class experience is largely determined by the productive relations into which men are born—or enter involuntarily. *Class consciousness is the way in which these experiences are handled in cultural terms: embodied in traditions, value systems, ideas, and institutional forms.* (Thompson 1966, pp. 9–10, emphasis added)

By asking, 'being hungry (or being sexy), what do people do?' (Thompson 1991, p. 262), Thompson launched a scathing attack against the then commonplace practice of Marxist historians, who in varying degree, entertained a simple 'animal' response to hunger (ibid., p. 226). This includes Hobsbawm and Rudé as well, who by assuming 'riots' as 'rebellions of the belly' (ibid., p. 186) were forced to swallow its supposed antonym: 'rebellions of the mind'. It should, however, be pointed out that Thompson did not reject the determinism of productive relations in the final analysis, nor did he undermine materialism altogether. As he explains

> it is of course true that riots were triggered off by soaring prices, by malpractices among dealers, or by hunger. But these grievances operated

within a popular consensus as to what were legitimate and what were illegitimate practices in marketing, milling, baking, etc. This in turn was grounded upon a consistent traditional view of social norms and obligations. . . . (ibid., p. 188)

His formulations were yet to be informed by gender and race relations. *The Making of the English Working Class* remained a biography of the white heterosexual male working class. Such sensitivities had to wait till the closure of the decade of the sixties, as it were, when the polarization against the U.S. intervention in Vietnam would explode in the movements of what is popularly known as '1968', all over the world.

The central thrust of '1968' was, on the one hand, to make the US realize the limits of its hegemony and, on the other, to force the organized Left, styled after the Bolshevik approach to the seizure of state power in the name of the dictatorship of proletariat, to re-write the script of struggle and change. As a result, the people, and not a party or a programme, emerged as the leitmotif of every political discourse. A range of issues, hitherto barely considered, sprang up and significantly broadened the meaning of radical politics. Class, consciousness, subjectivity, ideology, power, democratic struggle, etc., began to be debated in the light of gender relations, racial experiences, ecological consequences and alienation that enveloped not only the workers but other disparate sections of humanity. The Universal Hero was declared dead, the 'grand narrative' of Capitalism and Communism both were decried. Gramsci's *Prison Notebooks* became available to the English reader for the first time in 1971 (Hoare and Nowell Smith 1971) wherein a critique of Bolshevism was provided from within the Marxist tradition.

Rodney Hilton in his studies of the peasants of the late Medieval period abundantly reflected upon the changing language of social science (Hilton 1971, 1973, 1975). He criticized social scientists for their tendency to 'de-historicize' and 'de-class' the peasant experience (Hilton 1975, pp. 4–12) and argued that medieval peasants did occasionally show a consciousness of class. This consciousness, however, was a 'negative class consciousness in that the definition of class which was involved was that of their enemies (the nobility) rather than of themselves' (Hilton 1973, p. 130).[6]

[6] As students of Modern Indian History know, Ranajit Guha (1983) uses this notion of negative consciousness (which is actually derived from Gramsci) with a

Hilton's departure from the Marxist stereotyping of the peasantry led him to make two grand assertions: peasant movements as class struggles were consequential to medieval social change and development; and by this he turned Marx and several Marxists on their heads: 'the assertion of freedom against feudal subordination was not, as is often supposed, a specific contribution of the bourgeoisie', rather, the result of the struggles 'of the peasantry of the feudal era'. He continued, 'one of the most important . . . legacies of medieval peasants to the modern world is the concept of the freeman, owing no obligation, not even deference, to an overlord' (ibid., p. 235).

A similarly grand assertion appeared in James Scott (1976, 1977, 1985, 1990), who turned everything for which the peasantry invited the wrath of the Marxists, into its strength and virtue. One of the many criticisms about the peasants was that they cannot look beyond their family farm. Scott turned this assumption into a virtue by describing it as the peasantry's decisive strength over the proletariat. Admitting the relative isolation of the peasantry from the cultural and institutional life of the state and its ruling elites, Scott held that it made the peasantry as a class more immune compared to the proletariat. Owing to its proximity to the same, the proletariat remains more vulnerable to ruling class propaganda and ideology. Using the Gramscian notion of hegemony, Scott argued that the very embeddedness of peasant political organization in pre-existing social ties meant that it was less likely be co-opted by the negotiating agencies of the state. To reiterate, Scott (1977) refuted the claim that, being close to their traditional roots, peasants were less equipped to revolt: '(T)hat the social values of the peasantry are pre-capitalist may give its rebellions a quality of tenacity and moral cohesion—in the sense that the struggle to restore or defend customary rights may evoke a more passionate commitment than the struggle to create a new order' (ibid., p. 271).[7]

Since the peasantry is removed from the moral, social, economic and political centre of the state, it is able to maintain a cultural/critical

---

fair amount of success in his studies of 'elementary' aspects of peasant insurgency in colonial India.

[7] As Barrington Moore put it so eloquently (1966, p. 505), 'the wellsprings of human freedom lie not only where Marx saw them, in the aspirations of classes about to take power, but perhaps even more in the dying wail of a class over whom the wave of progress is about to roll'.

distance from the ideological universe of the state. On these grounds it is conceivable to reject the classical Marxist anxiety about the peasantry being reactionary, as it owns the means of production. The relative economic autonomy of the peasantry, in fact, empowers it to resist the ideological hegemony of the rulers more effectively than the wage-earning industrial proletariat. Scott, however, did not conclude from this that the ideological universe of the peasantry is totally unconnected from that of the state or the local elite. He merely, and correctly, assigned a relative advantage to the peasantry over the proletariat in this regard.

Along with the moral economy thesis, Scott developed a focus on a vast and relatively unexplored middle ground of peasant politics between passivity and open collective defiance, the 'everyday forms of resistance'. Under this rubric he explored everyday weapons of the weak: sabotage, foot-dragging, pilfering, slander and so forth.

Functionalists warn, however, that a resistance that takes place 'every day', and/or what is 'allowed' by the elite every day may not be of much consequence. After all, the argument goes, how shall we know that by allowing a degree of defiance the elite is not creating a safety valve? This is reminiscent of Claude Levi-Strauss' remark (1963, p. 13), 'to say that a society functions is a truism, but to say that everything in a society functions is an absurdity'.

However, it is correctly pointed out that in the 'moral economy' literature there is a tendency to treat the past and tradition in an ambiguous way, as if the transition has been from a calm past to a tumultuous present. Instead, the movement should be viewed from 'a disordered past to a disordered present' (Roseberry in Hanagan and Stephenson 1986). Scott has been criticized for romanticizing peasants and for his arbitrary assumption of the existence of a moral order in traditional society (supposedly based on mutual rights and duties between the lord and his peasants), the violation of which created a rupture in the social/cultural tissue. Scott's critics argue that traditional society might have been based on plain and simple exploitation (Popkin 1979; Adas 1980; Skocpol 1989). However, this argument can be made only if one constructs an ethereal realm where economy and morality are disjointed or if one assumes that 'traditional' systems of exploitation were standing on plain and crude coercion. Adas' argument, for example, that Burmese peasants under British colonialism revolted not because their traditional subsistence ethic was being threatened, but because they were frustrated with the market (that was glutted with rice, causing problems to peasants), shows a failure to perceive the interlinkages between subsistence ethic, colonialism and market forces. Did Scott (or others employing the 'moral economy' thesis) ever imply that 'shared norms' must be understood in terms of the 'traditional', or, that 'shared norms' could not be flexible reactions to new/changed structural conditions?[8] If not, then this kind of approach is merely an uncritical reproduction of economic reductionism and is totally consumed by the reasoning of 'the rebellion of the belly'. Charles Tilly (1975) among others, adeptly showed that 'food riots' occurred not so much where people were hungry, as where they believed others were unjustly depriving them of food to which they had a moral and political right. Moore's (1978) work on the social bases of obedience and revolt is another notable example.

One final point in this regard. Weller and Guggenheim (1989) have argued against the moral-economy school on the ground that 'food-riots, social banditry, and the rest of this repertoire are not contests for state power; they are responses to local conditions' (p. 12). We hear in this the echoes of the Marxist-Leninist tradition, in which the demolition of the state has been the pivot. Weller and Guggenheim imagined different 'local islands' which, when added together, apparently made up a closed unit called the state. This kind of reasoning resonates with the ideas of Hobsbawm and others who impose a hierarchy on resistance, where 'local' struggles are placed lower down on the scale.

My study is counterpoised against this historiographical development and moves away from the tyranny of proving revolutionary consciousness and capabilities, judged through success or failure in seizing state power. The effort is to gain a sense of ways in which kisans of colonial Bihar perceived their realities and the languages in which their resistance was articulated.

In reviewing the historiography of Indian peasantry, an evaluation

[8] Ralph Thaxton (1989 [1982]) uses moral economy arguments to reconstruct the story of the Chinese peasantry and Revolution. Abandoning the 'political mobilization' theory that made the revolutionary consciousness of peasants contingent on the Chinese Communist Party and its leadership, Thaxton shows that there was two-way interaction between the party and the rural poor who were constantly recasting their Little Traditions in the light of everyday changing realities.

of Ranajit Guha's *Elementary Aspects of Peasant Insurgency in Colonial India* (1983) forms the starting point as no single work on modern India has invited more attention. Arguing sharply against the Marxist and the nationalist narratives of social formation/nation-making for their elitist paradigm, Guha and his colleagues, writing for *Subaltern Studies* (since 1983 when the first volume came out) called for situating the subalterns as the active subjects of their own projects. The retrieval of subaltern voices was aimed at replacing their representation in the elite register of freedom struggle with acknowledgement of the relative autonomy of their cultures. Distancing itself from Hobsbawmian search for 'full' and 'pure' class consciousness, the group advocated the need to recast the intellectual tools required for doing history and encouraged the search for alternative sources along with a critical engagement with the archives.

Despite the fact that Ranajit Guha embarked on the project of restoring subalterns as subjects of their own histories, the very spirit of *Elementary Aspects* appears to be burdened with a series of dialogues with the ghosts of Lenin, Lukacs and Hobsbawm. Guha invites the ghosts, by a presumed compulsion to show that peasants too had a sense of political organization, solidarity, and an identity of their own (though the latter was negatively arrived at, à la Hilton). In the chapter entitled, 'Territoriality', he tries to explain the failure of peasant movements to travel beyond their own limited vicinity due to peasant 'habit of thinking and acting on a small and local scale', instead of questioning the Bukharinesque problematic in the first place. To our dismay, Guha does not even look into what 'could have accounted for the spatial circumscription'.[9] Under the spell of these ghosts, by the time the dialogue ends, Guha finds (or does he?) his vocabulary considerably corrupted. Peasant thoughts appear to him as 'disjointed perceptions' carrying merely a 'trace of consciousness' (Guha 1983, p. 27); what is worse, it is 'unquestionably false consciousness' (ibid., p. 268), thanks to the 'backward . . . material [and] spiritual conditions' (ibid., p. 265) of the insurgents. So Guha concludes that their politics was 'less sophisticated' (ibid., p. 170), 'relatively immature' (ibid., p. 265) and 'half realistic and half fantastic' (ibid.).[10] Part Leninist,

[9] See Dipankar Gupta (1985, p. 13). Gupta locates the root of the problem in Guha's anthropological naivete.

[10] Dipesh Chakrabarty (1985, p. 365), in a damage control exercise, tells us that Guha did not propose 'to study "peasant consciousness" in its entirety, but only the

part Durkheimian, the aspects of insurgency he studies, are 'elementary'. How did this happen, when this is precisely what Guha wanted to demolish in his book? The reason does not lie so much in his anthropological naivete, as in his inability to unlearn the Marxist language he grew up with. Guha did not succeed in making a clear break from the Bolshevik model of radicalism that routinely decried the 'localism' of the peasantry. Not then. He arrives as a tour-de-force in Indian historiography only with his 'Prose of Counter Insurgency' and 'Chandra's Death' (1983 and 1987).

It is generally accepted that not all contributors to *Subaltern Studies* retain the methodological rigour of Guha or Gyanendra Pandey (1984) or, as desired by Gayatri C. Spivak (1988). What is striking is the fact that asymmetry of quality is at times allowed to run in a direction opposed to that of the project. To end this historiographical detour, one example is taken up for further discussion, in consonance with the concerns of this book.

Whether valorization of community, or romantic and convenient slippage into 'timelessness' of cultures and traditions of subalterns, Partha Chatterjee's essays (1983, 1984) reflect one of those unreflecting moments we are referring to. According to Chatterjee, the 'peasant-communal ideology' enjoyed an authority which was prior to that of any single kisan over the entire collectivity and mediated existing power relations. Thus, as a legitimate political arbiter, it carried subversive potential force which could travel well beyond the world it inherited. The communal ideology functioned on a shared set of beliefs which, in turn, were coded with religiosity and political ethics. These were apparently timeless values of duties and obligations, authority and obedience. What we, in fact, observe here is a harmonious and consensual island where the division of labour, and, consequently, relationships of power had not penetrated the community of the kisan. But Chatterjee knows that the communal affinities carried 'possibilities of manipula-

---

consciousness of the insurgent peasants' and that Guha qualified his remark by adding that only 'relatively' the insurgent peasants showed purer consciousness. As I have sought to demonstrate, the privileging of moments of insurgency to 'dormant' moments is problematic. No appropriate sense of 'peasant consciousness' can be availed unless the points of ruptures are studied in continuum with that of lull. Guha's preference for insurgent peasants may well be a residue of that historiographical concern which looked and hoped for a Bolshevik type of Revolution everywhere.

tion' by the many constituents of a community. He therefore argues that 'the point which distinguishes the communal mode from other modes or organizations of power is this: here is not a perception of common interests which compels organizations to achieve unity; there is rather the *conviction* that bonds of affinity *already exist* which then become the *natural* presupposition for collective action' (Chatterjee 1984, p. 343, emphasis added). What was the basis of that conviction? Whatever happened to the division of Indian society along caste lines? My work attempts to show that the contours of any collectivity were never stable; they were constantly being redrawn as the actors had different per-ceptions of their lives, and prepared themselves in different ways for change.

Historical studies on the kisans of colonial Bihar have rarely addressed the problems raised in this book. The Kisan Sabha as an organization; Swami Sahajanand Saraswati as a charismatic leader of kisans in twentieth-century Bihar; the uneasy relationship between the Sabha and the Indian National Congress, are some of the themes explored. However, little exists by way of explanation of the culture of kisan politics, particularly through a focussed enquiry into political languages as and when they evolved.

THE ARGUMENT

Each chapter is an exposition of a language of politics available to the kisan, not in the sense of elite discourse, but language as a form and expression of life, informed by and informing, the consciousness of kisans. The book begins with a brief sketch of British agrarian policies. The introduction of the Permanent Settlement Acts in 1793 had a direct bearing on the lives of kisans in several ways, the economic impact of which has been explored in several studies. Many issues which cropped up later had their roots in the rather arbitrarily derived assumptions and conclusions of the Acts. The East India Company's search for subordinate allies introduced a newly-crafted zamindari system in the rural arena, which proceeded to enhance its legal and extra-legal powers to dominate the kisans. The Company's inability and reluctance to take into account the customary rights of kisans and its reliance on modern legal paraphernalia further compounded the problems of kisans. As the policies underwent several amendments, it becomes possible to observe the changing dynamics within rural Bihar.

The second chapter is an appraisal of 'Migration' and 'Crime' as they constituted the two major articulations by kisans against changes imposed on their lives. After establishing the scale of migration, an assessment is made of its impact on the socio-cultural register of Bihar, through the voices of women whose husbands migrated. This required a shift in emphasis from emigration to seasonal migration. Along with quotidian hardships, women who were waiting for husbands to return had extra burdens to bear: 'male anxiety' demanded their complete chastity and faithfulness, which is reflected in folksongs. Many of the songs appeared to have been strongly influenced by the Bhakti tradition, which seems to have been used to rechannel the female libido towards godly devotion. The linkages between memories of migration and women's militancy in future kisan struggles are also touched upon.

The section on crime includes a survey of changing views on crime and criminals, followed by a discussion on the religious and moral referents of crime in popular imagery. The chapter ends with a discussion on 'cattle-thefts', as these were not only the 'most popular' crimes, but also the particular favourites among lower caste groups, unlike the 'riots', that have attracted so much attention from historians (despite their comparatively rare occurrence). The latter were by and large confined to upper caste kisans with some resources. Cattle-thefts were also the first major efforts by kisans to create new kinds of collectivities in the face of new challenges of the times. The sheer scale of cattle-thefts goes to prove that discourses on crime, along with migration, emerged as the clearest articulations of kisan politicization in nineteenth-century Bihar.

In the third chapter on rumours and 'stories', we hear late nineteenth-century dissenting kisan voices, clearer than ever before. Kisan collectivities expressed through migration and crime aspired to break new ground, to travel as far as they could, and to bring as many as possible into their fold. Inimical undercurrents vis à vis the Raj and the zamindar, which used to surface occasionally during moments of near-total erasure of codes of power, gained in strength. Imageries of 'the death of the Empire' and collapse of the zamindari system, began to stir the consciousness of kisans. Rumour, as a tactical art of speech of the weak who were denied an open platform to air their thoughts and desires, was used to prepare a 'public sphere' of sorts before kisans made 'mass-movements' a generalized affair. Gandhian mass movements significantly borrowed from nineteenth-century expressions of conflict and distress as articulated in rumour. As a social text without an individual author, rumour functioned as a script of 'public opinion' and thrived on religious metaphors.

The fourth chapter concerns the religious matrices around which colonial domination and anti-colonial resistance were being worked out. 'Re-discovery' of the *Gita* by nationalist leaders in the twentieth century, strongly suggests the quest for a new language of politics. 'Language as a repository of action' is beautifully exhibited in the reinterpretation of the text, as Gandhi and Sahajanand found in the *Gita* moral and philosophical support for their ideas and actions. Many central categories of politics of the times derived their meanings from the new interpretations of the *Gita* which were being made available by the leaders. Needless to say, the process of constructing a language of mass politics was not arrived at unilaterally by the leaders, as the imprint of the people affecting the leadership is too obvious to miss.

The fifth chapter explores the religious articulation of kisans; their acceptance and rejection of elite construction of the language of mass politics; and the emergence of a new language which failed to find a favourable space in the discourse defined by the political leadership. Regarding the religious language of politics, we see a distinct framework evolved by kisans, whose religiosity was neither devoid of a critical consciousness of the world they lived in, nor shy of incorporating the secular or the material in their devotional yearnings. In fact, the kisans carefully reworked a tradition that allowed for a space where devotion could be blended with the mundane discontent they braved in their everyday lives. The chapter ends with an enquiry into the emergence of a political language around issues of caste identity and exploitation, and which failed to receive recognition as such by Congress leaders as well as those of the Kisan Sabha.

The conclusion reaches the point where a denial of this language is not only no more possible, but has become one of the most important issues around which national politics is defined and played out.

THE REGION, THE PEOPLE

Bihar and Orissa formed a part of Bengal *suba* under the Mughal Empire. In 1912 Bihar and Orissa were separated from Bengal and in 1936 Orissa was separated from Bihar. The field of this study lies between the Chotanagpur plateau and the Himalaya, comprising rich valleys traversed by the river Ganga and its tributaries. The 'Bihar' of our discussion excludes the Chotanagpur plateau which is the abode of the major *Adivasi* ('tribals') population of the province. Chotanagpur, played an important, though seldom cited, part in the struggle for freedom, and given its geography, economy and languages, formed a region in itself.

In the districts of Darbhanga, Saharsa, Purnia, Bhagalpur and parts of Munghyr and Muzaffarpur, the language spoken is Maithili with its ancient literary tradition.[11] In Gaya, Patna and parts of Munghyr the language spoken is Magahi (derived from Magadh, the seat of one of the greatest empires of ancient India). In Saran, Champaran, Shahabad and parts of Muzaffarpur the language spoken is Bhojpuri.

Along with being the centre of origin of many anti-Brahmanical philosophies, Bihar was also home to certain orthodox Hindu sects, which survived because of the deep-rooted caste system of the region. The community was dominated by Brahmans, Bhumihars, Rajputs and Kayasthas (the four upper castes), though numerically, the intermediate castes (see Appendix I) were much stronger. The upper caste dominance was rooted, apart from traditional social precedence, in control over land, and administrative and professional positions. More often than not, the caste location corresponded to economic position and vice versa.

A word on the key terminologies of the book. I have preferred the term 'kisan' to 'peasant', 'tenant', and 'share-cropper', not only because the term 'kisan' is used in all the languages spoken in Bihar, but because it has many other advantages as well. Unlike 'tenant' or 'share-cropper', it does not privilege the economic identity of the person. Because it is a word found in all the languages spoken in the plains of Bihar, it invites a glimpse into the cultural world as represented by those languages. 'Kisans' were always members of particular caste groups. In fact, the majority of them were lower caste Hindus. 'Peasant' on the other hand is too general and too alien a term to provide us with any cultural specificity about the person referred to.

The kisans of these pages held marginal holdings, which were barely

[11] I have discarded the conventional distinction between language and dialect. The latter is called so because, it is argued, it does not have a script of its own, hence inferior. If we agree that the chief purpose of a language is to make communication comprehensible, and not essentially to create and maintain a graphic record of utterances, then the distinction between the two becomes redundant.

enough for survival through the year. Owing to British agrarian policies even these small holdings were gradually slipping out of their hands. For similar reasons, the local expression 'zamindar', has been preferred to 'landlord'. Zamindars in Bihar overwhelmingly belonged to upper castes and consequently enjoyed many privileges *in addition to* those stipulated by legislative or legal provisions.

In exploring the mentalités of the kisan, political organizations and movements and points of rupture per se take a back seat. The purpose is to reconstruct the specific environment that gave rise to particular kinds of thought processes among kisans. Studies which privilege the event or the movement over the cultural ambience in which it is enacted, often work on a rather narrow canvass. The pace and intensity of the event, or, sometimes just the details of it, give very little time to the observer to comprehend the event in its totality. An ideal situation would be to look at the event from different angles with a longer time-frame, which would not be feasible within the scope of a single book.

The task of writing a cultural history of politics, of which the actors, the un-lettered kisans, did not leave behind 'written records' or memoirs, meant forsaking the 'beaten track' and looking for unconventional sources, which include songs, proverbs, stories, myths and anecdotes.

Translations and transliterations are entirely mine.

CHAPTER 1

Recasting the Revenue Regime: Agrarian Policies at a Glance

> According to the provisions of (the Regulation XXXV, passed on the 27th March, 1795, to recover his arrears of rent) . . . the distrainer could in the presence of police officer forcibly open the out-door of the ryot's house and even enter the zenana [the inner part of the house where women lived].
>
> —RAM NARAYAN SINHA, 1968

> Nowhere in contemporary India is the gulf between articulated ideals with respect to agrarian reforms and solid accomplishments more conspicuous than in Bihar.
>
> —F. TOMASSON JANNUZI, 1974

> All knowledge is rooted in a life, a society, and a language that have a history; and it is in that very history that knowledge finds the element enabling it to communicate with other forms of life, other types of society, other significations. . . .
>
> —MICHEL FOUCAULT, 1970

British agrarian policies in India epitomize the maxim that to rule is to know, and to know is to construct. The East India Company conquered Calcutta in 1757 and in successive stages acquired the grant of *diwani* (the right to collect revenue) of the entire Bengal presidency by 1765. Since then and until it evolved a far more 'stable' mechanism to extract agrarian revenue, the Company went through a series of hair-splitting debates. The over-riding concern of policy-makers was to refrain from uncertainties, in terms of formulating and following a certain revenue policy and also the realization of revenues from the land. The difficulty of arriving at a consensual policy was due to a lack of knowledge about local traditional practices, besides their own ideological differences concerning the method and ultimate purpose of the exercise (Ranajit Guha 1963).

For British officials who were sent to collect revenue without real knowledge about the agrarian world of India, it was 'a journey into the unknown in more than one sense' (ibid., p. 13). Even those who were acquainted with its English counterpart were of no help:

> At every step they came up against quasi-feudal rights and obligations which defied any attempt at interpretation in familiar western terms. The hieroglyphics of Persian estate-accounts baffled them. It was *only a part* of the difficulty that they could not easily master the languages in which the ancient and medieval texts relating to the laws of property were written; *for tradition recorded only in memory and customs embedded in a variety of local usages wielded an authority equal to that of any written code.* (ibid., emphasis added)

Some colonial scholars too expressed similar sentiments.[1] However, ignorance, as Guha correctly points out, was only a part of the problem. It took over a century for the British to acknowledge and initiate the process of procuring information about the customary rights of kisans. The reason probably lies in the fact that the British knew from experience that custom could be a volatile site of claims and counterclaims and thus, of conflict, as it primarily rested 'at the interface between law and agrarian practice' (E.P. Thompson 1991, p. 97). A similar point was made in relation to the English Enclosure system by Searle (1986, p. 120): 'Custom . . . was not something fixed and immutable, carrying the same body of meaning for both social classes. On the contrary, its definition was highly variable in relation to class position, and accordingly it became a vehicle for conflict. . . .'

Thompson's gloss of Bourdieu's (1977) concept of 'habitus' to

[1] B.H. Baden-Powell (1892, pp. 402–3) in one of the most masterly accounts of the British land policies in India, remarked that:

> There was no hand-book of ancient law to guide the Collectors in understanding the history of landholding, to direct their attention to the origin of the *villages*, the units composing the great estates, or to explain what those aggregates of cultivators meant, in the light of a comparative study of early custom and institutions. *Their* only conceptions of landholding was embedded in the English landlord with his tenants. (emphasis in the original)

explain custom is incisive: 'Agrarian custom was never fact. It was ambience. It may be understood with the aid of Bourdieu's concept of 'habitus'—a lived environment comprised of practices, inherited expectations, rules which both determined limits to usages and disclosed possibilities, norms and sanctions both of law and neighbourhood pressures' (Thompson 1991, p. 102).

As we shall note in subsequent pages, it was the authority of customs and memory over the mentalités of kisans, thoroughly schooled in the tradition of *shruti* (oral), since the very beginning of languages available to them, that proved to be the proverbial Achilles heel for the British. Time and again the authority of newly codified laws which preferred the sanctity of the written word to spoken accounts were defied by Indian kisans.[2] Notwithstanding the fact that these instances of defiance more often than not worked against them, kisans almost regularly disregarded the paramountcy of the modern liberal courts and their exponents. The knee-jerk colonial reaction against kisan perceptions of British law carried a heavy modernist overtone, flavoured with a disdain for indigenous cultural practices. Sir Henry Maine (1871), a historian and an influential mind of the metropolis, for example, thought that 'the Roman law is . . . fast becoming the lingua franca of universal jurisprudence' (Maine 1871, p. 361). Understandably, he had no hesitation whatever in asserting that the popular aversion to British laws resulted from the primitiveness of Indian society (ibid., p. 115).

The Permanent Settlement of Bengal was introduced in 1793 to get rid of the uncertainties of revenue extraction and to guarantee stability to the empire. As mentioned earlier, there was no consensus among the policy-makers over the way to proceed. Two factors apparently held the divided policy-makers together: their aversion to the existing agrarian policies (followed hitherto by the Company since 1765) and their unstinted veneration of private property. Though there was no unity among them on the question of the uses of property—some believed that it 'would strengthen the pillars of society', some thought it would principally stimulate agriculture—'they all shared the belief that a sound administration must have the security of landownership as its basis and nothing but a Permanent Settlement could ensure this' (Guha 1963 p. 17).

[2] Cohn 1987 has some comprehensive essays on British laws in India as a site of cultural confrontation.

'The period of Darkness and delirium' gave way to the refashioning of Bengal 'after the image of Whig England'.[3] The following are some of the ground-breaking changes set in motion by the Permanent Settlement Act.

Warren Hastings had introduced what was his contemporaries called the 'farming system', according to which estates were auctioned at the end of each term of settlement and then farmed out to the highest bidders for leases not exceeding five years. Since the results were disastrous, Hastings' critics decried the absence of any sense of permanence and farsightedness in his policy. As a result, the decennial settlement that Cornwallis had begun in 1789 was declared permanent in 1793, ending all previous periodic fluctuations in procurement for good. The Company settled the rights to collect revenue with the traditional zamindars who, as the coming years so vividly confirmed, gave their loyalty to the British Company and to the Crown in return for the royal gift that they had received. The revenue was fixed with the government while the raiyati rental (to be collected from the tenant-peasants) went up on one pretext or another. Proprietary status was conferred on zamindars with rights of inheritance and transfer of their estates subject to payment of fixed revenue to the government in perpetuity. In case of default, their lands were to be auctioned to the highest bidder, which could have been the government itself.[4]

'The assessment for ever' was targeted towards restoring stability and prosperity in the old landed aristocracy, which in turn was expected to improve agricultural output and alleviate the conditions of toiling tenants. Cornwallis was aware of the ruthless criticisms of John Shore made in 1789, when the decennial settlement was first announced. However, Cornwallis was persistent in his advocacy of permanence of assessment, for he assumed that the genuine proprietor[5] would develop as a 'gentleman farmer' once modern education was imparted to him and his comforts were secured. 'Secure in their proprietary rights they would have no hesitation in investing their wealth in land. Since

[3] Guha 1963, p. 17. Also Eric Stokes 1959.

[4] For details on the policy provisions of the Permanent Settlement see, Baden-Powell 1974; Ram Narayan Sinha 1968; Girish Mishra 1978; Robert Eric Frykenberg (ed.) 1969.

[5] On this question, Cornwallis wrote with brutal frankness in a circular dated 18 September 1789:

the demands of the Government upon them would be moderate and subject to no further alteration, they should in their own interest apply their profits to improve agriculture' (Guha 1963, p. 172).

In reality, nothing of this kind happened because the raiyats' interests were at best peripheral to the discourse, that had distinct ulterior motives. As Cornwallis admitted:

> Independent of all other considerations, I can assure you that it will be of the utmost importance for promoting the solid interests of the Company that the principal landholders and traders in the interior parts of the country should be restored . . . that a regular gradation of ranks may be supported, which is no where more necessary than in this country for preserving order. . . . [A.B. Keith (ed.) 1922, p. 159]

That in zamindars the Empire had found reliable allies was acknowledged even by the staunch British critics of the Permanent Settlement. Bentinck, for example, admitted in 1829 that though the Permanent Zamindari Settlement had proved to be a complete failure in many other essentials, it 'has this great advantage . . . of having created a vast body of rich landed proprietors deeply interested in the continuance of the British dominion and having complete command over the masses' (ibid., p. 12).

It was not that the Permanent Settlement altogether eschewed the rhetoric of protecting the tenants. The *patta* system (a document recording the terms on which a cultivator/tenant holds his land) was aimed at installing fixity of rent and putting a check on zamindars' whims to increase rents and evict tenants. Similarly, there was a ban on imposing *abwabs* (literally, cesses, but much more than mere illegal ways of increasing incomes) and tenants were also given the right to make final production decisions. Zamindars were further denied the right to collect transit dues and to administer civil cases. The latter decision was, in fact, celebrated by some contemporary commentators as a sign of depriving zamindars of their feudal privileges (Guha 1963,

---

I am fully convinced that the zamindars have the most unquestionable proprietorship in land. . . . I am also convinced that *even if they did not have the right to the proprietorship of the soil, the well being of society would compel us to acknowledge it in them.* I do not even consider it necessary to pass a judgement on the grounds of their claims to the proprietorship of the soil. (quoted in L. Natrajan 1953, p. 11, emphasis added)

p. 171). But zamindars continued to hold their 'informal courts' irrespective of the provision of the law against it (Yang 1989, p. 162).

Tenants remained vulnerable. All the provisions of the Act were declaratory in nature; nothing was binding on zamindars. This was probably what John Shore had in mind when in 1789 he opposed 'the proposal for declaring the Decennial Settlement permanent' in the following words: 'We know from our experience, what the zamindars are; and I am not inclined, in opposition to that experience, to suppose that they will at once assume new principles of action, and become economical landlords and prudent trustees of the public interests' (quoted in Sinha 1968, p. 62).

Shore's major objection touched the heart of the matter: the Settlement was being sought without knowledge of the interests and rights of the parties concerned. Only zamindars' rights were recorded with some amount of certainty while all attempts by Company officials at procuring either evidence or records of tenants' rights had miserably failed, as we have already noted. Cornwallis knew that further regulations were needed to safeguard the welfare of tenants, but he postponed them for the future (ibid., pp. 63–4). For the time being, he felt that it would be sufficient if tenants moved the courts, taking recourse to the judicial process in cases of zamindari excesses.[6]

That this belief was ill-grounded would be an understatement. Peasants could neither afford the expenses nor did they have faith in these new temples of justice that honoured written words more than oral accounts. To the people who grew up in the tradition of '*Pran jaye par vachan na jaye*' (Life may be lost but not the honour of the given word—a very popular line from Tulsi's *Ramcharitmanas*, which is collectively sung and read till today in the villages of Bihar), it meant a tremendous change in their belief system—that by a stroke of law a piece of paper acquired more importance than the tradition-based 'word' (*vachan*).[7]

[6] Letter from Governor General to Court, 6 March 1793—quoted in Sinha 1968, p. 64.

[7] So much so that a document itself began to signify the authority that was oppressive. There are many instances when insurgent kisans destroyed printed and written records of debts, rent-rolls, bonds, deeds, etc. (Guha 1983, pp. 51–2). Even in present-day rural Bihar adults rebuke the children when the latter draw lines in front of the house or on the wall or in the courtyard, either inadvertently or in play (for example, *ghar-ghar*), because to them these crooked lines represent debts in

This seems to provide a plausible explanation for the conclusion of the collector of Shahabad, T. Brooke, that the failure of the *patta* system was due more to the 'disinclination of the raiyats to receive them, than in the landlords to grant them' (Hubback 1928, p. 22). Hubback, though, differs from Brooke but confirms our assertion even more strongly. He remarks that tenants did not receive *pattas* because they 'were afraid that the pattas would be taken as meaning that they held their lands at the discretion of the landlord. . . .' Implicit in their refusal to accept a *patta* could be the belief that in so doing they would be able to deny the authority that it carried. However, the fear it represented in its initial years is difficult to miss.[8]

To sum up, the Permanent Settlement erected the stage on which future agrarian dramas were to be enacted. The belief in the principle of private property as a sure and solitary guarantee of stability, peace and prosperity, and unflinching faith in the zamindar as the agent to avail these, became the guiding spirits of the script. In the background lurked the ghost of traditions and customs of raiyats constantly threatening to disrupt the show. The show was indeed disrupted many a time, but of that later. For the moment it would suffice to conclude

---

curred by them. To understand the connection one only has to have a rough knowledge of the indebtedness of the peasants in the post-Permanent Settlement era. Adults religiously wipe out lines drawn by children in their precincts as if they were actually wiping the slate of borrowing clean. The lines become synonymous with scribbles in the register of the moneylender: illegible and dangerous. The non-lettered peasants took generations to pay-back even a paltry sum borrowed from the *sahukar* (the money-lender) or the zamindar, thanks to those scribbles. It meant the fear of losing lands, so vital to their lives.

[8] It is indeed possible to render a different, but not contradictory, meaning to this act. By refusing to honour the *patta* system, peasants were adamant in not acknowledging any decreed changes in land rights. Non-literate societies respond differently to writing depending on the context. See Goody (ed.) 1968 for a discussion on Islamic Africa where at times letters/words acquired quasi-spiritual/devotional dimension. A similar response could be seen in Sido and Kanhu's description of their *darshan* ('seeing') of the 'Thacoor' where the latter passed on his message to fight the Sahibs and the Mahajans (money-lenders) in writing (Guha 1983, pp. 54–5). Never before in South Asian tradition do we hear of prophetic messages delivered to a devotee in writing on a piece of paper. The apotheosis of the graphic form of expression instantly worked as an appropriation of the power the British had installed in written words.

that the Acts of the Permanent Settlement, as a clear departure from past practices, constructed to achieve the permanence of rule for show-men trained in the late eighteenth-century West European school of Progress and rooted in the doctrine of freedom of contract, failed to take into account the peasants' pasts.

CONTINUITY AND CHANGE IN POLICIES AFTER PERMANENT SETTLEMENT

Contrary to the claims of policy-makers, the Settlement could not check rack-renting by the zamindars. To make matters worse, many of the legislations introduced after the Settlement increased the powers of zamindars and further crippled the raiyats. Within years, the devastating results of the Act became too glaring to be ignored even by the British Parliament: '[T]he Permanent Settlement has produced more distress and beggary, and a greater change in the landed property of Bengal, than has, perhaps, happened in the same space of time, in any other age or country, by the mere effect of legislation.'[9]

Agrarian policies after 1793 and before the transfer of power (1947) are customarily divided into two phases, up to 1857 and after that date.[10] Metcalf (1963) is of the opinion that in pre-1857 years there was a genuine tension between those who championed laissezfaire (i.e. free dealings in land by the zamindar) and those who sympathized with the interests of tenants and their traditional rights in land. The 'Mutiny' of 1857, however, forced the English to realize that traditional elites were still a force to reckon with and thus acknowledge the inadvisability of interfering with their prerogatives. Hence the view that any lasting reform could only come from within Indian society

[9] *Fifth Report*, House of Lords (1812), quoted in L. Natrajan (1953, p. 9). Seven years later, Lord Hastings, a great admirer of Cornwallis, had the following to note:

> Never was there any measure conceived in a purer spirit of generous humanity and disinterested justice than the plan for the Permanent Settlement in the lower provinces. It was worthy of the soul of Cornwallis, yet his truly benevolent purpose fashioned with great care and deliberation, has, to our painful knowledge, subjected almost the whole of the lower classes throughout these provinces to the most grievous oppression, too, so guaranteed by our pledge that we are unable to relieve the sufferers. (P.C. Roy Chaudhury 1966, pp. 566–7)

[10] See Metcalf 1963; Rothermund 1978; Rakesh Gupta 1982.

and only with the support of the influential (native) classes. To strengthen his argument, Metcalf recalls Charles Wingfield, the Chief Commissioner of Awadh. The Commissioner was opposed to tenant right on principle and considered it 'an invasion of the rights of property' (Metcalf 1963, p. 78). Rakesh Gupta (1982, p. 6), however, maintains that in the first phase the zamindars were given enormous powers to collect the rent from the raiyats causing hardships to the latter. In the second phase the imbalance thus created was sought to be corrected, at least partially.[11]

On 29 August 1799, the Government of Bengal passed Regulation VII, known as *haftam* or *Qanun haftam*.[12] This regulation enabled zamindars to distrain the crops, cattle, and personal property of defaulting raiyats and tenants for arrears. The formality of serving fifteen days notice before the attachment of the defaulter's property was also done away with. Further provisions were made to ensure that the defaulter did not abscond with his moveable property.

Symbolically, at least, the most damaging element of the regulation was the one that forced open the zenana, the *antah-pur*, or female apartment, the innermost space of the peasant household. Now in the presence of an official, the distrainer, the zamindar, could take away the outer door, the *chaukhat*, or *darwaza*, that stood between the inner and the outer world of the raiyat. Unable to guard the zenana, and, allegorically, the women of the house, he was henceforth naked. The humiliation of not being able to protect the *izzat* (dignity) of his household must have weighed heavier than the pain of all cultural injuries put together. As this was a male world, it was exclusively *his* duty to protect the honour of the womenfolk of his household. There was no economic rationality behind this new regulation, for the price of a door could hardly compensate for the arrears of rent. If anything, it was first and foremost a cultural assault on the stubborn kisans; and it

[11] The difference could probably be explained in terms of their varying perceptions of the nature of the 1857 uprising. Metcalf holds the traditional view in which the landed aristocracy had a crucial part to play. The 'revisionist' school, however, rightly pays significant attention to the role of the peasantry and other lower classes. Scholars of the latter school explain shifts, if at all, in post-1857 British policies in the light of peasant 'disturbances': notable among them were Santhal Rebellions (1855), the 1857 Revolt, Pabna Uprisings (1870s), Deccan Riots (1870s), and those which followed the famines of the early 1880s.

[12] For details, see Sinha 1968, Chapter VI.

hurt them. Being the mirror image of the enemy as far as the chauvinistic order of things was concerned, the British probably knew this only too well.

The rule, known as *kurki zabti* in popular parlance, lives vividly in the minds of the people of the region in the form of a socially abusive term. The persistence of its memory concurs with the fact that a socio-cultural onslaught was considered probably far more damaging than any degree of exploitation in the realm of economy. More often than not, it proved to be a much stronger mobilizer. As Guha remarks in the case of the mid-nineteenth-century Santhal uprisings, 'in one of those unpredictable leaps of consciousness, prestige suddenly assumed for them an importance exceeding that of money . . .' (Guha 1983, p. 143).[13]

In any event, 'the law was passed in the bonafide belief that tenants were at fault, that the hands of the landlord needed strengthening, and that his power would be exercised fairly, and that the courts would give relief if needed' (Baden-Powell 1892, p. 635). We have already noted people's aversion for the law courts. Together with the inevitability of its abuse, 'this law produced the most evil results. . . . [I]t is difficult to read its monstrous provisions without indignation', remarked Baden-Powell (ibid., p. 636). Within a year, A. Tufton, Magistrate and Judge of Behar, found out that there were two hundred tenants in jail under the *haftam* rule. Upon enquiry he learned that 'all [complaints] were false' (quoted in Sinha 1968, p. 112). He called the act 'a most daring robbery'. Regarding the hope of redressal from a court, Tufton sums it all: 'One man whose cause was under investigation plainly told me that my requiring his attendance was adding to the loss he had sustained, and that the best thing I could do for him would be to let him return home' (ibid., p. 113).

The *diwani adalat* (usually translated in contemporary texts as a court for trying revenue and other civil 'causes'[14]) was notoriously expensive, primarily due to its time-consuming procedures. Zamindars, fully aware of this fact, took optimum advantage by dragging tenants to courts. C.F. Sealy, the Judge of Tirhut, wrote to the Acting Registrar to the Court of Sadar Diwani Adalat that 'there was scarcely a *bigha* of

[13] Similar observations have been made by Mukherjee and Yadav (1980) for peasant movements as late as the 1970s.

[14] Notice the semantics of imperial concern: the complaints lodged in the courts were 'causes', not cases.

land that had not become a subject of dispute because of the promulgation of Regulation VII of 1799' (ibid.).

Qanun haftam, however, made it necessary for zamindars to appoint patwaris who would be responsible for the maintenance of accounts and provide the court with relevant information in cases of litigation. This too proved to be a farce as far as the welfare of tenants was concerned, since patwaris were to be appointed and paid by the zamindars! Zamindars could easily make the patwaris party to the framing of tenants. In addition, not all zamindars could be forced to appoint patwaris. This is poignantly brought out in the following song composed by Shivsharan Pathak of Champaran around the beginning of the twentieth century:

> राम नाम भइल भोर गांव लिलहा के भइले
> चंवर दहे सब धान गैंड़े लील बोअइले।
> भाई भइल अमील के राज प्रजा सब भइले दुखी
> मिल-जुल लूटे गांव गुमास्ता हो पटवारी सुखी।
> असामी नावं पटवारी लिखे, गुमास्ता बतलावे
> सुजावलजी जपत करसु, साहेब मारन धावे।[15]

> [The village now belongs to the *Angrez* who insists on the cultivation of indigo. The lowlands are washed away, the highlands of paddy have been turned into indigo fields. *Amlas* rule the roost, the subjects are unhappy. With *gumasta* they are out to loot and the patwari prospers. Tenants' names are identified by the *gumasta* and recorded by the patwari. Our property is seized and confiscated by the tahsildar, the saheb (Englishman) rushes to beat us.]

Hubback (1928) recommended abolition of the patwari system, but the Board of Revenue continued to believe that 'it would be useful for . . . granting rent receipts to raiyats and helping proper valuations of the crops in *danabandi* (a produce rent system)' (Gupta 1982, p. 14).

By 1811 it was officially accepted that the law of distrain was disastrous for tenants, and, presumably as a corrective measure, Regulation V of 1812 or the *qanun panjam* was introduced (ibid.). It was a feeble attempt to fix *pargana* rates and abolished the ten-year limit on leases. The time frame for the latter was now to be arrived at by mutual

[15] Compiled in Shri Durgashankar Prasad Singh 1958, pp. 161–2.

agreement between zamindar and tenants.[16] Certain changes were also made in relation to the attachment of tenant property. It was made binding on zamindars to hand over their demands in writing to the defaulting tenant before attaching his property. Ploughs and plough-cattle were exempted from distraint and sale.

The political philosophy of the agrarian policy, however, did not change much. The state refused to intervene between the zamindar and the raiyat. In the absence of records of tenants' rights and laws requiring written proof, zamindars could freely oppress the tenantry. The state was not interested in procuring any kind of tenant rights of record, nor did it take any steps to bring rapacious zamindars to book. To worsen the situation further, as it were, the Court made a raiyat liable to action if he complained against the zamindar but failed to prove charges. By *qanun panjam* even the half-open door of justice was closed for the raiyat (Natrajan 1953). In other words, the state was just not there when its laws were being openly violated, for it knew who the law-breakers were and how crucial they were to the survival of the Empire.

Cosmetic alterations apart, the policy ran on the same track up to

[16] The mutual settlement, popularly known as *kabuliat*, was a misnomer. The tenants were forced to show up at the zamindar's office, *kachahari*, and were detained until they signed the *kabuliat* for the rent on zamindar's terms (Sinha 1968, p. 114). Sometimes the forced rate of rent used to be twice as high as the old rent (*The Administrative Report of Bengal for 1872–3*, pp. 146–9, quoted in Dhanagare 1986, p. 38). During the same period of Pabna and Bogra uprisings, 'the peasants in large numbers seized and destroyed the agreement forms-kabuliyats' (p. 39).

These *kachaharis* were places of torture and even the lynching of tenants. People in rural Bihar today remember these *kachaharis* as sites where parading tenant women naked or raping them was routine. Official documents do not speak on this issue. But the fact that a people chooses to nourish a particular memory is in itself a strong enough case to demand a sympathetic hearing from historians. Some guesses could be made on the account that the Government in 1859 had to legislate against this practice of zamindars forcing attendance (Gupta 1982, p. 18). The Act of 1885, by making any enhancement out of suit illegal, further attacked the 'ritual practices' at the *kachahari* in the name of *kabuliat*. Showing up at the zamindar's *kachahari* was a part of the quotidian ritual required for underlining and thus reproducing the power relations. When the Act of 1885 allowed the raiyats to send their rents by money-order, the zamindars vehemently opposed the Act for one, it gave raiyats a chance to not pay the rent in full, at least temporarily; secondly, it removed the raiyats from the site where the superordination of the former was routinely enacted.

the introduction of Act X of 1859 which provided for a considerable remodelling of the tenant law.[17] The most crucial provision was the division of cultivators into four classes:

> (1) Those who had held their lands at fixed rates of rent since the time of the Permanent Settlement. (2) Those whose rent had not been changed for twenty years. They should be presumed to have held their lands since the permanent settlement. (3) Those who had held lands for twelve years. They were conferred the right of occupancy under which the rent could be enhanced for certain specific reasons, and by a certain procedure. (4) Those who had held the land for less than twelve years. This class did not get any right, but allowed them (unless they were protected by local custom) in the position of mere tenants-at-will. (Gupta 1982, p. 18)

The Act once again required tenants to prove in court the duration of their holdings. If they could do so, the Act was certainly a departure from the previous legislations. But the tenant had little documentary evidence; zamindars rarely granted rent receipts and patwaris or any other officials were barely functioning at the village level (see Mishra 1978). Baden-Powell (1892) sums it up succinctly, 'it gave or professed to give, the raiyat a right which he could not prove . . .' (p. 647). The Secretary to the Government of Bengal, S.C. Bayley, noted in 1877 in his dispatch to the Commissioner of Patna Division that '[W]hat is most wanted there is to provide some ready means of enabling the raiyat to resist illegal distraint, illegal enhancement, and illegal cesses, and to enable him to prove and maintain his occupancy rights where the law gives them' (Yang 1989, p. 164). It was the same story over again, and it makes one wonder if there is any merit in the claim that after 1857, policies tended to turn pro-tenant. The significance of the Act, perhaps, rested in its legal scope, which was more far-reaching than all the previous Acts and Regulations taken together. Not that the tenants had begun to exercise their legal options, all of a sudden, so as to send alarms to the right quarters. However, the Settlement was almost eighty years old and if the tumultuous 1870s was any indication, things were not looking as bright for zamindars as they had before. It was easy for zamindars who knew the laws to see the tilt of the policies increasingly turning in favour of the tiller. In 1878, hundreds of them

[17] Baden-Powell (1974, p. 641) calls it the 'first "modern" tenant law'.

got together to form the Bihar Landholders' Association (ibid., p. 27). The very next year, exactly twenty years after the Act of 1859, once again there was an enquiry, only to admit the flaws of the Act, like a ritual admission of guilt. The enquiry revealed that 'less than one per cent of the sixty per cent who, according to estate rent rolls, had lived and worked in the same area for more than twelve years were in possession of the same plots. Landlords had thwarted the aim of the law by shifting their raiyats to other plots' (ibid., p. 165).

The government realized the need to assure the 'people who plough and sow' of the 'fruits of their industry' which had eluded them in the absence of protection and permanence of holdings and incessant enhancement of rent.[18] As a result came the Bengal Tenancy Act of 1885, that was to be the basis of British agrarian policies untill 1950 when the Permanent Settlement was unsettled for good by a stroke of legislation.

The main thrust of the Act of 1885 was directed towards placing occupancy raiyats in a comparatively strong and secure position requiring them to pay a moderate rent. Unlike the provision of the Act of 1859, the new Act did not require a raiyat to hold *all* his lands for twelve years in order to become a 'settled raiyat'. If he held *any* piece of farm land for twelve years in a village, he was entitled to occupancy status for *all* the lands he held, or might in future hold in that village. No enhancement of rent could take place by 'mutual contract' between him and the zamindar; an enhancement suit was needed for that purpose. And once the rent was increased, no further increment was allowed for the next fifteen years unless the zamindar claimed and proved improvement in the land.

Even a defaulting tenant could not be evicted except in the execution of a decree. Distraints too were curtailed, since now they were possible only through the civil courts. More important, notwithstanding the distraint, tenants were permitted to reap the crop. In an oblique admission of the abuse of the legal apparatus, the Act imposed a minimum three-month interval before the zamindar could bring a new rent suit against his tenant.

A highly significant aspect of the Act was its gesture toward local customs and usages: '[N]othing in this Act shall affect,' it maintained,

[18] *Selections From Papers Relating to the Bengal Tenancy Act, 1885*, Calcutta, 1920, pp. 7, 11; quoted in Mishra 1978, p. 154.

'any custom, usage or customary right not consistent with, or not expressly or by necessary implication modified or abolished by its provisions' (quoted in Banerjee 1981, p. 278). But the local customs and practices were to be recorded, to whatever little extent, only when the Survey was undertaken by the government in the first decade of the twentieth century. None the less, to some scholars, it was nothing less than a virtual repudiation of the post-Permanent Settlement practice of principles of English law.[19]

To conclude, the legislative enthusiasm of the British notwithstanding, the tenants' condition did not improve with time. In fact, as some scholars have argued, the second half of the nineteenth century was indeed the 'landlord's paradise'.[20] There emerged a far better regulated symbiotic triangle between Empire, zamindar, and money-lender. With improved communication and transport facilities, added by the ever growing tentacles of bureaucratic control, the land, produce, and markets were increasingly linked to the whims of the international market. The logic of the latter demanded more commercially viable crops. A lack of adequate credit institutions propelled money-lenders into unprecedented prominence. Not that moneylending was not significant earlier, but with the provisions of the Permanent Settlement, money-lenders were now seeking lands from defaulters instead of a part of the crop as they did previously. No legislative juggling was of any help. No wonder, in many nineteenth-century peasant uprisings, the triumvirate of sarkar (the British Government), zamindar, and sahukar emerged in league against the kisans and were identified so by the latter. The interlinkages of repression conceptualized in the following folksong also reveal kisan perceptions:

फिकिरिआ मरलस जान।
करजा काढ-काढ़ खेती कइनीं
मर गइले सब धान।
बैला बेच रजवा के देनीं
सहुआ कहेला बईमान।

[19] See, for example, Anil Chandra Banerjee 1981, S.B. Cook 1993, or Baden-Powell 1974.

[20] The expression is taken from Barrington Moore, Jr. 1993 (1966), p. 353. Also see Metcalf 1962. This view can be found in Metcalf's other writings on the subject as well.

> [Anxieties are killing me. Took loans to till the land. Alas, the crops perished. Had to sell the bullock to pay the rent to the state or the zamindar. The money-lender is accusing me of being deceitful. (Ram Talika Singh, Garahani, Bhojpur, 31 January 1996)]

The purpose of this chapter was not the obligatory sketch of the 'economic background' against which kisan 'responses' could be read. This is a familiar way of 'doing history', as 'Cause is made to stand in as a phantom surrogate for Reason' (Ranajit Guha 1983, p. 47). The practice of externalizing elements of consciousness from kisan mentalité emanates from the unit of thought that flourishes on a Liberal diet of Enlightenment. The latter in due course becomes a euphemism for colonial domination over those who were, of course, not endowed with (West) European Reason, Rationality, and Objectivity. This is what some scholars have called 'cultural difference' that was strategically deployed as a 'civilizational lack'; and, hence the legitimization for the colonial enterprise.[21]

[21] See Frantz Fanon 1986 and Homi Bhabha (who develops on Fanon) 1994, especially Chapter III.

CHAPTER 2

Migration and Crime: The Craft of Survival and Protest

> As a figure in a dream dreamt by an unknown sleeper, he appears to act autonomously, at times unexpectedly; but everything he does—unless he revolts—is determined by the needs of the dreamer's mind. Abandon the metaphor. The migrant's intentionality is permeated by historical necessities of which neither he nor anybody he meets is aware. That is why it is as if his life were being dreamt by another.
>
> —JOHN BERGER in *A Seventh Man: The Story of a Migrant Worker in Europe*, 1975

For an Empire of private property erected on the principle of collusion between sea merchants and local landed gentry, almost every attempt by the tilling and toiling millions to survive became a subject of suspicion, treason, and crime. In officialdom crimes were regarded as the first concerted voice of dissent. There was also kisan ridicule of and satire on the dominant. The cynicism, mockery, and laughter of the nineteenth century would probably throw equal light on the dissenting minds. But this is a far more difficult story to tell since instances of derision or mimicry were not as earnestly recorded as openly 'criminal' endeavours were. To write a story of this nature would therefore require far greater speculative indulgence than usually permitted. Unconventional sources are too scanty to be of any help.

Most of the people forced to migrate were either marginal peasants who also worked on others' lands for wages, or landless labourers, some of whom might have tenancy rights over land.[1] However, a clear note of protest in large-scale migrations, which resulted primarily from the unsettling effects of the Permanent Settlement, is conspicuous by its absence. Understandably, the effort was to project economic Reason as the cause of the mass undertakings of migration in the nineteenth century. A chorus of 'pull and push factor', or the rationality of 'supply and demand' of job opportunities is not essentially incorrect, but it inevitably suppresses the cultural pangs that followed in the wake of migrations.

Colonial scribes were not at their best when it came to recording quotidian kisan muttering of disenchantment, disillusion or dismay. Not at least until the beginning of the twentieth century, not in comparison to their meticulous research and documentation of the rebellions or mass movements. The reason largely lies in their perception of what constituted a threat to the survival of the Empire. Nor are the indigenous sources of much help for the interregnum. The annals of Nationalist historiography ritualistically begin either with the rise of the Mahatma on the political horizon of the nation-in-making or nationalize the memory of the nineteenth-century explosive upheavals to manufacture a pre-history of the former (Guha 1982). We are left with little choice but to rely on voices entangled in one-sided official narratives of crime, migration, 'rumour mongering', etc., in order to write about a history of moments between two points of rupture, namely, the nineteenth-century 'uprisings' and the twentieth-century 'mass movements'.

These moments are often rendered dormant without pausing to explain what holds the space/distance between any two points of explosion. In other words, one must account for not only the production and sustenance of visible ruptures, but also for quiet periods that actually produce the ideological adrenaline for the former. A disagreement with this formulation could only be sustained at the cost of declaring explosions as 'spontaneous' acts of irrational/emotional fit,

[1] '[I]n 1930, when the Royal Commission collected twenty life histories of jute workers [in Calcutta], there were thirteen workers who had almost no income from land. The Labour Investigation Committee of 1944 also noted that there were some workers who had small plots and others who had just tenancy rights. The Jagaddal survey found that 41.3 per cent of the workers owned some land but almost 60 per cent had very little or no land' (Samita Sen 1999, p. 67).

devoid of ideology, 'rebellions of the belly' as opposed to rebellions of the mind.[2]

MIGRATORY MOVEMENTS

Emigration has always arisen mainly from the difficulty of finding an adequate livelihood in one's native place. . . . In most areas, pressure on the land has been increasing for a long time. . . . The loss of land through indebtedness, the need or desire of a landlord to his own cultivation, quarrels, the death of the title-holder and other causes, bring fresh recruits to this class [of labourers]. Among those who retain tenancies, various changes may operate to render a holding insufficient for those dependent on it. An increase in the number of members of the family, a rise in rent, the growth of debt, all contribute to force the agricultural worker to abandon his ancestral occupation. (*Report of the Royal Commission on Labour in India*, 1931)

To move away from the immediate site of exploitation is an 'option' that has historically been sought, all over the world, with varying degrees of success. Migratory movements may not offer long-lasting respite from everyday drudgery, but the temporary relief that they provide is of great importance. People who exercise this 'option' do so in a desperate move for survival. To leave the place of domicile for an unknown destination is certainly a difficult decision that cannot be taken ordinarily. It must involve, therefore, a cautious evaluation of things in an extraordinary situation.[3]

It is customary to assign varying degrees of importance to seasonal migration, permanent emigration, and desertion. Seasonal migrants return to their 'original' place and not all members of a household may move. A permanent emigrant moves to settle somewhere other than his/her place of origin, and so there is an effort to move collectively, with as many family members as possible. Therefore, the sense of being uprooted is total. Desertions, on the other hand, are depicted as forced,

[2] These are E.P. Thompson's phrases from 'The Moral Economy of the Crowd in the Eighteenth Century', 1991.

[3] There are also scholars to whom migration was 'rural households' releasing 'the surplus adult men' to urban centres. See for instance Samita Sen 1999, pp. 55, 67. Sen's preoccupation with women's labour somehow lends her a rather curious understanding of the political economy of the time. See her Chapter II (pp. 54-88).

or non-voluntary (Yang 1989, p. 181). They are said to often carry the propensity of 'avoidance protest'.[4] The voluntary–non-voluntary dichotomy echoes the language of economics where 'pull' factors are supposed to cause migration, but 'push' factors explain desertions.

The distinction may not be wholly untrue. A permanent displacement is surely more unsettling than seasonal migration. However, this in itself may not essentially mean that a higher degree of consciousness is involved in such acts. If we view the issue from the vantage point of a woman, or of a family, the problematic begins to unfold newer dimensions. In en masse migrations, the family may remain intact; husbands and wives are together, so are the children with their parents.

More often than not, male members undertook seasonal migrations in our area of study, while women and children were forced to stay back and wait for their return. The separation may have been far more traumatic when the existing power hierarchy in a village made women's positions vulnerable. In rural Bihar, for instance, 'jokes' about the wife conceiving while the husband was away are commonplace. Speculation about the identity of the biological father of the child becomes a collective preoccupation in the form of incessant gossip. The pressure on a woman to stay faithful and prove her fidelity is added to the overall grief of separation. There have been some works on certain parts of Africa where historians have seen the frequent dispatches of 'medicinal' herbs sent by male migrants to their wives, to guarantee latter's fidelity, as signs of labourers' homesickness.[5] It might be equally worthwhile to diagnose 'male anxiety' and focus on the pain of the women waiting for their respective spouses braving the pressures of 'remaining faithful'. Research on this theme is yet to be taken up in studies of migrations in Bihar.

Folksongs are almost routinely cited in studies on migration to show the pathos of women whose husbands are far away, but often only to spice up, or add an exotic flavour to, the overall story. The feminine trauma of loneliness melts into the hands of male narrators only to become sheer frills of the central story. The folklorist who collects and translates these songs (for sociologists and historians), invariably

[4] See for example, Adas 1981; Asiwaju 1976; Irfan Habib 1963; Anand Yang 1989.

[5] See Gordon 1977 and Murray 1981.

ignores—and thereby suppresses—even the most explicit male biases in them. How women themselves can begin to internalize and reproduce those biases is another point often neglected.

According to the Census of 1891, by the end of that decade, over 2,26,000 people had migrated from Bihar to the districts of Bengal alone.[6] One-third of the total emigrants of Gaya district went to Calcutta (Samita Sen 1999, p. 66). Of the total immigrants in Assam 45 per cent, i.e. 2,75,000 labourers, came from the Santhal Pargana and Chotanagpur between 1885 and 1900.[7] '[T]he number of persons absent from their districts at the time of the [1911] census [was] 279,000 more than in 1901' (L.S.S. O'Malley 1913, p. 172). Around this time in south Bihar the emigrants equalled 8 per cent of the total population, a ratio double that of north Bihar (ibid.). Calcutta and other towns of Bengal were the chief recipients, 'three-tenths of the absentees from Patna, Gaya and Shahabad being enumerated there' (ibid., p. 182). The tea gardens of Assam were also destinations for Biharis living south of the Ganga: they numbered 46,000 according to the 1911 Census, of which 15,000 were born in Shahabad, 13,000 each in Munghyr and Gaya and 5,000 in Patna (ibid.).

Except Champaran and Purnea, where immigration exceeded emigrations due to the sparse population and vast tracts of unclaimed land, immigration was on the rise in all the districts of north Bihar. The Census of 1891 returned the following figures:

> . . . in Saran the immigrants . . . [N]umber no less than 284,000 or one-eighth of the population. In the remaining three districts the number varies from 168,000 in Bhagalpur and 176,000 in Darbhanga to 195,000 in Muzzafarpur, the percentage of the total population being 8, 6, and 7 respectively. (ibid., pp. 181–2)

Of all the districts in north Bihar, Saran topped the list of emigration throughout the nineteenth and the early twentieth centuries.[8] 'Saran not only had a high population density, but its southern thanas, from

[6] The figure is derived from *Census of India, 1891*, vol. 5, pp. 106-44.

[7] I am grateful to Rana Pratap Behal for permitting me to use this information from his unpublished paper, 'The Emergence of a Plantation Economy: Assam Tea Industry in the Nineteenth Century', *Occasional Papers*, NMML, vol. XXI, 1985, p. 23.

[8] For an extensive survey of Saran, see Yang 1989.

TABLE 1: MIGRANTS FROM BIHAR TO BENGAL, 1891

Districts of Bengal	*Male*	*Female*	*Total*
Bardwan	8,513	3,633	12,146
Bankura	788	194	982
Birbhum	2,368	834	3,202
Midnapur	1,909	615	2,524
Hugli	4,463	1,677	6,140
Howrah	13,942	4,049	17,991
24-Parganas	19,271	9,870	29,141
Nadia	3,839	936	4,775
Jessor	1,693	322	2,015
Murshidabad	6,589	4,280	10,869
Kulna	1,790	158	1,948
Dinajpur	13,000	5,563	18,563
Rajshahi	4,007	2,485	6,492
Rangpur	22,549	1,420	23,969
Bogra	6,737	880	7,617
Pabna	5,316	758	6,074
Darjeeling	8,060	1,324	9,384
Jalpaiguri	12,529	4,216	16,745
Dacca	15,484	1,579	17,063
Faridpur	4,282	440	4,772
Bakharganj	2,161	293	2,454
Maimansingh	15,626	977	16,603
Chittagong	754	169	923
Noakhali	149	20	169
Tippera	3,974	185	4,159
Chittagong Hill Tracts	76	7	83
Grand Total	17,9869	46,884	2,26,753

Percentage of Male Migrants: 79.32
Percentage of Female Migrants: 20.67

SOURCE: *Census of the Lower Provinces of Bengal, 1891*, by C.J. O'Donnell, Calcutta: Bengal Secretariat Press, 1893.

which outmigration was the heaviest, were the most crowded and demanded higher rent rates than the relatively nonmigrating northern areas' (Yang 1989, pp. 195–6). Recurrent floods made things worse for those on the margin.

In addition to internal migration, there was consistent effort on the part of British agencies, governmental and private, to recruit indentured labourers for their colonies abroad after the abolition of slavery in the British Empire in 1834. 'The shortage of agricultural labour arising out of the virtual refusal of the liberated slaves to work in the sugar plantations of Mauritius, British Guyana, Trinidad and Jamaica threatened the existence of the sugar industries there.' (Panchanan Saha 1970, p. 1). By the middle of the 1840s, India had become the major source of workers for the West Indian sugar colonies (ibid., p. 17). The number of hill coolies from Chotanagpur, Shahabad, Bankura, etc., gradually declined, partly due to heavy mortality at sea and partly because of competition for labour from the tea districts of Assam (ibid., p. 29). Yet, the number of Indian labourers who went to Mauritius, British Guyana, Trinidad and Jamaica in the nineteenth century neared 7,00,000 (ibid., p. 1).

In Mauritius alone, the Indians numbered over 2,25,000 by the end of the nineteenth century (Kuber Mishra 1981, p. 36). The 1911 Census put the figure of overseas emigrants from Bengal at 11,667 of which 'more than half came from Bihar, 3473 being residents of Shahabad and 1109 of Patna' (O'Malley 1913, p. 174). The records of emigration from the districts of Bihar (and Bengal) are misleading principally because most of the emigrants recruited from Calcutta and other districts of Bengal were labourers from Bihar who had come there in search of jobs. For this reason, their number does not appear in the district records for Bihar.

Internal/seasonal migration, as the tables suggest, was the preferred option despite government's consistent effort to recruit people for the colonies. Hunter's volumes on the different parts of Bihar confirm the trend represented in Table 2. Lower-caste people overall emigrated in much larger numbers than people from higher castes, but in north Bihar the latter dominated. As a reason for the emigration of the lower caste people, 'feudal and social oppressions' have been cited (Saha 1970, p. 47), 'but the causes of the emigration of the upper caste Hindu population cannot be explained only by social oppression or feudal exploitation' (ibid., p. 48). What is even more puzzling is the fact that scholars concerned with the issue of migration are yet to realize and raise this problematic. Saha, in general, states that 'the great Sepoy Mutiny of 1857-58 indirectly worked as an impetus to

TABLE 2: MIGRATION ABROAD

Destination	*High Caste*	*Low Caste*	*Muslim*	*Total*
		SARAN (1869–74)		
Mauritius	351	247	224	812
Demerara	374	292	181	847
Trinidad	84	83	52	219
Surinam*	45	20	16	81
Jamaica	90	94	57	241
		TIRHUT (1869–74)		
Mauritius	152	111	90	353
Demerara	146	130	93	369
Trinidad	27	32	18	77
Surinam	26	24	13	63
Jamaica	21	33	21	75
		SHAHABAD (1869–74)		
Mauritius	707	2425	487	3,619
Demerara	377	1631	281	2,289
Trinidad	147	573	93	813
Jamaica	76	393	85	554

NOTE: *Figure available only for 1872–4.

SOURCE: W.W. Hunter, *A Statistical Account of Bengal*, vols. XI, XII and XIII, 1976 (rpt), first published 1877.

emigration among a considerable number of high-caste Hindus in those troubled years' (ibid., p. 75). This explanation too is not of much help. As the table shows, the high-caste migration in larger numbers continues well after the troubled years of 1857. More importantly, this does not tell us why the high caste members of Shahabad, Gaya and Patna did not migrate in larger numbers: there, the uprising of 1857 was much more widespread than in any district of north Bihar.[9]

This riddle brings us face to face with the state of migration studies

[9] Needless to say, this requires further research. Yang's (1989) book which is a marvel of empirical investigation, remains insensitive to this problematicprimarily because his method cannot handle the collectivity that caste carried in the nineteenth century. See my review of this book, 1996.

in the country. Most studies, according to a review of publications between 1948 and 1970, remain preoccupied with macro-level movements and ignore the local landscape (see Anand Yang 1989). As a consequence we do not have information on many crucial issues. Unless we take up micro-level studies, we shall never know about the nature of dynamics at the village or district level. Whether it was the relative high density of population in the region, or the upper stratum was weaker compared to its central and southern counterpart, and whether the upper castes in the north were more mobile and relatively better equipped to take risks than the upper castes of central and northern Bihar, are questions that remain until we can refocus our studies towards people and their environment.

MIGRATION AND WOMAN IN FOLKSONGS

> गवना कराई सइयां घर बइठवले से
> अपने लोभइले परदेस रे बिदेसिया।[10]
>
> [After marriage my husband ensconced me in his house and himself got lured by foreign lands.]

Historical treatises, are almost invariably inadequate in their analysis of the cultural meanings of migration, which remained by and large a male enterprise. As the figures on migration to Bengal (Table 1) indicate, female migrants were 20-odd per cent of the total number of migrants. While husbands were away, women were left to fend for themselves in more than one way. Their pangs of separation, along with their response to 'male anxiety', found expression in songs. These songs remain scattered and uncatalogued, posing a fierce challenge to interlocutors in the field. For instance, in some cases it is possible to guess that women could not have written them. Women's yearnings in most of these folksongs are male representations, because they were authored by men. Thus such songs present a problem of representation. In the process of depicting women's pangs of separation, for example, male composers often voiced their own anxieties and concerns, which were invariably loaded with patriarchal values and flattering to the male ego. The preoccupation with female yearnings was geared to-

[10] Bhikhari Thakur composed this Bhojpuri song for his play, *Bidesia*. Cited in Shri Durgashankar Prasad Singh 1958, pp. 221–2.

wards safeguarding existing patriarchies. As a result, we rarely come across songs that depict male longing. Even so, such songs are a far superior source for understanding lived experience than the routine notes of an administrator or chronicler. It is possible to read these songs critically to learn how society was affected by the sudden exodus of male population. What John Berger says about stories is also apt for folksongs: they constitute 'daily history' allowing 'the whole village to define itself', to become a 'living portrait of itself: a communal portrait, in that everybody is portrayed and everybody portrays . . . [it] is constructed . . . out of words, spoken and remembered . . . [I]t is a continuous portrait; work on it never stops' (John Berger 1979, p. 9).

The qualifier, extremely relevant in our case, is that there does not emerge a single harmonious portrait, as there are always many artistes with various thoughts and tastes. Let us turn to some of these songs.

रे बदरा मति बरसु एहि देसवा
रे बदरा बरसु ललनजी के देसवा
बदरा हुनके भिंजाव सिर टोपिआ रे बदरा।
एक त बैरिन भेल सासु ननदिया
दोसर बैरिन तुहुं भइले रे बदरा
मति बरसु एहि देसवा।[11]

In this song, composed in *malar* form in Maithili (the lingua franca of the larger Darbhanga in north Bihar), the woman asks the cloud not to rain:[12]

O cloud, do not rain here
Go to the land where lives my man
Drench his hat
Already, my mother and sister-in-law are hostile to me
O cloud, be not my enemy too.
Do not rain here.

In the following *chaitawar*, she laments that the tormenting month

[11] Cited in Rahul Sankrityayan (ed.) 1960.

[12] Sankrityayan (1960). There are songs specific to months and seasons. They can be found in almost every form/style of Bihari folk-lore: *chaita/chaitawar, phag/phagua/holi, jhoomar, sohar, malar, kajari*, etc. They also appear in *nirgun, nachari/alchari* and *barahmasa* which are sung throughout the year, anywhere, any time of day.

of *Chait* (March-April) has already arrived, but her husband's letter has not.

नइ भेजे पतिया।
आयल चैत उत्पतिया हो रामा
नइ भेजे पतिया। (वही)

The following Magahi song (spoken in Patna, Gaya and parts of Bhagalpur), has the woman at a loss not knowing how to cope with the fact that her beloved is away:

गत-गते बिरहा के पेंसल अगिनियां
करिआ बदरिआ में जइसे चंदनियां
बिसरे बिसरल न बतिया, सुरतिया
कइसे के सुधि बिसराऊं हे
कहमा पिया केरा गांऊ हे। (वही)

[Slowly . . . the fire of separation cuts into (my being)
Just like the moon enters the cloud
Try hard as I may, I can't
Forget his words, his face
How do I banish him from my head?
Who knows which hamlet he lives in?]

In the following Bhojpuri *nirgun*, we hear of the difficulty faced by a woman in raising her son alone as the husband has gone to the East:[13]

पिया मोरे गइले रामा पुरुबि बनिजिया
कि देके गइले ना, एक सुगना खिलौनवा कि देके गइले ना।
तोरा के खिलइबो सुगना दूध-भात कौरवा
कि लेके सुतबो ना, दुनो जोबना के बीचवा कि लेके सुतबो ना।
घरि राति गइले, पहर राति गइले
सुगवा काटे लगले ना, मोरे चोलिया के बनवा कि काटे लगले ना।
अस मन करे सुगवा भुइयां ले पटकिती
कि दुजे मनवां ना, मोरे सामी के खिलौनवा कि दुजे मनवा ना।[14]

[13] In the plains of Bihar, 'moving to the East' was a euphemism for the large-scale migrations to Bengal in general and Calcutta in particular.

[14] Ibid. With some variation Singh (1958, p. 178) accredits this song to one Jagardev about whom, he admits, not much is known.

[My lover has gone for the business in the East
And left me a parrot to play with
I'll feed you milk and rice
I'll cuddle you in my breasts as we sleep
As the night climbs on
The parrot pecks at my blouse
I feel like flinging you, then I do not
After all, you are my lord's toy.][15]

The husband often returns with a *sautan*, another wife, in these songs.

पिया मोरे गइले रामा हुगली सहरवा से लेई अइले ना
एक बंगालिन रे सेवतिया, से लेई रे अइले ना।
सवती के ताना मोहिं लागेला जहरवा, कहरवा डाले ना
मोर कसकत छतिया, कहरवा डाले ना।

[My beloved went to Hugali city and brought back a Bengali *sautan*. Her snide remarks are like poison, they kill me. My breasts throb (with unfulfilled desire); I am tortured.]

Some songs carry explicit sexual yearnings and responses to (and, thus, inversion of) 'male anxiety'. The responsibility of straying is handed over to the husband who stays away:

अमवां मोजरि गइले लगले टिकोरवा से
दिन पर दिन पियराला रे बिदेसिया।
एक दिन बही जइहें जुलुमी बेयरिया से
डाड़ पात जइहें भहराई रे बिदेसिया।

[The Mangoes have come up.
They are beginning to ripen.
One day a stormy wind may blow away everything.][16] (Singh 1958, p. 221)

[15] *Sugana*, *sugawa*, or *sugga* literally means a parrot; however, in folksongs it is often used as a metaphor for son. In our context, however, it is suggestively ambivalent; the parrot is simply a 'substitute' for the husband in whose absence the woman may pass her time talking and playing with it. 'Tota', another Bhojpuri word for parrot, as a common metaphor for the (male) lover, and 'maina' for the beloved, are found in many legendary love-stories. In all the stories they go through a highly testing time before the happy ending arrives; sometimes it requires another life, another birth. Taken as son, parrot's pecking at the brace of the blouse, therefore, is supposed to convey a child's insistence for milk.

[16] The mango is a common metaphor for the breast.

The warning is loud and clear. Unfulfilled yearning could very likely result in the woman's infidelity for which she alone is not responsible. Contrasted with songs by other male composers, there is a remarkable difference as this song hints at women's agency; she does not merely pine away. Perhaps such a possibility was envisaged by Bhikhari Thakur, who by profession was a female impersonator and could transgress the male world. Patriarchies limited the understanding of most male composers to the extent that they were unable to comprehend woman's emotions and desires, despite claiming to represent women's agony. How the woman would survive when the man left, was the refrain. Once again the centrality of man in the woman's universe was re-iterated.

Sometimes patriarchies use the trope of bodily pain:

नथिया के गूंज टुटि गइल रे देवरा
मोर नइहर में अनाड़ी सोनरवा।
रात अन्हारि पिया डर लागे
पिया परदेस कड़के मोर छतिया।

[The pin of my nose ring has broken off, O *devara*
The goldsmith at my mother's is no good
The night is dark, I am scared
My heart throbs . . . you are in another land.] (Sankrityayan 1960)

At the subconscious level, a thorn in the foot, a nose-ring or an earring—all conjure up images of pierced woman's body. They are also markers of patriarchal control. The 'thorn in the foot' is a widely used metaphor; to pull it out, the husband must come back. The thorn as a phallic symbol signifies male control over the 'straying' foot of the female. It could be an allegoric expression of infidelity and the resultant pain of guilt or shame. Similarly, the broken pin of the nose-ring or the loss of an earring can also be read as threats to woman's marital status. They act as metaphors for broken reins, or the disappearance of the harness, due to which the woman is scared in the dark of the night. The allusion to the goldsmith in the natal home suggests that going back to the parents' place is no solution. Rather patriarchy remains intact and she stays on in the marital home. In the absence of her husband, the husband's younger brother must take charge to remove the fear.[17]

[17] The *devar* has always been confidant of the woman with whom there is no avoidance as in case of relationships with male agnates older than the husband. The

To read the pin of the nose-ring as a phallic symbol is not a speculative exercise as the shifts from the breaking of the ring to the unfeasibility of going to the natal home, to the coming of the night and the consequent fear which must be assuaged by the younger brother-in-law, occur almost abruptly. And yet there is a logic and taken-for-granted manner within which these shifts become possible. Patriarchy remains in place.

MEMORY OF MIGRATION: WOMEN IN FUTURE LAND STRUGGLES

The scale of migration and its sociological impact on everyday life is reflected in an extensive range of folksongs. Their quotidian pervasiveness proves, on the one hand, the trauma of separation and on the other, women's desire to express it. The forms *nachari* in Maithili and *alchari* in Bhojpuri are said to have derived their names from the Hindi word *lachari*, which literally means, helplessness (Sankrityayan 1960, p. 151). And what could have been a better script for this form than separation of husbands and wives brought forth by migration?

Although it is difficult to show a running thread between these experiences and women's militant participation in the struggles for secured tenancy during the 1930s, it might well be that the memory of separation that was kept alive, fuelled their future struggles. It might have added to women's resolve, and this was forcefully exhibited in their non-violent resistance against arbitrary rent hikes and evictions by zamindars. The 1930s was also a decade when it was no longer feasible or safe for males to sustain and carry forward peaceful struggles. Migration could have influenced women's role in future land struggles in yet another way.

That seasonal (male) migrations took place during the lean period of agriculture and the migrants returned during the peak season to attend to agricultural work is nothing short of a myth.[18] Most migrant work-

---

physical and emotional proximity underlying this relationship has usually enjoyed cultural legitimacy in Hindu north India.

[18] *The Report of the Indian Industrial Commission, 1916–18*, Calcutta, 1917–18, uncritically accepted the 'findings' of the *Report of the Indian Factory Labour Commission of 1908*, according to which the workers from Calcutta mills returned to their respective villages to harvest the crop.

ers returned during the months of May and June, which had hardly any agricultural activity.[19] In the region, rabi season is well over by May, and June is too early for the kharif.[20] What this entails is that most jobs (except ploughing, probably every other productive activity) in the field were done by women, which in turn must have boosted their confidence and enhanced their relationship with the land, in addition to imparting a sense of belonging hitherto quite unknown to them. Various contemporary documents establish women's predominance in agricultural work.[21] In militant struggles for land in the 1930s, it can thus be concluded, women were not merely fighting to protect a 'supplementary income'. The kisan women of Bihar are likely to have realized that their lives and fortunes revolved around the possession of land and remembered that the prevalent patriarchal norms made a single woman's life, that too without access to land, miserable.

CRIME

It is exactly in a rural society, where any open, identified resistance to the ruling power may result in instant retaliation . . . that one tends to find the acts of darkness. . . . [E.P. Thompson (1991) in 'Patricians and Plebs']

In the month of November, after the Rubbee is sown crowds of Gowallahs [Ahirs], Dosadhs and even Rajputs leave their homes ostensibly on a pilgrimage, but in reality on thieving expeditions: the weeding & c of their field is carried on by their wives and younger offspring[s], and when the rubbee is ready to be cut, the campaign is over and back they all come with their spoil. ['Yearly Statement for 1854', quoted in Anand Yang (1989)]

[19] See B. Foley 1906, particularly para 83.

[20] Samita Sen (1999, p. 73) makes this argument forcefully with additional information on famine relief operations of 1896–7. She ponders why male migrants returned during the lean season of agriculture, but provides no answer. One possible reason could be to negotiate tenancy deals for the coming year. Details of tenancy are finalized in the months of May and June. This reiterates that landlords changed tenants frequently, enhancing the latter's insecurity and anxieties. Second, it should have been relevant to Sen that this helped continue the practice of decision-making by the men of the family, even when they were not there most of the year to do agriculture themselves.

[21] See, for instance, *The Census of 1911; Bihar and Orissa District Gazetteers*, Saran (1930); Stevenson-Moore's report on *The Material Condition of Small Agriculturalists and Labourers in Gaya* (1898).

Peasants' recourse to 'crime' during testing times has become an important issue in academic enquiry since Eric Hobsbawm's *Bandits* (1969), preceded by yet another provocative study, *Primitive Rebels* (1959).[22] Along with George Rudé, Hobsbawm advocated the need to identify the 'social' elements that pushed the rural/urban poor to pursue measures not favourable to the law. Taking a brave step forward from the prevalent 'commonsensical' belief couched in the jargon of modern criminology, Hobsbawn and Rudé invited historians and social anthropologists to cull out the radical/political from the 'criminal' endeavours of the people. The ideological thread may be found running as far back as the essays of Hobsbawm published in *Labouring Men*, where he refused to treat machine-breakers as mindless creatures devoid of political ideology.

In the 1970s, criminality was discussed even more sharply, with the focus on political ideology and law. E.P. Thompson and his colleagues at the University of Warwick undertook local studies of rioters, smugglers, and poachers to redeem the historicity of crimes from getting lost in the quagmire of official criminology.[23] Since law mediates class relations and, in turn, class relations find expression in the forms of law, crime had to be viewed at the locus of ideology (Thompson 1975). Yet other adherents to the 'moral economy' thesis point out that the eroding traditional patronage system in the wake of the capitalist onslaught resulted in a spurt of agrarian crimes. According to this school, the traditional mechanism of extraction used to function with a promise to protect the peasantry under a mutually agreed code of morality. The 'benevolence' of the feudal lord in turn demanded regular payment of rent and services from the peasant. A breach from any party was the moral justification for the other to protest. This immediately sought to undermine economically reductionist arguments.[24]

[22] One of the first essays, of this generation, linking crime with bloated prices in England was by R.B. Rose 1961.

[23] See Hay, Linebaugh and Thompson 1975; Thompson 1975a and 1978.

[24] See Scott (1976, 1986). Dale Edward Williams (1976) also argues against economic reductionism. Lewin (1979) appeals for caution against romanticization of social banditry for it was still (a) very much located within the structures of patronage and (b) it was 'traditionally circumscribed by a political system which was still patrimonial'. For views opposing the 'moral economy' thesis, see Langbein (1983); Dale Edward Williams (1984). The last two, in my opinion, construct an extremely narrow definition of politics and the elites' interest in formulating policies of control in England.

In his extremely thought-provoking study of punishment in the modern European annals of discipline and power, Michel Foucault moves away from the leading concerns of Marxist scholars of the period, including social historians at the University of Warwick. In order to comprehend the structure of historical crimes, he focuses on 'punishment as political tactic', a technology to put the future in order rather than taking stock of a crime committed in the past; and is accredited with having discovered that the human body itself is invested by power relations.[25]

However, for Foucault power becomes simply a strategy constituting its own objects. His concept of power allows very little room for resistance on the part of those on the margins of socio-cultural resources. None the less, his explanation of how the penal regime thrived on human sciences, or how legal apparatus was supposed to have been erected on the basis of 'scientific' knowledge, not only stands the test of time but goes even further in studies of criminology and science, and their ideological foundations. His exploration of the human body at the centre of modern epistemology of crime, morality, insanity, and redemption or control of the criminal and the mad is remarkable: 'But the body is also directly involved in a political field; power relations have an immediate hold upon it; they invest it, mark it, train it, torture it, force it to carry out tasks, to perform ceremonies, to emit signs. . . . [T]he body becomes a useful force only if it is both a productive body and a subjected body' (Foucault 1979, pp. 25–6).

Criminology and Empire

As far as socio-economic interpretations of crime in the 1960s are concerned, they were no novelty; since attempts in this direction were already in place within eighteenth-century scholarship.[26] Commenting on justice, police, revenue and arms, Adam Smith noted that 'nothing

[25] Frantz Fanon wrote with similar concern about the human body as the site of power relations in the modern world. His insistence on racism as the very axis of colonial ideology could not have sustained itself without bringing the human body to the centre of the discourse. It is ironic that Foucault, who comes only a decade later on the French intellectual horizon, does not even acknowledge Fanon and his work.

[26] The next two paragraphs on the relationship between crime and economic conditions in England are based on David J. Pyle 1983.

tends so much to corrupt mankind as dependency, while independency still increases the honesty of the people' (Pyle 1983, p. 4). Underlying the spirit of the political economy of his time, Smith stated that the establishment of commerce and manufactures, which produces independence, was 'the best police for preventing crimes'. Implicit in his assumption was the belief that once the wheels of commerce were in full swing, common people would be able to secure a better wage, leading to a law-abiding life.

Writing around the First World War, W.A. Bonger identified the sixteenth-century philosopher Thomas More as the first thinker to have explained the occurrence of crime in terms of existent economic circumstances. About the reason why common people indulged in thefts, the author of *Utopia* had remarked: 'neither is there any punishment so horrible, that it can keep them from stealing, which have no other craft whereby to get their living' (ibid.). Loathing the havoc wrecked by the introduction of Enclosures system,[27] More wryly remarked, '(G)reat and horrible punishments be appointed for thieves, whereas much rather provision should have been made, that there were some means, whereby they might get their living, so that no man should be driven to this extreme necessity, first to steal, and then to die.'

Beccaria-Bonesana, an eighteenth-century Italian criminologist, singled out 'the right of exclusive property', the source of 'misery and despair', as the major cause for crime. Later in the nineteenth century the proponents of historical materialism and class struggle made good use of this tradition. Fredreick Engels (1892) echoed it in *The Condition of the Working Class in England in 1844* as he wondered: '[A] class which bears all the disadvantages of the social order without enjoying its advantages, one to which the social system appears in purely hostile aspects—who can demand that such a class respect this social order?' (Engels 1892, p. 5). A number of scholars in the nineteenth century

[27] In sixteenth-century England, 'Enclosures', developed as systematic 'encroachments made by lords of manors or their farmers upon the land over which the manorial population had common rights or which lay in the open arable fields. Propelled by the prospect of profits to be made either in selling wool or by leasing their lands to those who did and thereby increasing their rents, the lords of the manor found a variety of legal and semi-legal methods to deprive the peasants of their rights to use the common for pasture of their cattle, the collection of wood for fuel, and the like' (Barrington Moore 1993, p. 9).

focused on the growing disparities in wealth between classes to explain the criminal/anti-law persuasions of the common people.

Towards 1900, however, a paradigmatic shift appears to have occurred in English thought on crime. Ironically, when the threat of criminality appeared to be ebbing in England, the earlier tradition of construing criminality as a problematic in the realm of morality was withdrawn (Weiner 1990). 'With the rise of natural science and its increasing implication to human behavior' criminality was 'de[-]moralized' to witness the emergence of a (new) science of criminology (ibid., p. 228). In reconstructing its boundaries, the new approach fixed the world of criminality, as it declared crime to be a 'natural phenomenon'. From now onwards, criminals were distinct from the non-criminal majority; they had become pathological cases. Henry Mandsley, a prominent scientist of the late Victorian era in whom the new criminology found a persuasive spokesperson, said 'criminal acts, like lunatic acts, did not issue from the will of their perpetrators, but were the outcome of physical causes over which they had no social control' (ibid., p. 232).

The rise of positivist criminology in the West was at the very centre of the chaos (assuming it is possible to know the centre of a chaos). Refuting any connection between economic condition and crime, authors like Lombroso, Ferri, Garofalo and others started hammering 'anomalies of the skull, brain, viscera, sensibility, reflex activity . . . intelligence and feeling, especially of the moral sense and the peculiarities of the criminal dialect and literature', not to mention, 'civil status, profession, residence, social class and education' (Ferri quoted in Pyle 1983, p. 5). Similarly, Cesare Lombroso (1835–1909) was of the view that criminals were indeed a different sub-species of man, with a distinct mental and physical make-up. He included the 'asymmetry of the face; excessive dimension of the jaw and cheekbones . . . ears of unusual size . . . excessive length of arms' in his list of physical abnormalities that indicate mental deficiency. Correspondingly, as it were, Bentham advised tightening the penal reign ever so tightly as he concluded: 'Individuals pursued pleasure and avoided pain. If some individual chose to perform criminal acts in the pursuance of pleasure, this must be because there was insufficient deterrence (or pain) attaching to those acts' (ibid., p. 6).

The colonial accounts of crime in India and the measures to

check them further complicate the issue. In the 1840s, W.H. Sleeman (1788-1856), a Lieutenant-Colonel in the Bengal Army, wrote about 'colonies' of 'hereditary dacoits'.[28] In 1871, the Criminal Tribes Act was passed, according to which certain social groups were dubbed as 'criminal tribes'. A Law member of the Governor General's Council clarified:

> It means a tribe whose ancestors were criminal *from time immemorial, who are destined by the usage of the caste* to commit crimes, and whose *descendants will be offenders against Law, until the whole tribe is exterminated* or accounted for in the manner of the Thugs. . . . *Reform is impossible*, for it is his trade, his caste, I may say, his religion to commit crime. (cited in the *Report of the U.P. Criminal Tribes Enquiry Committee*, 1948, p. 9, emphasis added)

The stereotypical caste system came in handy, in two ways, to the colonial rulers. It reproduced the difference between the worlds of the colonizer and the colonized and quite significantly, helped coin a euphemism for racism. Since the stereotyping is inextricably linked with 'epistemic formation'[29] of the subject to be ruled, the importance of such utterance is immense.

At first glance this appears very much like pre-emption of an ideological somersault that the Empire was to undertake three decades after the passing of this Act. Resurgence of biological racism in European thought, by the turn of the century is meaningless in the South Asian context since it never appears to have left it in the first place. This is important because Sleeman's narrative on 'hereditary criminals' precedes the 1857 Revolt which is sometimes taken as the marker of a major shift in the governmentality of the British empire by some of the scholars of the colonial discourse in South Asia.[30] Right through the century, and well into the twentieth, we come across the use of racist epithets like 'hereditary criminal class/caste/tribe', 'habitual criminal', 'predatory castes' (see, for instance, volumes of Hunter), etc., in the administrative discourse.

[28] *Report on Budhuk Alias Bagree Dacoits and Other Gang Robbers by Hereditary Profession*, 1849.

[29] The expression is Michel Foucault's who, ironically enough, remained race-blind. Once again we may note Foucault's ignorance of Frantz Fanon who was forcefully theorizing European epistemic formation precisely on account of its racist foundation.

[30] See, for example, Jenny Sharpe 1993 and 1993a. Also, Mrinalini Sinha 1995.

Considering the phenomenon that colonial relations required a different vocabulary of control, it does not seem logical that the Empire would give up the strategic space for manipulation by declaring criminality 'racial', 'biological', or 'natural'. For once it is rendered biological, there hardly remains space for human intervention, and that could be fatal for the legitimation of imperial presence. The Empire must project all hindrances as manageable, all diseases curable, all sinners redeemable, and all wrongs as correctable.

This makes one wonder why genetic racism resurfaced in colonial discourse when the fight against slavery seemed to be over. In South Asia, the caste system, especially as the metropolis constructed it, seems to have done the trick. Hereditary crime referred to the notion of hereditary profession, passed ostensibly on the very principles of caste. That is the reason why the colonial body of knowledge took recourse to economic explanations for the occurrence of crime. For sure, economic reasons looked reversible; they certainly appeared possible to minimize. No wonder that imperial gazetteers are so generous in acknowledging economic havoc as the major culprit for unceasing crime. Rightly, the popular among them were the fallacious policies of what was called the Permanent Settlement. At times, we also encounter official remarks which hang at the abyss of helplessness: '[I]n 1908 there was an increase of thefts and burglaries, due directly to the prevalent scarcity. These crimes are *inevitable and practically impossible to detect*' (*Bengal District Gazetteers: Bhagalpur*, 1911, p.146, emphasis added). To project economic crisis as the sole cause of crime is also to deny in it the political element. As we said with Guha (1983) in the beginning of this section, for the powers that be, Causes must be made to stand in as a phantom surrogate for Reason.

At this point we would suggest that anthropometrical epithets spilled in the imperial records of administration were probably nothing more than a linguistic slippage—an act fairly understandable since in England itself, where the administrators were being schooled, the vocabulary of criminology was undergoing a sweeping change. This of course is not to argue that racism was absent from the colonial mind. What we are arguing is that the shift towards genetic explanations of recurring crimes was strategically not available to the Empire that aspired to have as much control over the subject population as possible. The reconstructed contours of the caste system provided all the ambivalence that might have been needed to reproduce colonial control.

In fact, as Bhabha (1994, pp. 66–84) argues, ambivalence remains central to imperial stereotyping. The depiction of 'India' as 'fixed and normalized as an unchanging text' (Sharpe 1993, p. 30), at any point of time, is to negate, among many other things, the 'paradoxical mode of representation' that colonial discourse always pursued in order to produce and 'fix' the difference.

Crimes in the Popular Register

Bubhukshitah kim na karoti papam; Kshina narah nishkaruna bhavanti
[What is criminal for the hungry? the weak are unkind.] ('Shantiparva', —*Mahabharat*)

In perfect good faith, and all unconscious of its incongruity, he ['the Indian'] will pray devotedly in the morning to some tutelary deity for the success of his crops, and that very evening will ask divine blessing on the dacoity he is about to commit. (Augustus Sommerville 1929)

These passages, though taken from two different kinds of sources—one arguably the most popular scripture of the Hindus of India, the other a typical colonial commentary couched in a curious mixture of contempt and condescension—confirm one fact, that the hard pressed in rural India did not fall short on religious/moral referents when it came to committing 'crime' in order to live. The poor had no strong moral qualms about violating legal boundaries since they thought they had the religious sanction to do so from the highest authority that mattered. Legal actions were hindrances at the most; they could not have been decisive deterrents for the gods, who, if unable to protect crops (from drought, flood or the greedy mahajan and the tyrant zamindar), were seen as morally responsible for the success of all other para-agricultural endeavours of the faithful. To propitiate the god/*devta/devi/thakur/devi mai*, differently as the Almighty was known, was what was supremely important. It was left to the colonial administrator-ethnographers to grapple with the riddle of the existence of religious sanctions for crime:

In the courtyard of their houses there is a small *pindi* dedicated to Ram Thakur, on which they sacrifice . . . animals. . . . They have a priest (*bhagat*), who officiates for them at various domestic ceremonies, and also on special occasions, when the Dharhis set out on a thieving expedition. (*Bihar and Orissa District Gazetteers: Monghyr*, 1926, p. 185)

The poor remembered the story of the renowned rishi Vishvamitra who, driven by hunger, had to steal a piece of meat (a portion of dead dog's leg, to be precise) from the house of the *Chandala* who had employed him to guard his hut (narrated by kisans of numerous villages in interviews conducted between October 1995 and January 1996). This legend is significant, for it exonerates the most heinous crime possible in popular discourse: a Brahmin sage (1) working under a Chandala, (2) stealing (3) his master's (4) dead, not even killed by himself (5) dog's (6) leg. Ironically, to assuage his hunger, the rishi committed not one but six crimes, which were regarded within the Brahmanic discourse as low and therefore 'shudra' in nature. Hunger, thus legitimizes the most reprehensible crimes, blurring even class-caste distinctions. We must view crime in rural Bihar in this moral milieu; as Ranajit Guha pithily sums up, 'meaning is controlled by the use of language in situations, crime in the new social context comes to signify an integral part of a comprehensive system of defiance—a *parole* in a new *langue*. . . .' (Guha 1983, p. 93). Nothing reflects this moral matrix of defiance better than the following remark of a rather innocent colonial in-charge of law and order:

> There is undoubtedly evidence that the people are not as a rule inclined to aid the police in investigations. . . . As to the attitude of the people in regard to investigation of offences and the detection of the offenders, there can be no doubt that it differs widely from the attitude of the people of England. The people of India are not generally actively on the side of law and order; unless they are sufferers from the offence, their attitude is generally at the very best one of silent neutrality, they are not inclined actively to assist the officers of the law. (*Report of the Indian Police Commission 1902–3*, p. 22)

Crimes in the Official Register

The changing socio-economic register of nineteenth-century rural Bihar recorded crimes on a fairly regular basis. There were crimes of many kinds: rioting, dacoity, trespassing, burglary, cattle theft, affrays, etc.; with varying intensity; luring members of all castes and creeds. Preparing a lengthy statistical account of the province in the 1870s, W.W. Hunter maintained a separate entry for crime. Officials and commentators of the time coined phrases such as 'agrarian crimes', 'agrarian murders', 'rent crimes', 'agrarian riots', 'lootings' and so on.[31] The link between economic hardship and 'individual' crimes (as opposed to group or gang crimes) was frequently accepted in the official discourse. Disputes over rent and/or ownership of land were considered 'commonsensical' reasons for unlawful avocations of the village folk. The administrative report of Bengal (1899–1900) returned the crime figures for the last decade of the nineteenth century with the following note: 'The figure for reported cognisable[32] crime rose at a bound in 1897 on account of the famine. . . . The total for non-cognisable crime is considerably lower than that for 1898 or 1896. The fall in some districts is attributed to the completion of settlement proceedings which have removed land disputes—a very fruitful source of non-cognisable complaints.'[33]

Much earlier, '[T]he authors of the *Fifth Report* (1812) took it for granted that dacoity (another indigenous word that entered English dictionaries) spread in Bengal following the Permanent Settlement'.[34] The latter is also faulted on the ground that it erases 'the mental structure of paternalism', extremely essential for controlling illegal activities in the pre-democratic epochs, by destroying the traditional landed elites, the earlier in charge of law and order [McLane, 'Bengal Bandits, Police and Landlords After the Permanent Settlement' in Yang (ed.) 1985, p. 46].

The districts of Munghyr and Purnea saw three cases of rioting in

[31] The frequency and pervasiveness of 'looting' is reflected by the fact that the word 'loot' made its way into English dictionaries. See Arnold 1979, p. 112.

[32] ' "Cognisable offence" means an offence in which a police officer may, in accordance with the express and specific provisions of law, arrest without a warrant a person accused or suspected of such an offence: section 2(c) of the Criminal Procedure Code. Cognisable offence also means an offence in respect of which the police can take up investigation suo moto and without being required to obtain prior permission of the magistrate: section 156 of Criminal Procedure Code. All other offences are non-cognisable, i.e. police can take up investigation of such offences only on the order of a competent magistrate . . . and cannot make any arrest in such a case without obtaining a warrant from a competent court.' Mukherjee 1995, p. 13.

[33] *Report on the Administration of Bengal 1899–1900*, pp. 26–7.

[34] *The Fifth Report from the Select Committee of the House of Commons on the Affairs of the East India Company, 1812*, pp. 39–40, 65–6, and 71, cited in John R. McLane 1985, p. 30.

TABLE 3: CRIME IN THE LAST DECADE OF NINETEENTH CENTURY

Year	*Cognizable Crime*	*Non-Cognizable Crime*	*Total*
1890	1,17,443	1,16,554	2,33,997
1891	1,26,472	1,19,072	2,47,544
1892	1,46,185	1,21,624	2,67,809
1893	1,37,898	1,21,490	2,59,388
1894	1,40,902	1,18,070	2,58,972
1895	1,36,777	1,25,685	2,62,462
1896	1,47,433	1,29,439	2,76,872
1897	1,85,061	1,25,770	3,10,831
1898	1,71,993	1,29,935	3,01,928
1899	1,67,642	1,22,786	2,90,428

SOURCE: *Report on the Administration of Bengal 1899–1900.*

1865, which rose to 12 and 34 in 1872 and 1874 respectively.[35] There were 437 cases of theft in 1865; 561 in 1872; and 1350 in 1874 (ibid.). 'The cases of housebreaking [in Saran] increased from 1,192 in 1870 to 1,223 in 1871, and to 2,505 in 1872' (Hunter, vol. XI, p. 346). The rise was explained in terms of the 'large destruction of crops by floods' (ibid.). The situation went from bad to worse as time went by. Owing to severe crop failure in 1903 and endemic shortage of irrigation facilities, 'an outbreak of grain looting occurred in Banka subdivision and lasted for three days . . . till a heavy fall of rain came and put a stop to it'. Byrne continues, '[t]he grain dealers had formed a combination to put up prices and the people of the locality would not endure it any longer' (*Bengal District Gazetteers: Bhagalpur*, 1911, p. 146). The level of extraction from the peasants was so high that even a slight change in their incomes could spell disaster:

The suspension of mining operations in the coalfields rendered large numbers without a source of livelihood. The statewide dacoity figures doubled from 213 in 1917 to 408 in 1918. Hazaribagh and Bhagalpur districts together contributed two thirds of the total. In 1919, there was an almost 100 percent rise in dacoity (815) over the previous year's figure

[35] W.W. Hunter, *A Statistical Account of Bengal*, vol. XV, 1877, p. 162.

which had included about 100 'technical' cases of dacoity connected with the Shahabad bakrid riots. (Sudhir Kumar Jha 1995, p. 238)

In fact it rarely happened that a *Fortnightly Report* carrying news of price rise or unfavourable weather for harvest did not follow up with news of increased agrarian crimes.

Cattle-thefts: A History Unwritten

Among all modes of extra-legal survival, stealing cattle was probably the most favoured. Its modus operandi centrally involved 'the practice of restoring the stolen animals on payment of blackmail [*sic*]'.[36] Considering that disposal of stolen cattle would not have been easy, repeated frequency of cattle-theft suggests that the owner preferred to pay the ransom and get the cattle back rather than to rely on 'inefficient' legal apparatus, namely, the police, and lose them for good (ibid.). The Report acknowledged that 'so long as the custom of paying blackmail continues unchecked . . . the risk of detection [will be] very small'. And yet the figure available for persons convicted or bound over for stealing cattle outnumbers those for dacoity and murder taken together.

'Gaya . . . [and] Shahabad exceed[ed] all other districts of Bengal in the extraordinary prevalence of the crime of cattle-stealing' (Hunter, vol. XII, p. 129). Cattle-theft was on the rise in Bhagalpur and the Santhal Pargana districts as well. From 1871 to 1874, the number of thefts, 'both ordinary and cattle thefts, numbered . . . 526, 516, 405 and 567' (Hunter, vol. XIV, p. 211). In Darbhanga district 243 people were convicted or bound over in cattle-theft from 1893 to 1902, while those taken in for murder and dacoity for the same period numbered 73.[37] Similarly, in Champaran district the people convicted or bound over in cattle thefts numbered 302 while the number of people caught for dacoity and murder was 227 and 19 respectively (*BDG: Champaran*, p. 10). The high number for dacoity was nothing unusual since the district thanks to its geographical terrain, was notorious for dacoity. From 1901 to 1911, 56 people were convicted/bound over in murder and dacoity cases in the district of Muzaffarpur while there were

[36] *Report of the Indian Police Commission 1902–3*, p. 160.

[37] *Bihar District Gazetteers: Darbhanga, Statistics 1901–1902* (*BDG* hereafter), p. 10.

225 cattle-thieves convicted/bound over in the same period (*BDG: Muzaffarpur*, 1913, p. 13). In the same decade, Saran convicted/bound over 94 persons involved in murder and dacoity while there were 275 people convicted/bound over in cattle-theft (*BDG: Saran*, p. 11).

Given this picture, it is somewhat curious to note that the phenomenon of cattle-theft has not caught the attention of historians in the way that riots have.[38] Certainly riots were more 'spectacular' than cattle-thefts. As acts of 'direct' confrontation 'involving force [riots] required at least two antagonists with sufficient economic and social standing to mobilize a few *lathials* (clubmen)', argues Yang (1989, p. 215). No wonder, 'the faces in the crowd were generally of people with some degree of resources' (ibid.).

This line of reasoning supports Yang's unspoken faith in Hamza Alavi's (1973) 'Middle Peasant Thesis', which in turn appears to have been borrowed from Barrington Moore, Jr. (1966) and partially from Eric Wolf (1969), and his larger concern with illustrating controls of the local elites over village-life.[39]

Cattle-theft on the contrary, brings different actors, with meagre resources, on to the political landscape. The people who indulged most in this particular art of survival came from poor economic backgrounds and lowly social status. Hunter's remarks about them are of interest: 'There are four classes in Gaya District, who may be considered as habitual criminals—namely, Goalas, Dosadhs, Babhans and Doms. Cattle-lifting and grain thefts are the special crimes of the first class; lurking house-trespass, of the second; riot and affrays, of the third; and thefts, of the fourth' (Hunter, vol. XII, p. 130).

Of these four 'classes', Babhans who specialized in rioting were, not surprisingly, the only ones from the upper bracket of the caste hierarchy. Goalas, 'the most obnoxious caste in Bihar' (Bourdillon, quoted by Hunter, p. 131), were also the most populous caste not only in the province but also in each district. According to census reports from

[38] See Yang 1989 (pp. 212–24); Arnold 1979, 1979a; Guha 1983.

[39] Both Wolf and Moore emphasize the need for the guidance and support of the village elders in order to 'give shape' to the peasants' sense of injustice. See Wolf 1969 and Barrington Moore 1966. These two, particularly the latter, were among the most influential sociological readings of the 1960s. Hamza Alavi 1973 demonstrated a classic Leninist legacy in his advocacy for an enlightened leadership to mobilize the peasant populace.

1891 to 1931, they constituted between 8 and 11 per cent of the entire population. Together with Dosadhs and Doms, they accounted for nearly 16 per cent of the population. Musahar, the eleventh most populous caste in Bihar (*Census 1931*, p. 247), could be another addition to this list of petty offenders (see Hunter, vol. XI). The focus on social locations in terms of caste is crucial since the process of depeasantization more or less followed the caste hierarchy: the lower one was in the social ladder, the greater the possibility that s/he would lose control over the land. In contrast, upper caste raiyats were 'usually prepared to fight their landlord if he attempt[ed] to oppress them'.[40]

In other words, what is illustrated in the incidence of cattle-theft is the response of the weaker sections of the population to the changing socio-economic environment of the time. The act did not require resourceful/upper caste peasant intervention. Nor was it necessary to gather in broad daylight to return the gaze of the rich upper caste peasants, so to say, as in the case of a riot, in order to make a political statement. To do that would surely mean snapping the cultural signs that so firmly held the power equations in rural Bihar. Cattle raiding was certainly not an everyday occurrence. For if the cultural deposits of the ruling elite are plundered everyday, the elite cannot remain one for long.

Individual quile was sufficient to keep the act going. To remember John Berger once again: 'In the dark, lest he be seen, a man plots—slowly, obstinately—his own revenge. The dark he does this in, is like a kind of sleep: there is room for only one person in it. The village is vindictive' (1975, p. 90).

There were time trusted networks, that helped disposal of the booty, without which the economy of cattle-theft could not have carried on. When the colonial chroniclers describe the native 'cowboys' as 'obnoxious habitual criminals' they also acknowledge, albeit unwillingly, the success of this enterprise along with their helplessness to curb and control it. To announce that there were certain castes specializing in this craft, almost automatically underlines the collectivity inherent in it.[41]

[40] Stevenson-Moore, Settlement Officer, quoted in *BDG: Muzaffarpur*, 1958, p. 192.

[41] It is important to clarify here that by using certain facts from imperial records to substantiate our argument we do not necessarily subscribe to its racist values. We take Hunter's characterization of certain castes as 'habitual criminals' and

In certain districts, like, Shahabad, Gaya, and Patna, there were also 'gangs' of cattle-thieves (see Hunter, vol. XII, p. 129). Throughout the province even today, approximately within a 10 km. radius, there can be found a *chor gaon* (village of thieves, or 'bandit villages') which are remnants of pre-Independence times.[42] These are invariably villages of lower and/or intermediate castes with marginal accessibility to land and related productive resources. In the collective memory of the present inhabitants of these infamous villages, cattle-thefts and small scale burglaries have been a part and parcel of villagers' survival strategies.

It appears that the entire village did not turn into a *chor gaon* overnight, but to nullify the wrath of zamindars of surrounding villages and their *lathaits* (toughs), it was tactically useful to take up this profession as a collective rather than individual pursuit. That is the reason one rarely finds a *chor gaon* of mixed caste population, especially where upper castes predominate, unless upper castes were to take up thieving, which would have been more an exception than a rule. 'It also helped in disposing off the stolen animals. You can enter a house and look for

---

'experts' in certain professions only as indicative of their specific socio-economic locations. Goalas, for example, specialized in cattle rearing and cultivation. Doms rarely ever possessed land. If a good number of the former took to cattle-theft (and the latter to theft in general) it was only understandable.

[42] The concept of *chor gaon* is not to be found in official accounts. I 'discovered' them during my conversation with the villagers of different districts.

From October 1995 through January 1996 I travelled in six such villages in Bhojpur (part of earlier Shahabad), two in Patna, and three in Jahanabad (a part of the erstwhile Gaya district) and talked to a number of peasants in the age group 50 to 80 (most times I either had to take their words or exercise my own guess since very few of them could recall the year of their birth, let alone the date). I am particularly thankful to Debi Dayal Singh, age 60, of Bhangawatipur and Sambhu Nath Singh, age 50-5, of Demhan, both from Bhojpur district; 'Azad Baba' [literally, 'Free Grandpa'], age 70, of Jahanabad and 'Kariwaa' [the black boy], age 62 (luckily, he remembers that he was born in the year of *Bhayanak Bhookump*, the dreadful earthquake of 1934) of Shahpur, Patna. Kariwaa is a Dusadh, an untouchable, and says he lives on earnings in the night, as he put it so wryly: I am not permitted to touch anything except people's things in the night. 'Azad Baba' is Koeri, an intermediate caste and a 'whole timer' with an 'Ultra Leftist' party of Bihar. Debi Dayal Singh and Sambhu Nath Singh are Yadavas, another intermediate caste, and have lands enough to survive through the year ('*Khaye peeye bhar jamin ba*').

your stolen buffalo, but you cannot search all the houses of a village [to do the same]. . . . No body has *aukat* [wherewithal] to doubt everybody . . . [of having stolen the cattle].'[43]

What is even more striking is that people from 'weak villages' (meaning where a particular lower caste was in minority) would always look to establish matrimonial relations in one of the *chor gaons* in order to 'empower' themselves ['to multiply the number of *lathis*' (clubs/thick bamboo sticks) is the expression often used].[44] Empowerment was not realized in the sense of an open confrontation with the locally powerful, as this was rare. What was more common was for individuals to link up with their relatives in a *chor gaon* to harass the rich, the upper castes and zamindars 'in the darkness of night'. A favoured 'tekanik' (technique), other than lifting cattle, was to destroy the crop. Sometimes the standing crop of the perceived enemy in the area would be cut during the night simply for fodder.

Though official records are silent about which classes and castes were the major targets, the oral accounts available in the villages of Bihar are clear that the lower and the intermediate castes who took this profession were ensuring their survival, which was becoming increasingly difficult. In support of their case, kisans in a number of villages of Shahabad district (Bhojpur and Rohtas today) fondly recall one Pirthi Singh, a veteran thief of the Yadava caste, who in their accounts appears as nothing short of a Robinson Crusoe. The singularity of caste configuration of a *chor gaon*, the near perfect discrimination in selecting the target—all point to its well-defined political character. No wonder a *chor gaon* or people's kinship links with *chor gaons* became a matter of concern for the propertied sections of society.

Needless to assert, cattle-theft became a particular expression of political consciousness and thus of politics itself, for those who participated in it. As is well known today, the language of politics of the underprivileged is rarely the language of the politics of the privileged.

[43] I owe this insight to Saraju Yadav of Ramgarh, Bhojpur (Shahabad). (He insisted that I must give the name of his village as 'Ramgarh' and not 'Teen Gharawa' (meaning 'a hamlet of mere three houses') as the upper caste people of the area pejoratively do.)

[44] This was confirmed by the kisans of all the villages I went to. In *chor gaons* such as Jokata, Demhan and Bhangawatipur, I also got a chance to speak with a number of kisan families which had recently entered into such alliances with 'weak' villages.

As should also be clear from this line of reasoning, it is erroneous to equate differences in language of politics with the absence of politics itself. Stealing of cattle must be seen as one of the tactics of survival; it was not a passive act. What cattle-theft perhaps did not aim at accomplishing was the open inversion of authority employed in everyday sign-systems; but, then, this could be or was attempted only in moments of open insurgency when the outcome of a failed inversion ceased to frighten the insurgents. What the economy of cattle-theft did accomplish, however, was that by its almost unstoppable currency it generalized dissent in a fairly large section of the population. The disgust and annoyance of the colonial narrators against 'habitual' cattle-thieves are testimony to this fact. In fact, if the later colonial scribes are to be believed, the Babhans, the leading rioters in Bihar, à la Hunter (1877), had begun to be considered one of 'the most law-abiding castes' (*Census of India, 1911*, vol. V, Part I, p. 555). This total somersault in perception took place in a period of just over three decades. This should be read as cattle-theft having become an everyday irritant for colonial law and order machinery and its lackeys among the colonized. Property, sacrosanct as it was to both, was ever more vulnerable, as a trusted civil servant who served the Empire for over three decades, noted in 1920:

> It can never be the interest of the landlords to desire weak government, even if it be national government. . . . They are well aware of their stake in the country, and know that, in the words of a letter written last April by the Maharaja of Darbhanga [the biggest zamindar of Bihar] to two large landholding associations, their 'very existence depends' on the protection of property and the maintenance of law and order. . . . (Lovett 1920, p. 245)

Law and order indeed were central to the very existence of the propertied populace. For the poor it was altogether a different story, as Sahajanand was to remark in the post-Depression period: 'thieving does not have to be preached (or taught) to the hungry and the poor' (*Chori ka updesh kisi bhi bhookhkhad ko nahin dena padata*).[45]

[45] Sahajanand Saraswati 1940, p. 35

CHAPTER 3

Rumour: Beyond Muffled Murmurs of Dissent

In this chapter we look into the articulation of dissent through rumour: rumour as a language of kisan politics, a language of aspiration to reconstruct a political collectivity which would be more confident and directly confrontationist in nature, a language of indulgence in 'fictive realities'; in brief, rumour as the language of collective dreams. As a much clearer voice of dissent than 'crimes' and 'migrations', rumour in the hands of Bihari kisans aspired to create a *janmat* (public opinion) against the powers that be, decades before direct political engagements became a general vocation or national passion.

We will try to discern the thoughts and desires that coalesced into ideologies that could travel far and wide, breaking given (and constructed) territorial barriers. Not much exists by way of empirical narratives or factual accounts of the travel itself. Not enough attention has been paid to reconstruct the political articulation that went before the spread of modern nationalist politics. This chapter examines what may be tentatively called the re-formation of a political collectivity through rumour, before mass movements became a generalized affair. An enquiry into rumour as a political language may open up a rarely investigated area of politics that has a direct bearing on the way kisans conducted politics in late nineteenth- and early twentieth-century Bihar.

The validity of this problematic rests on two assumptions. First, there always exists a collective, a political and a social, not eternal or static, but one which is a chronicle of human interventions, and always changing. If British imperialism gradually succeeded in creating a huge umbrella of subordination in the entire country, there might have been counter-efforts at constructing political communities that were at least larger than a village and/or a zamindari, if not big enough to envelop the entire subcontinent. Of course, a collectivity constructed sharply in reaction to the Raj would not have been the only collectivity available. The 'traditional', the 'indigenous', the pre-British collectivities must have been as real as they are difficult to reconstruct today. Second, the success story of Gandhian mass movements must be explained in terms of their receptivity and the cultural milieu that prevailed before Gandhi arrived. The Gandhian movement cannot be cause and effect at the same time. Nationalist historiography's efforts at explaining the success of mass movements through Gandhi's personal charisma is tautological and thus unsatisfactory. More so, since the Nationalist imagination fails to note or chooses to suppress the tension that persisted between elite 'mobilization' and popular participation.[1] Mass movements do not happen in a day, or out of the blue. It is in order to know the cultural resources of the kisans which were more conducive to Gandhian ideas, compared to others, that the issue of pre-Gandhian collectivity acquires immense methodological and political importance. The argument could become more forceful if it could be shown (a) that there were certain pre-Gandhian antecedents that made some of the Gandhian articulations possible and (b) that even during the period when Gandhian articulations were in vogue, there were audiences for non-Gandhian formulations, continuing from the pre-Gandhian phase.

However, to tell the story of kisan politics in nineteenth-century Bihar through rumours has certain obvious problems. Rumours were elusive to the official scribe as they thrived on orality and anonymity. For a researcher therefore it entails a relative paucity of evidence. The research becomes less frustrating as one comes to the 1920s when print had begun reproducing many of the rumours circulating in that period more regularly. What is interesting is that the spurt in printing did not eliminate or minimize the importance of rumour on its own.

[1] In the nationalist historiography, for example, there is a tendency to emphasize or even exaggerate the break that Gandhi's arrival affected: Gandhi here acquires a kind of superhuman quality and his acts of mass mobilization an inexplicable pied-piper performance. Any historiographical effort to demystify Gandhian success in mass politics will have to examine the political languages of peasants available to Gandhi, and the innovative use he made of them.

Rumour perhaps faded only when those who had employed it as a specific language of politics became confident with the new language that emerged with the spread of mass politics.

A note on the origin and carrier of rumour is in order. A successful rumour is one whose source is not known, and the author remains removed from official surveillance. In that sense a rumour is a text without an author. Since a rumour acquires many hues during the process of its transition, and its carriers actively participate in its social production, it is a multi-authored text. The desired destination of a rumour is its dissolution into a commonsensical wisdom, a public opinion.

Scholars concerned with the 'birth of a public' by and large remain prisoners to West European specificity where market and the print media are said to have played a pivotal role in producing the former. From Georges Lefebvre (1932) to Habermas (1974) to Benedict Anderson (1983), this line of thinking seems to have had an unassailable dominance. Interestingly, narratives of 'the birth of a public' strongly resemble those of 'the nation'. The resemblance is so strong that to many the distinction remains elusive. No wonder then, that a narrative of nationalism in Europe, which is almost invariably an elitist narrative, also conceives of a public which is bourgeois. The non-Western world experienced different realities. C.A. Bayly, who also remains confined to elite India is however, rightly of the view that the Indo-Islamic world had a very clear sense of 'public' and that the '(p)ublic opinion—the weight of reasoned debate—was not the preserve of modern or western polities' (p. 181). Using the word 'ecumene [analogous to Habermas's "public sphere"] to describe the form of cultural and political debate which was typical of north India' (p. 182), Bayly focuses on Indian oral tradition, which creatively co-existed even after the advent of print. To make the case, he recalls the tradition of religious debates, i.e. *shastrarth* in the Hindu tradition, or the use of the *masjid* to address the gathered brethren of Islam before the muezzin called for prayer.[2] Wendy Singer (1997, p. 79) in her rich ethnographic account of Pandaul, Darbhanga, argues even more persuasively: 'the means of communication across space in the 1930s were similar to the means of communication across time from the 1930s to the present. In

[2] This was primarily a Middle Eastern phenomenon that had travelled to the Indian subcontinent.

both cases, key sources of communication were oral narratives that explained and historicized events by placing them into the context of the lives of their listeners'.

Thus the dense orality of the region and a flexible social communication based on it, did not need writing technology the way it was perhaps needed in the Western hemisphere in order to construct a public. However, it has become customary among social scientists to point out the low literacy rate in the province of Bihar to explain its oral tradition of communication. The rate of literacy was below 10 per cent as the district gazetteers of the period suggest. However, what requires reiteration is the fact that it was not so much the technology of writing or print which was lacking, but the need for them (in the Western sense). In any case, recent researches tend to show much more proximity of the people with the indigenous literati than has been hitherto accepted.[3]

Given this scenario, it is surprising that even recent research, that is reopening thinking on orality and social communication, is not paying enough attention to rumour as a form of political language. A few thoughts on the transmitters of rumour will be appropriate here.

Religious congregations, evenings with minstrels and bards, pilgrimages, weddings, match-making endeavours, funeral ceremonies, routine trips to local *haats* and bazaars, all were laden with opportunity for generating and circulating rumours. They all provided different avenues for people to exchange views, news, and information. Among these, the local bazaar is perhaps the most frequently referred to as the site where rumours originated. Across history the people at marketplaces have provided not only listeners and gossip mongers, but also a gathered audience (Bohannan and Dalton 1968, p. 17). In north India it is hard to imagine a market without a temple or a shrine. Similarly, every pilgrimage site invariably has a market. Many match-makings and weddings take place in the precincts of the temple at the market. Few funerary rites can be completed without a trip to the market. Thus what emerges is a gamut of activities that revolve around markets. This is true of all societies which undertake the activities we just mentioned. It is therefore not surprising that the market invariably

[3] Along with Bayly (1996) and Singer (1997), see Ajay Skaria, 1996.

became a site where a free *trade* in ideas could take place.[4] Guha sums up the strategic location of the bazaar:

> it is at the market-place where perhaps more than anywhere else in a pre-industrial society people gather regularly at frequent intervals and en masse for trade and certain forms of folk entertainment [*sic*], the socializing process of rumour too tends to operate most actively there . . . the verbal exchange which . . . constitutes the transitive function of rumour, comes to affirm its own identity as a type of popular discourse by virtue of its intimate association with economic exchange so essential to the life of the people. (1983, p. 258)

In Bihar too, rumour circulated easily from a bazaar. This however should not lead us to believe that the merchant, the petty trader, the speculator and the financier would be equally interested in a rumour, which was meant for the consumption of and further reproduction by a kisan. This is particularly true of political rumour. Here we may also want to differentiate between carrying and circulating a rumour inadvertently and actively participating in it. The latter cannot happen without it being made a conscious political choice. And there is nothing to suggest that, say, a petty trader and a speculator had developed a common cause against the zamindar and/or the Raj who were the main targets of the rumours of this study, in nineteenth-century Bihar. Nor can it be argued that they had forged an alliance with the kisan in an anti-imperialist struggle. At least not yet. If anything, rumours against traders, moneylenders and zamindars were the order of the day.

A Historiographical Sketch of Rumour

Ranajit Guha (1983) discusses rumour in connection with the 'transmission' of peasants' rebellious moments. Shahid Amin (1984) recounts it in order to explain how Gandhi and his messages were looked at by the peasants of Gorakhpur; how the 'Mahatma' was conceptualized in the mind of the popular. Sumit Sarkar's is the first effort (1984) at categorizing rumours and examining them methodically in order to

[4] Markets have many socially defined characters. In some communities mostly women go to market; in some it is the men. Cattle markets/fairs are almost universally shunned by women. In what specific way these differences would affect the kind of rumours we are concerned with is yet unknown.

'break out of the narrowly economic and . . . political' rhetoric of popular movements. In his exercise, Sarkar, like Amin, confines himself to the period when Gandhi had already 'arrived' on the national political stage. Like Guha, Sarkar's interest in rumours is to know subaltern militancy better. Unlike Guha, neither Amin nor Sarkar focus on a longer history of rumour to delineate its connection with people's consciousness. However, Sarkar does question 'the historical problem of the extraordinarily open nature of the "reception" of the Gandhian message' (p. 313) but never actually historicizes the problematic fully. So much for the historiography of rumour.[5] Let us now turn to the conceptual detail.

For psychologists and sociologists, for linguists and historians, the starting point about rumour is that it thrives in the society of oral tradition.[6] In a non-lettered culture 'word of mouth' becomes the only source for 'the dissemination of news' (Lefebvre 1973, p. 73). This belief is largely true. However, modern societies have not been able to rid themselves of rumour. On 21 September 1995, throughout India (and even abroad where believing Hindus resided) people woke up to hear that the idol of Ganesh (son of Shiva) was 'drinking' milk from his devotees. Hindus thronged nearby temples to offer milk. The spectacle lasted the whole day. A cobbler, an untouchable who mended shoes in front of a science institute in Delhi, tried in vain to explain, on national television, the trick of 'surface tension' and 'capillary action' that made milk 'disappear' in the mouth of Lord Ganesh. To spread a rumour on a pan-Indian level in one single morning, the help of all scientific gadgets available (telephone, fax, e-mail etc.) must have been sought. By 'word of mouth' a rumour can travel only a limited distance in a day; it cannot reach from India to Indonesia in the same morning. Stories about 'space ships' or 'aliens' invading the earth are another example of literate, modern and scientific community believing in rumour. In any event, why a pre-literate,[7] traditional society remains

[5] To this list one may add what is probably the first study of rumour in Modern India: J. Prasad, 'The Psychology of Rumour: A Study Relating to the Great Indian Earthquake of 1934', *British Journal of Psychology*, vol. XXVI, July 1935.

[6] See, for example, Lefebvre 1973; Lang and Lang 1963; Allport and Postman 1965; Vachek 1966 and Vansina 1961.

[7] It is not only a matter of being 'politically correct' to use 'pre-literate' instead of 'illiterate'. Historically, and culturally, written texts in the Indian subcontinent did

hungry for 'news', needs explanation. What was the use of 'news' for people who apparently could not even see beyond their fields? We shall return to this question shortly as it is related to the central concern, i.e. the collective quest after meaning.

It is not uncommon for official scribes to dismiss all rumours as lies. According to Guha, this reaction is an indicator of two things: 'a measure of the distance between a typical site of collective discourse and an ideal seat of official truth—between the bazaar and the bungalow, so to say', and 'an ill-conceived assimilation [of rumours] to news' (Guha 1983, p. 259). This is quite understandable. In rumours an official narrator finds merely a corruption of news; an additional irritant in the saga of control and subordination. Oman (1908) and Kaye (1888) are good examples.[8]

While expressing his annoyance over the distorted nature of news, Kaye however, put his finger on the subversive potential of rumour. For an alien regime where each murmur of the native meant some kind of plot against it, it was extremely important to know everything knowable. In such a situation, a rumour, distorted news from an unknown source, was nothing short of an ontological crisis.[9] Consider the imperial anxiety in the following passage:

> We know so little of what is stirring in depths of Indian society, we dwell so much apart from the people; we see so little of them, except in full dress and on their best behaviour, that perilous intrigues and desperate plots might be woven, under the very shadow of our bungalows. . . . But

---

find their way to people's minds and imaginations through oral media, for example, recitals, or, singing of popular epics, reproduction of legends and mythological stories through their repeated telling. However, this did not make society 'literate' as written texts were not *directly* available to the majority of the people. Of course, once it became available, it was open to popular interpretations, interpolations, and, thus, alterations according to the socio-cultural dynamics. The term 'pre-literate' stands in the middle of 'illiterate' and 'literate', as it were.

[8] They frequently refer to rumours as Bazaar *Gup* (Lies of the market-place).

[9] In relation to accuracy of news and rumour, it may be of interest to note Whipple's observation on *Aussage* (testimony). As early as 1909, Whipple reached the conclusion that 'the chief single result of the *Aussage* psychology is that an errorless report is not the rule, but the exception, even when the report is made by a competent observer under favorable conditions' (quoted in Lang & Lang 1963). Lang and Lang conclude from this that 'information that comes by way of the rumour channels is no different from any information communicated' (p. 56).

still less can we discern that quiet under-current of hostility which is continually flowing on without any immediate or definite object, and which, if we could discern it, would baffle all our efforts to trace it to its source. But it does not the less exist because we are ignorant of the form which it assumes, or the fount from which it springs. (Kaye, vol. I, pp. 257–8)[10]

Rumour: A Social Text without an Individual Author

Rumour is a text without an author. Unlike news where the source is identifiable and hence subject to censorship and control, a rumour belongs to the eternal fugitive, as it were, always on the run, always a step away from the law, the authority, the system. Kaye's anxiety is not unique; Lefebvre nearly half a century after him noted the same: 'for the government and the aristocracy, this means of transmission was a great deal more dangerous than freedom of the press' (1973, p. 73). The anonymity of/unknowability about the origin of rumour empowers people to communicate and defy surveillance and systemic control. It is an 'autonomous type of popular discourse', an unofficial pass needed to roam around without fear in the alleys of subordination and repression where curfew is unceasingly on.

This quality provides rumour with a great socializing power. Unlike news once again, where there is always a distance, a distinction, a hierarchy of sorts between communicator and audience, the rumour travels 'from a teller to a hearer who himself becomes a teller' (Guha 1983, p. 260). The power one experiences in the possession of information is transferred to the hearer along with the information (Peterson and Gist 1951). Rumour stakes a claim for absolute transitivity.

It is from this transitivity that rumour derives its extraordinary openness—yet another prerequisite for socialization. Contrary to an authored text which is limited in meaning or whose 'signified' can be controlled by the author, a rumour is always open and inviting to addition, subtraction, modification by its participants as it 'leaps from tongue to tongue'. About written text, Roland Barthes notes in 'The Death of

[10] That the author had to repeat the concern almost verbatim in the same volume (pp. 361–2), could well be due to the fact that he wrote in the backdrop of the 1857 uprising. Significant for our purpose is his observation regarding the anonymity of the origin of a rumour.

the Author': '[T]o give a text an Author is to impose a limit on that text, to furnish it with a final signified, to close the writing. . . . [w]hen the Author has been found, the text is "explained" ' (Roland Barthes 1977, p. 147). This is profoundly substantiated by a non-graphic, phonemic system like rumour, that owes its birth itself to anonymity. The many improvisations that a rumour undergoes makes it a unique text. At any point of time, it has no one author; *rumour truly is a multi-authored text*; the creation of all who believe in it and pass it on. It is a social text—collectively written, collectively read, and collectively comprehended.

Expanding on transitivity of rumour, Guha cites Lev Semenovich Vygotsky on oral speech in general and believes that the same is true of rumour too: 'The speed of oral speech is unfavourable to a complicated process of formulation—it does not leave time for deliberation and choice. Dialogue implies immediate unpremeditated utterance. It consists of replies, repartees; it is a chain of reactions' (quoted in Guha 1983, p. 261).

This prompts him to conclude that '(rumour) has all those qualities of speed, immediacy, disposition for *unreflecting response to stimulus*, etc. developed more fully within it than perhaps in any other type of *spontaneous* discourse' (emphasis added). Seduced by the theatrical urgency assigned to oral speech in Vygotsky, Guha juggles on the issue of spontaneity and ideology: 'Since rumour is "immediate unpremeditated utterance" (to quote Vygotsky once more), it is improvised within the rebel community not as a *conscious device* to rally the people, *but spontaneously*, without deliberation, that is *by the force of ideology alone*, so far as the insurgents themselves are concerned' (p. 262, emphasis added).

To see ideology inherent in spontaneity (and not in deliberation), may be the brilliant tactical move of a historian of peasant insurgency, but in Guha this remains largely unsubstantiated. He perhaps needed to be more cautious in his elaboration of the transitivity of rumour and celebration of Vygotsky. Compared to an authored text, no doubt rumour demands an immediate, quicker and spontaneous response, but the response does not essentially have to be 'unreflecting'. The spontaneity, that too of a subaltern populace, is never oblivious of the social and cultural codings woven around the existing power relations. Guha himself (1982) takes this position. As we saw earlier, being a collectively produced, shared and understood text, rumour realizes its meaning only in the social arena; it cannot breathe comfortably even for a brief moment in the state of unreflection.

Even if it is proved that at its point of origin, a private moment, a rumour was the result of some unreflected spontaneous discourse, once it starts rolling it becomes public by its acceptance, modifications, rejections, contestations, and so forth. It is important to recall Josef Vachek on spoken utterance in general: 'The function of the spoken utterance is to respond to the given stimulus (which, as a rule, is urgent) *in a dynamic way*, i.e. quickly, readily, and *with equal attention to both the intellectual and the emotional* factors of the situation that gave rise to the stimulus' (Vachek 1966, p. 153, emphasis added).

It is interesting to note that, like Vygotsky, Vachek too emphasizes the speed of the response to spoken utterance. However, unlike Vygotsky, he does not throw away the ideological or the conscious element from a spoken utterance. What is perhaps even more interesting is that Guha paraphrases the above cited quotation as well (see pp. 256, 257 and f.n. 92). He retains the urgency, emotionalism and dynamism, but, for some strange reason, overlooks its intellectuality. It is not as if Vachek does not give it the required emphasis. Guha, in fact, reiterates this opinion while showing his agreement with F. C. Bartlett (1977) similar views on 'effort after meaning', which is 'characteristic of every human cognitive reaction'. To describe the latter, Bartlett has phrases like: 'unreflecting', 'unanalytical', and 'unwitting' (cited in Guha 1983, p. 264). Guha repeats uncritically, 'Rumour . . . represents precisely such an effort after meaning' (ibid.).

J. Prasad, dealing with rumours around a sudden natural catastrophe of unprecedented scale, the earthquake of 1934, similarly invokes 'emotional disturbance' and 'emotional instability' as something that 'prepare the soil for the growth and spread of rumours' (1935, p. 6). 'With the return of emotional stability', Prasad concludes, 'rumours practically ceased to grow' (ibid.). Even if one concedes that this could be true in the case of such a calamity, the conclusion Prasad draws about rumours in general is difficult to sustain. One cannot push rumour—the collectively authored text—to the basement of reason called emotion. This too escapes Guha's critical eye. It would be of some interest to note that this line of reasoning did not differ from that of Kaye, 'in a state of panic men do not pause to reason' (Kaye 1888, p. 182) of whom Guha is so critical otherwise (Guha 1983, p. 268).

Further, is it not characteristic of the colonial, the imperial, the elitist, the official, the Orientalist, the Rationalist to distinguish arbitrarily between emotion and intellect and assign the former, as essentially lacking in the latter, to the colonized, the non-European, the 'irrational', the subaltern? The slippage has resulted from Guha's indulgent and yet eclectic reading of Vygotsky.

Before I move to the final frame of the argument, a quick clarificatory distinction between rumour and gossip is in order. Lang and Lang further a widely held opinion that unlike rumour, gossip is intimate, not public; that its boundaries 'are the same as those of an already established group'; 'that gossip usually remains within the circle in which it starts, whereas rumours are apt to spread farther' (1963, p. 68). Though these remarks are not necessarily incorrect, a closer look at the relationship between rumour and gossip may reveal new dimensions, particularly while reading them as collective expressions about the existing power structure. Keeping the repressive nature of the system in mind, it should not be difficult to imagine that gossip would most likely act as the first and safest outlet of people's anguish. Especially when cultural codes are not being openly violated, gossip functions as a form where muffled murmurs of disenchantment may take shape as a relatively better articulated dissent. As noted, with Guha (1982), a prose of insurgency is never composed in haste, since the risk in case of failure is tremendous; it simply is a question of life and death. In such a situation, gossip may serve as a medium of deliberation where people could weigh their chances. The closeness of a social circle in which an anti-authority gossip circulates, guarantees secrecy of the gossip which is vital in a repressive regime if it is ever to turn into an articulated discourse of dissent. Lang and Lang are unreflecting in their conclusion that gossip conserves the status quo (p. 69). This is ironic because they ingeniously remark in the same breath that 'whenever gossip goes beyond a closed circle and creates or supports cleavages—when it involves an issue whose truth is disputed—it becomes rumor'. This relationship between gossip and rumour is of crucial concern for a historical sociology of popular political culture. Gossip in the private domain functions as a forum where rumour, which is social in nature, is collectively comprehended (or miscomprehended). It helps rumour constitute a *janmat*, public opinion, among the pre-lettered subalterns. This proposition is now examined in detail.

Rumour: A Collective Quest after Meaning

The relationship between mass movement and political culture is not a well-studied field in South Asian scholarship. To explain the acceptance and success of Gandhian mass movements, some historians rely on the charismatic leadership of Mahatma Gandhi and the mobilizational acts of the Indian National Congress. The argument of the traditional Left hinges on the assumption of increasing consciousness of segments of the population, especially the working class. The growth of radical consciousness is seen as unilinear and dependent on the enlightened party and leadership. Colonial historiography, as can be expected, peddles the theory of the 'conspiracy of the few' and 'aspirations of the local elites' to explain anti-colonial mass movements. In its critique of elitism inherent in all the three schools mentioned earlier, Subaltern Studies stresses on the plurality of dreams and aspirations encapsulated under the rubric of 'freedom struggle', and on the zig-zag ways in which progressive consciousness spreads among the people.

None of the above-mentioned schools has rigorously engaged with the task of mapping the changing political contour of the masses: how does one understand the receptivity of ideas pertinent to and required for a mass movement in the sense of a changing cultural praxis? If one finds lacunae in the elitist historiographies and wants not just to juxtapose popular initiatives with those of the elite, but to study them dialectically(?), one has to understand the ways in which forms and facts, thoughts and ideas of pre-Gandhian mass movements affected and changed Nationalist/Gandhian mass movement. In other words, one must grapple with the historicity of Gandhian idioms and metaphors, tactics and strategies. It is not enough to explain their grand arrival in terms of Gandhi's individual charisma: 'many of these rumours were very consciously spread by the local leaders, who took advantage of Gandhi's charismatic appeal to give additional impetus to the agitation. . . . But what matters is that *the peasants believed them because Gandhi's name was associated with them*' (Pouchepadass 1974, p. 84, emphasis added).

This tautological statement begs a crucial question: why Gandhi's name meant to the peasants of Champaran what it did. Shahid Amin analyses Pouchepadass in some detail in his study of the deification of the Mahatma by the peasants of Gorakhpur district (1984), but he too is not interested in examining the pre-Gandhian political language of the peasants of Gorakhpur and its interplay with the changing grammar and vocabulary of national politics. It is not merely a matter of the subjective choice of the author for, as we shall attempt to show in this chapter, the interplay directly takes us to the choice and receptivity of the Gandhian language of politics.[11]

Rumours as Narratives of Resistance

> A particular rumor is the most elementary manifestation of a shared perspective. The rumor process refers exclusively to those unorganized and fugitive efforts to arrive at definitions when social orientation is necessary, but there are important gaps in the structuring of the relevant cognitive field. Collective definitions arise through the rumor process. (Lang and Lang, 1963, p. 52)

Had rumours been simply 'the bazaar *gup*' or 'the lies of the market-place', as the official scribes described them just after the uprising of 1857, the colonial regime would not have worried about them the way it did. Desiring permanence of rule, the British incessantly wanted to know what the subject population thought and dreamt of. The imperial intelligence knew that it was vital to keep its ears glued to the hustle bustle of the bazaar if it wanted to have 'some idea of the standpoint from which they [the people] regard the actions of their foreign rulers' (Oman 1972, p. 218).[12]

The uprising of 1857 was one such occasion when the need for a social re-orientation guided people to look collectively for a new definition, a new meaning of the Empire. Rumour was the medium through which they could communicate with others. Since 'rumor

[11] Sumit Sarkar's essay in the same volume gives many methodological insights for researchers. It is one of those scholarly pieces that are not written to *answer* but to *raise* questions. Ranajit Guha's (1983) work remains the sole effort in the genre which explores the pre-Gandhian, what he calls, *Elementary*, political thought-processes of the subalterns. Even though he remains preoccupied with insurgent moments, his chapters on *Negation and Transmission* are examples of speculative history writing *par excellence*. However, on rumour Guha stops way short.

[12] That Kaye too reaffirmed this line of reasoning is obvious from his detailed treatment of the rumours circulating at the local bazaars in regard to the sepoys' discontent.

is rife when uncertainty, disenchantment, and an air of uneasiness pervade any collectivity', it is bound to 'reflect a certain critical orientation to social authorities' (Lang and Lang 1963, p. 68).

'In early 1855 it was rumored that the government of Bengal would by legislation prohibit the rite of circumcision among the Muslims.' (J.C. Jha, 1985, p. 15). The rumour about the cartridges being greased by the fats from cows and pigs, which supposedly triggered the Revolt of 1857, could affect only those who were in military service. Kaye noted that there were other pollution rumours which were affecting the entire community. He mentions the rumour about polluted food: ground flour, ghee, *English* bread, salt, country sugar, and drinking water, which automatically concerned the entire population. Guha is right in his conclusion that they were not separate sets of rumours but variations of the same rumour (1983, p. 262). The colonial authorities were quick to realize this 'shrewd unifying stratagem' of the people. What Guha concludes from this is that 'improvisation contributes directly to the efficacy of rumour for rebel mobilization' (ibid.).

There is something more to be read in the 'unifying stratagem' of the people manifest in their imaginative improvisation. It was an attempt to create a community of dissent, a community of 'Hindus' and 'Muslims', of sepoys and civilians, united in their efforts to oppose imperial rule. Before there were clubs of the local intelligentsia, concerted campaigns of the lettered middle class officials and newspapers to rally the masses against British rule, the masses might have relied on rumours to propagate discontent and conflict. Rumours were directly related to the formation of *janmat*, a discourse of the 'public sphere' of the plebeians. It is in this sense of constructing a *janmat* that a collective definition acquired political meaning. Improvisations of a rumour provided with the space where individual feelings of anger and animosity against the Raj could be employed to attain a popularly cognizable language of conflict accessible to a much larger public.[13] A

[13] There are some strong reasons why we choose to use *janmat* instead of 'the public sphere' to refer to the collective of dissent being constructed through the process of sharing rumours. Though it was Immanuel Kant who first gave the idea of the bourgeois public sphere, the phrase gained currency only after J. Habermas' *Structural Transformation of the Public Sphere* (1989) became available in English.

The category of the public, in his framework, resulted from the long-run socio-economic changes eventually precipitated by the dreams of a highly successful and

janmat arrived through shared rumours means nothing short of the ideology of the people in times when mobilization, propaganda, and free associations are not the norms of the day.

Janmat

The relationship between rumour and *janmat* has historically been so strong in pre-Gandhian Bihar that in all its major languages, Bhojpuri, Magahi, and Maithili, the demarcating line between rumour and *janmat* barely exists. A single word, *hawa*, is used even today to refer to both, rumour and *janmat*. Let us consider some examples.

1. *Hawa palat gayeel* (Bhojpuri); *Hawe palat gellai* (Magahi); *Hawe palait gell* (Maithili). All the three expressions mean: '*the public opinion*' swung unfavorably.
2. *Hawa uda delan sa ki* . . . (Bhojpuri); *Hawa uda delakai ki* . . . (Magahi); *Hawa ura delkau ki* . . . (Maithili). All the three expressions mean: it was 'rumoured' that. . . .

---

self-conscious bourgeoisie. The latter through its reading clubs, patriotic societies, discussion circles, coffee house debates, etc., broke ground for 'voluntary association' of the people. In the medieval monarchic frame social associations were fixed and limited to those with higher legal and hereditary status. The emergence of a self-confident, but non-regal, bourgeoisie aspired to create a space that would concede to it the role of leadership in the coming century.

However, Habermas essentially limits his concern to the bourgeois public and its sphere. In the process, he reposes too much faith in its rational discourse. As Geoff Eley so succinctly summarizes, the elitism of this sphere neglects 'the ways in which [it] blocked and consciously repressed possibilities of broader participation/emancipation *and* ignores alternative sources of an emancipatory impulse in the popular radical traditions' (1992, p. 306). Eley explains: 'In particular, Habermas' oppositions of "educated/uneducated" and "literate/illiterate" simply don't work, because . . . the liberal public sphere was faced at the very moment of its appearance by not only a "plebeian" public that was disabled and easily suppressed but also a radical one that was combative *and* highly literate' (p. 305).

Though it remains a contentious issue how far the plebeian of India or Bihar, or for that matter, of Europe, was disabled, and how easily suppressed, it is this public sphere of the plebeians that concerns us.

Another contemporary work, though relatively less known, is that of Reinhart Koselleck 1959, English tr. 1988. For a comparative appraisal of Koselleck and Habermas, see Anthony J. La Vopa 1992.

3. Similarly, in Hindi, *aisi hawa chali hai*, means: 'such is the public opinion'; while, *yeh sab hawa hai*, means: these are all airy-fairy, rumours.
4. The colloquial expression, '*zamindar ko dekhate hi unki hawa nikal gai*', literally means: they felt deflated the moment they saw the zamindar. But what is being conveyed is that they were dumbfounded or clueless not knowing what to do once they saw the zamindar.

There are many similar instances in which *hawa* is used in the sense of wisdom and opinion. The *hawai kila* (or, Qila; literally, the castle in the air) which is often pejoratively used to refer to an unattainable dream, could well mean a vision, a utopia, an idea.

What is perhaps most remarkable about the usage of *hawa*, in both its senses, rumour and opinion, is that it unfailingly brings out the dynamic, ever changing and shifting nature of things. Like air, an opinion is always on the move. So is rumour. They are processes in continuum, living breathing discourses of human thoughts and actions. No wonder then that *hawa* is also used to connote the entire environment in which one lives.

Equally interesting is to recall the etymological unity of the words *afwah* (Arabic) and *afsana* (Persian), rumour and fiction. They, etymologically speaking, are not burdened with elitism, unlike their English counterparts in which fiction is a fine form of art while rumour is deplorable. In Hindustani, both demand a skill to create. Both share a similar yearning to reach the unknown, as if they were voyages into the deep sea of desire. However, this does not make them unreal. They *are* indeed the present, subtle sounds of discontent with the present.

It is precisely in this sense that we could fathom the imperial fear of the native inclination to imagination. In a situation like this, to imagine is to escape the tyranny of the present.[14] It is a denial of the authority in the sphere where it matters the most, people's heads. It was to this realm of the colonized that Kaye (1888) wanted the British to have access. Henry Maine hit the nail on the head as he wanted the natives to be denied this lethal weapon right away (I shall discuss Maine

[14] It goes without saying that light on this aspect comes from Frantz Fanon 1967; Mannoni 1972); Césaire 1972 and Memmi 1967.

in some detail in the next chapter). It indeed was a difficult task as the Raj learned to its greatest dismay. It was nothing short of capturing the soul, arresting people's will to dream. Those who conversed in the language of rumour, who were first to wish the death of the Empire, were convinced of its hidden potential.

Almost universally, we find in rumours the very first pronouncements of the death of the Empire. Be it the Xhosa uprising of 1856–7, or, Zulu revolts of 1905–6 in South Africa, or, the Belgian Africa of 1920s when Simon Kimbangu rose to deliver the Black race, or, the Maji Maji revolt of 1905–7 in Tanganyika, or, Mau Mau uprising in Kenya (1952–6), the number of anti-colonial struggles employing rumour to rally people, is fairly large and it might just be the case that with continuing studies we might find rumour the universal medium of communication under circumstances which are alien, discriminating, and repressive.[15] Interestingly, the early declaration of death of the Empire is invariably couched in religious metaphors, the inherited political vocabulary of the people.

It is not uncommon to find some disarmingly sharp but 'false-consciousness' variety of readings of 'sacralized political sphere' of this genre. Marx, as Talal Asad notes (1993, p. 46) in his thought-provoking anthropological account of religion, viewed religion as 'a mode of consciousness which is *other than consciousness of reality*, external to the relations of production, *producing no knowledge*, but expressing at once the anguish of the oppressed and a *spurious consolation*'. As explored in the following pages, this variety of understanding takes an awfully narrow view of not only knowledge and consciousness but even of reality. In such a genre of reasoning, reality (and thus knowledge and consciousness of it) becomes an abstracted thing which could apparently be contemplated without sensitivity to its cultural locus. Implicit is the assumption that there is only one reality (and, by implication, knowledge and consciousness of it), which has been discovered in the nineteenth-century West European laboratory of materialism.

According to Coquery-Vidrovitch (1988), '(A)t a time when the traditional societies were increasingly losing their control over temporal affairs . . . when the ancestral methods of warfare had become ineffective, Messianism appeared to endow them with new force'

[15] See Coquery-Vidrovitch 1988; Isaacman 1976; Gwassa and Iliffe 1968; Comaroff 1985 among others.

(p. 178). It was 'a flight into the imaginary' (p. 189), 'the last resort of a powerless society whose weapons had failed' (p. 188). 'Their recourse to the supernatural clearly revealed the conflict between the ideology of the rebellion and the economic and cultural realities in a rural society whose dispersive social organization countered all attempts at fundamental change' (ibid.). Once again, to a Marxist, this is a familiar way of relegating religion to the corner of 'false consciousness'. The instrumentalist framework too is clearly at display here. Coquery-Vidrovitch would have us believe that religion was called upon by the African people to rescue them when their 'ancestral methods of warfare had become ineffective'. But what was the ancestral method of warfare? Was it ever possible for an African to conceive it outside the halo of his/her religion? To pose the question differently and provocatively, is it possible to make sense of Coquery-Vidrovitch's arguments outside the purview of orthodox Marxism?

Ranajit Guha appears to have exchanged the false-consciousness variety of understanding (his reference to 'self alienation' and 'self estrangement' notwithstanding) for an instrumentalist one: '(T)he mythopoeic [as opposed to the empiric] imaginations of the rebels endowed them with exceptional and indeed magical powers, a pathetic device by which a poorly armed peasantry compensated themselves in fantasy for what they actually lacked in military equipment and organization' (1983, p. 270). To illustrate the point, Guha cites prophetic rumours like the promise of charismatic leaders about bringing fire from heaven or, turning enemy bullets into water. It is interesting to note that similar rumour could be found in Tanganyika as well, where Kinji-Kitile Ngwele 'claimed to have the gift of immunizing warriors with magic water (*maji*) that would also transform German bullets into water' (Coquery-Vidrovitch 1988, p. 178). It cost many lives in Tanganyika and in Chotanagpur, Bihar. Why did people continue to believe it? Guha would promptly remind us of their 'pathetic device . . . [to] compensate(d) themselves in fantasy for what they actually lacked in military equipment and organization'. Those doubting Guha's Freudian fantasy should seek the answer elsewhere.

If we leave aside the instrumentalist reading of religion and focus, for example, on rumour as a linguistic metaphor rooted in a world-view, it would be impossible to think of any other medium in which people could have sought to mobilize themselves. They did not *assign* supernatural powers to their leaders, they always *saw* their leaders as a shade supernatural to them. It is not only in relation to, what Sumit Sarkar categories as 'miraculous total transformation' (1984 p. 312) that we find religious idioms invoked. Even in mundane, secular, and highly specific instances,[16] even when the anti-colonial movements had acquired a national character and were blessed with secular and Enlightened leadership, we can find similar language at work.[17] In fact, the Gandhian metaphors were primarily derived from religious sources. True, there was no single religious source, nor was Gandhi the only individual to rely on religion. The reason why Gandhi became more successful than others is because he emphasized sacrifice and purification of the self, which allowed him to withdraw movements, to the annoyance of many, and yet remain supremely popular.[18] In his scheme of things, every movement and every social act of the individual was ultimately tied to his self. In other words, if an act resulted in failure, the Gandhian explanation would be that there must have been some shortcoming still lingering in the self. Devotion and sacrifice must not have been enough. In other words, the failure of the Gandhian leadership was well accounted for, not as a tactical device, but in his system of satyagraha itself.

[16] One 'Bahadur' combined the two in his poem and asked God to take care of increasing taxes:

O Kanhaiya [Lord Krishna] where are you?
In the matter of the enhancement of taxes
the people have no voice, all their efforts become useless
You had promised to appear on such occasions;
why then do you not appear today?

(*Tarun Bharat*, 6 September 1923, D.I.G. (C.I.D.) Report on objectionable matters published in vernacular, F/n. 172/1923, Home Political Special, Bihar State Archives, HPS/BSA hereafter, Patna)

[17] During the 'recrudescence' of the Tana-Bhagat movement under the leadership of Sibu and Maya (in the early twentieth century), leaflets granting supernatural powers to them were distributed. The leaflets stated that 'the Germans are now masters of the world, that the zamindars' day is over, that no rents or taxes should be paid, the Marwaris [a merchant caste] should be driven out of the country for raising the price of cloth and Muhammadans for slaughtering cattle' (F/n. 421/1919, HPS/BSA). This tells us about the remarkable marriage between the sacred and the temporal. The sense of time captured here is impeccable—the rise of Germany in the international arena of power struggle, increasing Hindu-Muslim strife in the South Asian polity, sharpening animosity against the zamindars and the merchants and moneylenders, and the emergence of a sense of 'country'.

[18] This argument is taken from Sumit Sarkar (1984, p. 316).

The centrality of the idea of 'self-sacrifice' in the Gandhian scheme of things soon made it pervasive. It began to be expected from the rank and file as well. What was perhaps implicit or assumed in the nineteenth-century political endeavours became an explicit requirement. The lead article of the *Tarun Bharat*, 2 September 1923 (published in Patna), brought this out quite clearly in its welcome to Maulana Mohamed Ali on his release from jail:

> we could not come up to your expectations. At that time [when you were sent to jail] the bureaucracy [an euphemism for the Raj] was greatly afraid of you as well as of the Indians, but today owing to our cowardice . . . , it has become more audacious. At that time you, because of your patriotism and self-sacrifice, had taken us to the door of Swaraj; but today we have been thrown miles away from it.[19]

There is no reason why we cannot grant the same space to those who believed in the magical power of their leaders even at the cost of their lives. How can we know for sure that the 'blind faith' restored in the commands of the traditional leadership was merely an example of superstition and not of the sacrifice that a group demanded from its members to oppose a powerful enemy? It is often argued that the key to Gandhi's success lies in his forging of fearlessness in the masses.[20] If this is true, and I think indeed it is,[21] then what prevents us from admitting that the construction of a supernatural leadership was also an effort in the same direction? What else do the peasants in Shahid Amin's essay convey in their processes of deification of Gandhi? Amin looks in vain, so does Pouchepadass, for denials and clarifi-

[19] F/n. 172/1923, HP/BSA.

[20] A typical illustration of the phenomenon is captured by 'Bahadur' in his poem published in *Tarun Bharat*, 4 February 1923, 'You may call me guilty, but I am not guilty. You may well punish me but I do not deserve punishment. I do not deserve the gallows; I am not guilty. . . . How should I bow down before you for pardon? . . . Here, O, impostor. I do not entertain any hopes from you. I am a servant of God and am not your slave' (F/n. 172/1923, HP/BSA).

[21] 'Oh! Almighty God! Give me strength to die for my religion, to die for the whole world', Gandhi spoke to satyagrahis. 'Remember what Shri Krishna told Arjuna about the *Sthitaprajna* ("the man of steady intellect"—editor's note) in the second chapter of the *Gita*. There is no salvation in death when dying, there is salvation in death when dying willingly, when dying gladly.' Gandhi proceeded, 'God has given me strength to die for my country and for my religion' (*Collected Works*, 1967, p. 271).

cations from the Congress leadership of rumours which were adamant to make Gandhi nothing less than a Mahatma. To the contrary, local leaders contributed to further deification of Gandhi. Consider, for instance, Sardar Harihar Singh, of village Chaugain, Shahabad, who, participated in the Civil Disobedience movement of 1921 and was twice elected to the Legislative Assembly, who composed the following poem in Bhojpuri:

> धीरे बहु धीरे बहु पछुआ बेयरिया।
> घमवां से बदरी करहु रखवरिया।
> जुग-जुग जोहे जगत पुरातन
> धरती पर उतरेला पुरुस सनातन।
> नाहीं बरुए संख-चक्र, नाहीं गदाधारी
> नाहीं हउए दसरथ-सुत धनुधारी।
> कान्हे पट पीत नाहीं, मुरली अधर नाहीं
> साक्य-राजपुत नाहीं, बनल भिखारी।
> अबकी अंजब रूप धइले गिरधारी।

> [Blow slowly, O Western wind. O cloud, give respite from the sun. The man awaited by the whole world for millennia, has descended upon the earth. He has no conch-shell or *chakra* in his hands (he is not Lord Vishnu), nor is he with bow, (as Lord Ram) the son of Dasarath. No yellow cloth on his shoulder, no flute on his lips. He is like a beggar, but he is not Buddha either. This time the one who held a mountain on his finger-tip has taken a strange form!] (Shri Durgashankar Prasad Singh, 1958, pp. 228–9)

What is at stake here is the value of historical-sociology. If it aspires to be meaningful it must try to gain access to the world-view of those it wants to write about. It may never achieve the target, but the incessant effort to do so will help minimize the distance between the two worlds that lay between the observer and the observed.

Rumours in the Age of Print

By the 1920s, print had already become a powerful medium of communication. With the increasing efforts at vertical mobilization, the literate segment of population had begun to assume leadership in opinion making. This group had no moral compunction in borrowing idioms from elsewhere. It could be tactical, instrumental, and calculating without feeling the moral burden of doing so. This is not to suggest that there invariably was a water-tight compartmentalization between the language of this segment of the populace and that of the masses, who preferred religious, 'rumorous', and ambiguous utterances. As a result, we now often find local-level Congress resorting to religious expressions and reproducing rumours in their speeches. The newspapers, English and vernacular, gave them an unprecedented air of authenticity by simply reprinting them. *Home Political Files* are full of such instances, mostly recorded under the rubric of 'seditious speeches'. This entails a shift in the nature of rumour.

Rumour reproduced in speeches and print, and in some cases floated consciously by local leaders, meant that now it had found an author. However, it had not yet lost all its charm because not all rumours were spread by known and conscious agents. Despite charges of 'sedition' and persecution, rumours never ceased. And, finally, there still was a need for unauthored rumours because the attempt at vertical mobilization was far from complete or hegemonic; there indeed was a case to be made against the effort of this kind of mobilization itself. As mass movements grew in confidence, the Nationalist attempt at all-India mobilization against the colonial regime faced many class/caste/group/region-based challenges.

In its *Fortnightly Reports* for April 1919, Mcpherson wrote to the Secretary to the Government of India:

> Wicked stories are being spread. It is being pointed out to the Muhammadans that Hindus have differences of opinion with them on questions of religion its true [*sic*], but in the British they have a deadly enemy not only to their religion but also to their interests which are common with those of the Hindus. It is pointed out that the British having seized all their sacred cities they will soon open hotels in them where swine's flesh will be eaten and shops opened where swine's flesh and other meats will be sold.[22]

In the beginning of February 1921, one Ram Raksheya Brahmchari, a local Congress activist, addressed a gathering at Sitamarhi ground, invoking people to join the Non-Cooperation movement. Among other things, he told the crowd that

[22] Report dated 18 April 1919, F/n. 421/1919, HPS/BSA.

> [T]he Hindus want cow protection and the Mussalmans hate pigs, but the English men devour both cows and pigs. 18 lakhs [hundred thousand] of cows being simply their breakfast. The English men got Mandils [temples] pulled down and destroyed by the Hindus and Musjids [mosques] by the Mussalmans and got Ramayan burnt by the Hindus and Qoran by Muslims.[23]

The number of cows being devoured by the English increased to 20 lakh by the month of December in the speech of one Bhagwat Pandey.[24] The holy cow was put to yet another ingenious use. The same year, in the month of March, people of the Danaha region in Bettiah moved about village to village 'repeating idiotic stories'. The story was that the King, Gandhi, a Brahman and a cow had been put into a fire together and that the King was burnt up, but the others came out unhurt. A variant was that they had been put into boiling ghee, and another variant was that Gandhi had pulled the King out and that he had run off as fast as he could.[25]

The first version was the popular one. Wherever the story reached, people were asked to take it to the next five villages, on the pattern of *patias* (snowball letters).

The metaphor of the cow signified the nation in peril.[26] The insecurity of temples and mosques, the disrespect for the *Ramayan* and Koran, articulated popular resentment at the lack of freedom. The anxiety around religion as a whole shows the seriousness of the situation and the urgency to oppose the foreigner. Examples of this nature are plenty, recorded and popularly remembered. What is crucial here is to reflect upon whether or not they were novelties of the time, emerging and acquiring meaning in the Gandhian discourse and only in it, without any historical legacy whatever.

[23] Report of Sub-Inspector Ali Imam of Sitamarhi P.S., Muzaffarpur District, dated 7 February 1921. See F/n. 10/1921, HPS/BSA.

[24] F/n. 644/1921, Confidential, HPS/BSA.

[25] Confidential letter of D.I.G. Crime, F/n. 148/1921, BSA.

[26] To use the symbol of the cow to depict the nation was allegorical as well as real. *Gaurakshini Sabhas* (associations for cow-protection) had already begun to make their Hindu imagery of the Indian Nation into a movement. The Sabha's alleged goal, to save the cow from being killed for British consumption, was to provide them with a benign and politically correct appearance. Soon, however, it focused its political appeal against the Muslim who also happened to be beef-eaters.

The rumours of pollution, greased cartridges, food items mixed with animal fat, etc., floating around the uprising of 1857 were the precursors of some of the rumours in Gandhian times. That both major religions, Islam and Hinduism, were in danger was, similarly, no innovation of the Non-Cooperation-Khilafat movements. With Guha we have already noted the 'unifying stratagem' of the rumour process during the days of the 1857 uprising. This, the masses realized at the very first point of National upsurge that Hindu-Muslim unity was of vital consequence. No elite tutorship was required on this score.[27]

In other words, whatever be the significance of the religious metaphors in general and the question of Hindu-Muslim unity in particular in the Gandhian discourse, the debt to history is enormous. That the *janmat*, the discourse of the plebeians to create a collectivity, was central to the evolution of Gandhian language could be elaborated with the help of prophetic rumours.

Guha mentions a couple of prophetic rumours before and during the 1857 uprising which forecast the end of the Raj. These rumours were important as we noted earlier, in the sense that the death of the Empire could be envisioned, speculated, and desired only in the realm of gossip and could be shared with others only as a rumour. Towards the end of the nineteenth century, there was a similar rumour afloat in Bihar, according to which a saint had announced some thousand years ago that the British would conquer Hindustan but would be driven away from it in the year 1900. This was certainly an improvement on previous rumours, for it not only predicted the end of the Raj, but also made colonial conquest destined, a 'had-to-happen' kind of phenomenon and thus underscored the colonial supremacy often being orchestrated through its victory over the subject race. Put differently, it tended to neutralize colonial domination. A closer scrutiny of the grand promises floating during the days of Non-Cooperation movement reveal similar unspoken concerns.

Including Gandhi and Shaukat Ali, every Congress leader was talk-

[27] There is almost a consensus among Indian historians that the uprising of 1857 was as much a struggle for Deen (faith) as it was for Dharma: the Hindus and Muslims perceived the British as inimical to and destroyers of their religions and this perception found spectacular expressions. Proclamations issued by the rebel leaders have been profered as convincing proof of the Hindu-Muslim unity. See R. Mukherjee 1984.

ing about the attainment of swaraj by the end of 1921. The popular version, of course, had its own take on it: 'Congress is like a temple, which had been under construction for the last 35 years and the idol of the God (meaning swaraj) will be consecrated on 31st December. If we die in our attempt we will enter heaven and if we succeed we will gain swaraj.[28] This genre of political campaign belongs to the same prophetic tradition of the nineteenth-century rumours that sought to unite people by convincing them about the short life of the Empire. Despite differences in the way political space was available at these two different moments of colonial control, the political employed a strikingly similar method to arrive at a collective consciousness that was in conflict with the survival of the British regime. It is in this sense, that Shahid Amin could have been more cautious in assigning so many 'firsts' to the Gandhian moment:

> The enthusiasm Gandhi generated, the expectations he aroused and the attack he launched on British authority had all combined to *initiate the very first* moments of a process which, given other factors, could *help the peasant to conceptualize* the turning of his world upside down. This was an *incipient political consciousness* called upon, for *the very first time*, to reflect—albeit vaguely and intermittently—on the possibility of an inversion of many of those *power relations deemed inviolable until then*, such as British/Indian, landlord/peasant, high caste/low caste, etc. (1984, p. 25, emphasis added)

One will have little hesitation in admitting that Gandhi did create a political sphere that was congenial to a confident and fearless mass movement. However, history stands in firm opposition to Amin's assertion that it was due to Gandhi that the peasant could 'conceptualize the turning of his world upside down', or, that it was due to Gandhi that 'for the very first time' it became possible for the peasants to 'reflect . . . on the possibility of an inversion of many of those power relations deemed inviolable until then. . . .' Movements trying to invert power relations in the period before the Gandhian language of politics acquired currency, are many. The Subaltern Studies project was launched precisely on this point. Amin merely has to turn to the early volumes of the project.

In fact, even before 1921, the period Shahid Amin examines to

[28] One Bhagwat Pandey was reported to have repeated this rumour in his public speeches on 12 December 1921, F/n. 644/1921, Confidential, HPS/BSA.

formulate the popular perception of Gandhi in Gorakhpur, in order to arrive at the earlier-mentioned conclusions, the Commissioner of Patna reported some time towards the end of 1916, rumours in Gaya and Patna according to which the British Raj was to end by March 1917, and, therefore, it was not 'necessary to pay the land revenue due on the next March *Kist* [instalment]'.[29] This is also before Gandhi was persuaded to come to Champaran in 1917 to organize the peasants against the atrocities of indigo factory owners which gave vent to a different set of rumours, as mentioned by Pouchepadass (1974). This is even before belief in the attainment of swaraj could be popularized by the non-peasant leaders of the Congress. It very clearly shows the consciousness peasants had already acquired about the link between the Raj and the zamindars. This is further strengthened by the discussion on the refractory rent paying that had already developed among peasants as an everyday form of resistance in nineteenth-century Bihar (see Chapter 1).

If one looks at a couple of 'remembered' (unrecorded) 'experiences', the point can be made even more forcefully.[30] Frequently, people 'heard' that in a certain village (always too distant to be verified) recalcitrant tenants were thrown into the cage of the hungry tiger kept by the zamindar. In one village, it was said, the *Mast* elephant of the zamindar was let loose and it ran amok in the ranks of the protesting tenants, hundreds got trampled, and so on. Rahul Sankrityayan, a prominent leader of the Kisan Sabha in Saran district, recounts an incident of this nature in Amwari Satyagraha (24 February 1939). Along with several kisan activists, he had gone to harvest the sugar cane in the field of a kisan. The zamindar of the area had claimed that field as his own. The time to offer satyagraha was fixed and announced in the presence

[29] *Fortnightly Report*, 1 January 1917, F/n. 169/1918, HPS/BSA.

[30] The following argument is based on conversations between October 1995 and January 1996 with the following villagers of Bihar: Ram Talika Singh of Garahani Tola, Debi Dayal Singh of Bhangawatipur, Sambhu Nath Singh of Demhan, (Late) Keso Yadav of Pawana, all from Bhojpur district; 'Azad Baba' of Jahanabad, 'Kariwaa', of Shahpur, Patna, Ram Charan Sharma of Baheri, Darbhanga. Brief details of some of these people are given in Chapter 2. The 'stories' narrated by them were confirmed by many other kisans, including those of my village, Garahani Tola, Bhojpur. I specially thank Indrajit Singh of Mahatwaniyan village (Bhojpur) who is an archive personified of Bhojpuri culture.

of the police official. When the activists reached the place at the announced time, they were greeted by zamindar's toughs and his two elephants kept in an inebriated condition to trample the satyagrahis (Rahul Sankrityayan 1950, p. 512).

We may not ever come to know the 'truth' of most of these stories. However, it is a fact that keeping tame elephants was very much a part of the regal insignia, and its symbolic importance continues in some respect even today. And we do not know how many of the zamindars actually had tigers. What remains crucial is the association of beastly powers with the zamindari rights, legal and otherwise. The uncontrollability of a mad elephant (it always trampled the poor peasants) and the tiger's appetite for humans are mythopoeic. The zamindari was almost poetically represented by the brutality and strength of the tiger and elephant; the choice of symbols, assuming that they were purely fictive, conveyed nothing short of a jungle-Raj. The madness of the elephant was the allegory for the madness of the zamindar and the tiger's hunger for humans was the zamindar's hunger for rent—always insatiable. In the existing scheme of things, to satisfy him was possible only through meeting one's death. In any event, these rumours tell us about the recalcitrant tenants who rose in protest against the zamindar.

To these, numerous other 'stories' can be added, stories which were true but were probably exaggerated out of proportion. That tenants were often forced to sell their young children (often girls) to meet the rental demands of the zamindar, is one such story. It even found a place in Swami Sahajanand Saraswati and Rahul Sankrityayan's writings.[31] It has, in fact, assumed the aura of folklore. In the 1930s when the Kisan Sabha undertook a survey to enquire about the conditions of peasants in Bihar, not many cases of such sale of daughters were reported. The reason probably lies in the socio-cultural matrix of the province. It does not seem likely that merely a couple of instances would have shaped people's memory. The disrespect that a *betibechwa* (one who has sold his daughter) is subjected to in the male-dominated society of Bihar, might have prevented many tenants from reporting correctly. However, the very fact that there is a proper expression for it in the lingua franca of Bihar—*betibechwa*—means that the incident could not have been that rare.

[31] Sahajanand Saraswati 1940, p. 82; Rahul Sankrityayan 1973, p. 140.

One can further mention the notorious *dola* system according to which the palanquins (*dola*) carrying the brides of mostly lower castes were forcibly stopped by the zamindars' men and the brides had to spend the first night with the local zamindars. The practice was particularly prevalent in the Bhojpur region.[32] Sahajanand mentions one incident in which a tenant, upon failing to get milk for the zamindar, was asked to milk his lactating wife (*Kisan Kaise Ladate Hain*, p. 82). In yet another incident narrated to the Congress Enquiry Committee by a woman of Bithan village in Darbhanga district, the tahsildar ordered that a woman's thigh be tied to the thigh of her father-in-law (ibid., p. 93). The victim had failed to pay the rent. These incidents might have been rare, but the fact that they still survive in people's memory means that they formed a very crucial aspect of a popular knowledge system. The following folksong is testimony to the cruel realities faced by the peasant women at the hands of zamindars:

निहुरल-निहुरल अंगना बहरलौं
रजवा चलावे एक रोरिया ना।
'गांव के लोगवा राजा भाई रे भतीजवा'
दैया हमरा से कइसन ठठोरिया ना।
फूल लोढ़े गइलों मैं राजा फुलवरिया
रजवा एक रोरिया चलावे ना।
'का तू अए राजा रोरिया चलावेला
हमहूं त गांव बेटियवा ना।'
'जो तू हऊ गांव के बेटियवा।
त का करे अइलू फुलवरिया ना।
ऐहि रे समइया गोरी खेलि-खुनी लेहु
फिर तूं हो जइबु लरकोरिया ना।'

[32] 'There used to be a king Ranpal Singh, in Bhojpur, whose fiat it was that every newly-wed girl be initiated by him. The subjects found this revolting, but did not dare oppose him. One day Mahthin Dai, a bride, refused to go with the king, inviting an encounter in which the king was done to death. In the clash also died the husband of Mahthin who then chose to become a *sati*. As a memorial to her bravery, the people built a Mahthin temple in Behea in central Bhojpur' (Arun Sinha, *Frontier*, 7 January 1978).

This is not a tale from medieval times. Local people narrate that the Eastern Railway tracks were being laid when construction of the temple was still in progress. The incident therefore may have occurred around the 1880–90s.

Bending low, I sweep the courtyard. Zamindar, the tease, tosses a pebble in my direction (to catch my attention). Being from the same village as myself, you are no different from my brothers or nephews. Why, then do you flirt with me? I went to pick some flowers from the zamindar's garden; again he tries to catch my attention (by tossing a pebble). Why are you flirting with me? I am daughter of the village. 'If you are indeed the daughter of the village, how come you wandered into my garden? This is the age to have fun and games. After all, soon you'll end up as a mother'.] (Hiralal Tiwary 1980, p. 316)

Seen in the context of the *dola* system, the song points to the threat of molestation from the zamindar, which lurks even in a women's natal village, notionally the most secure of spaces. A peasant's daughter was considered like a fruit which could be readily picked by the zamindar at will. Through such stories, kisans understood and reaffirmed their social locations. In their remembering and telling, the kisan reproduced a consciousness about kisan-zamindar relations of the times. Exaggeration of such incidents should be seen in the light of kisans' desire to reproduce that consciousness.

Certainly, the Gandhian Congress ably read the pulse of the people and the time. The Gandhian language of politics was indeed pro-people *par excellence*. But it was not the case of the leadership creating the popular, as Amin would have us believe. The popular gave Gandhian politics a language that early Congress men and women had failed to acknowledge and learn. The popular was constructed through discourses that were often religious in nature and spread through rumours that were discrete and cunning. The space of improvisation that a rumour entails, provided it with a fluidity central to any communication process. If the version of rumour at Danaha that had Gandhi, a Brahmin, and a cow come out of a fire unharmed, very much in line with a popular Hindu belief that the soul of a dead person can cross the dreaded Vaitarini river on its way to heaven holding the tail of a cow, assisted by the mantras of a Brahmin, was the continuation of religious imageries, the other version in which Gandhi pulls the king out of fire tells us about the changing language of politics. The non-violence advocated by Gandhi had begun to gain access to the people's minds. There was no guarantee of its unilinear progress, nor had it achieved a cognitive universality, as Amin remarkably illustrates elsewhere (Amin 1996).

The changing concerns necessitated by a quest for a 'secular' nation did not have to destroy the religious images. The latter was only being enlarged and put to unprecedented usage. As a man from Bankipur, Patna, 'referred to the story of Joseph in Jail and exhorted the people to be mindful of the day of resurrection'. In the same breath, he told his audience that, 'Bishwanandji has proved by the shashtras [*sic*] that if the sacred thread be touched with a foreign cloth it will be desecrated'.[33] Or, as Ramvriksha Benipuri, a contemporary litterateur, a Socialist, and a Kisan Sabha activist, mentioned in his reminiscences, there was rumour that on the leaves of tobacco, the hair of both cow and pig had grown (Benipuri 1979, p. 55). Religion continued to give newer aspirations a language with which it could propagate arguments for swadeshi or issues of social reform, or swaraj.

To underline the need for a Hindustan that believed in *sarva dharma samabhava* (equal treatment to all religions), it had become crucial to invoke not only Hindu and Muslim images as was the practice earlier, but to include as many as possible; indeed, that was inherent in the hegemonic discourse of a pan-Indian nation, so much so that religion even appeared to subsume unfavourable episodes of history as well. As one Khalil wrote in his poem (which was being sung daily in the Bhagalpur vernacular schools):

> Oh, Mother India, victory to thee, victory to thee. . .
> May we be more brave than Bhim and patient like Arjun
> May there be rise of Akbar and Shivaji again
> May Gandhi live (may not die) and may Tilak come back again [*sic*]
> Says 'Khalil' O' Hindus and Musalmans, listen,
> Let all combined speak aloud 'Victory to the Motherland'.[34]

[33] F/n. 644/1921, HPS/BSA.

[34] F/n. 158/1925, HPS/BSA. The poem is significant for two particular reasons. Probably responding to the communal divide that had already emerged in the South Asian polity, it tries to play down the supposed *religious* rivalry between Mughals and Marathas. Secondly, it is one of the most rare poems in which a Muslim clearly invokes the imagery of the Motherland. As we know, the Hinduized version of the Motherland, popularized as Bharat Mata had made it increasingly difficult for a post-*Tabligh/Tanzim* Muslim to visualize the nation as such. *Tabligh* and *Tanzim* refer to a rather fundamentalist movement for purifying Islam and organizing Muslims. It arose in reaction to upper caste Hindu *shuddhi* and *sangathan* (purification and organization).

That the discourse of *janmat* provided Gandhian politics with a language of conduct could be observed through yet another set of rumours. We have noted rumours regarding the supernatural powers of the traditional leaders of the peasants around the 1857 uprising. Gandhi was attributed with similar qualities: 'He knows how to disappear. One day people even saw him riding the cloud. The English imprisoned him, the gate of the Jail was locked, but Gandhiji disappeared' (Benipuri 1979, p. 55). According to Ram Raksheya Brahmchari of Sitamarhi, as Kans could not kill Lord Krishna, so no power could kill Gandhi.[35] The construction of Gandhi as Mahatma was the people's signature on the National register of mass movements. However, we cannot overlook the fact that in the course of making politics sacred, the kisans did not miss the chance of airing their mundane, everyday sufferings. Pace Pouchepadass:

> Those rumors . . . reported that Gandhi had been sent . . . to redress all the grievances of the raiyats, and that his mandate overruled all the local officials and the courts. He was said to be about to abolish all the unpopular obligations which the planters imposed on their raiyats, so that there was no need to obey the word of any planter any more. A rumor was also in the air that the administration of Champaran was going to be made over to the Indian themselves, and that the British would be cleared out of the district within a few months. (1974, pp. 82–3)

This may not appeal to rationalist minds, but, that is how ran popular imaginations, the metis of the people: prophetic, ever hopeful, almost mystical. It was only logical that Gandhi became the hero of the masses for he himself was mysticism personified, seldom drawing his inspirational energy from the outer rational world. K.K. Dutta narrates one such incident. Opposing the Indian Criminal Law (Amendment) Bill No. I of 1919 and the Criminal Law (Emergency Powers) Bill No. II of 1919, Gandhi was 'somewhat at a loss as to how Satyagraha should be offered. But the idea "broke upon" him one night in a dream. . . .' (Dutta 1957, p. 290). And dutifully, he followed his subconscious. It is no surprise then that he who could follow the language of his dream would be the champion of those who lived each day precisely because they could dream.

The Raj realized the significance of a fugitive utterance very early.

[35] Report of Sub-Inspector Ali Imam, F/n. 10/1921, HPS/BSA.

As Kaye and Oman bring before us the picture of a fidgeting regime in the 1857 uprising, rattled by a series of uncontrolled and, indeed, uncontrollable rumours, they also hint at its efforts to counter them. The first rational reaction of the administration was to disbelieve them, dismiss them as lies of the market-place, or, 'bazaar *gup*' as they were sometimes referred to. It was only through time that the Raj learned the futility of its disbelief and began to look for methods to counter them effectively. By 1921, it had been a fairly established fact among the top administrators of Bihar that perhaps a rumour could be countered effectively only by a rumour. And in this regard, an official mentioned his helplessness to Mcpherson that the '*jo-hukumwalas*' ('yes men') were of not much use since they could pass a loyal resolution or print propaganda material, but they could not match the propaganda of those who relied on the spoken word.[36]

Rumour was an outlet for political aspirations of the people in late nineteenth-century and early twentieth-century Bihar. As they proved detrimental in the course of time to the larger interests of those who led the Congress, the aspirations found other fora where they could receive a sympathetic audience. It was only befitting to a plebeian discourse that was dynamic enough to try and break away from the hegemonic controls of the Congress. But that is another story.

One of the elements of rumour as explored above was its strong religious content. The following chapter looks into the readings of religion by Gandhi, the architect of the Indian National Congress and by Swami Sahajanand Saraswati, the most important kisan leader of Bihar in the first half of the twentieth century, as two different political languages. It attempts to show how each in his individual way, mined a single religious text to evolve his own distinctive political style and ideology.

[36] F/n. 648/1921, HPS/BSA.

CHAPTER 4

Re-working Religion: The *Gita* and the Quest for a New Language

In the preceding chapter, we discussed rumour to illustrate how a political language may evolve and function in a period when space for open politics is not easily accessible to the masses. The late nineteenth and early twentieth century rumours gave a glimpse of the early kisan resolve to pronounce the death of the colonial Empire and its primary social base, zamindari. The language of politics, not only of the kisans who produced and consumed these rumours (with others), but also of Gandhi and the Gandhian mass movements, was overwhelmingly religious. The Gandhian language of non-violent satyagraha appeared to be substantially informed by the nineteenth century lingua franca of the kisans rather than the latter being a passive construct of the former, as is often claimed in the official narratives of the Congress.

This chapter focuses on the colonal discourse on Hindu religion and the religiosity of Gandhian language and some of its key concepts which are central to a discussion on the kisan political language of the period. For example, notions of sacrifice, purification of the self, satyagraha, and ahinsa are pivotal to the Gandhian ideology of mass movement. And these concepts remain crucial for understanding kisan struggle as well, since no mass movement in colonial India could afford not to engage with Gandhian categories once the latter became so overwhelmingly available. The same was true for Gandhi, the individual, as well. One could disagree with him, as many did; but neither institution nor person could ignore him. Many of those who grumbled about him, occasionally or consistently, respected his sincerity and integrity.

The Kisan Sabha in Bihar drew its initial energy, intellectual and institutional, from the Gandhian Congress. Swami Sahajanand Saraswati, the founder of the Sabha, owed a great deal, along with many others, to Gandhi for their first lessons in active politics. As we know, the Sabha later broke away from the Congress and Gandhi. So did Sahajanand (to whom we shall return later). Their relationship, their language of politics, and their handling of religion per se, provide the matrix to evaluate the significance of some of these concepts in their praxis. In other words, acceptance, transformation, or rejection of Gandhian categories of mass movement together take us to the 'new' language of politics that was evolving during this period.

The first logical step in this direction is to map out the changes Gandhi introduced in the policies of the Congress in his efforts at conceptualizing the colonial regime. As subsequent pages will attempt to show, Gandhi traced the reason for Indian subjugation in its moral decadence. And for possible moral rejuvenation and action, he identified the *Bhagavad Gita* (popularly known as the *Gita*, a text written around the fifth century in the form of dialogue, and appended to the *Mahabharata*) as the most suitable Hindu scripture. Although Gandhi liberally borrowed from a host of religious and cultural practices, it was largely from the *Gita* that he enriched his concepts and vocabulary of anti-colonial struggles. The *Gita* was 're-discovered' in the late nineteenth and the early twentieth centuries, in the sense that many leaders, spiritual and political, saw in its message of ceaseless action (as opposed to renunciation) the key to India's rejuvenation and freedom. The deep religious orientation which allegedly tended to make Indian people aloof from worldly affairs and to strive for moksha (salvation) from the cycle of temporal births underwent a sea change. Instead, to do one's duty without desire of reward became the new mantra, the very essence of moksha. Sahajanand too wrote a commentary on the *Gita*.[1] The way Gandhi and Sahajanand read and interpreted the *Gita*, provides us with a clue to their different approaches to political action and emancipation along with the basic religiosity of their language of politics.

The endeavour of the Mahatma and the Swami, in a way, addressed the core of the intellectual dilemma of the time, i.e. how to make

[1] *Gita Hridaya* (Hindi, 'The Heart of the *Gita*'), Buxar: Shri Swami Sahajanand Saraswati Smarak Nyas, 1988 (2nd edn.).

voluntary political participation a mass affair, a social wisdom and a collectively internalized avocation. While Gandhi believed in healing the psychological and social wounds of a nation, so that it could fight for its freedom, Sahajanand in his endeavour questioned the cause of these wounds and wished to eradicate them, thus earning the label of a 'radical Swami'. At the risk of oversimplification, the difference can be summarized in the following way: Gandhi saw swaraj, the attainment of political freedom from external rule, as elementary to the upliftment of the entire society, while Sahajanand sought to eradicate the exploitation of kisans, the most populous segment of the subcontinent, as the basis of victory over colonial forces that were decisively supported by the zamindari system. In order to gain swaraj, it was imperative for Gandhi to unite all sections of society, kisans *and* zamindars included. The antagonistic elements were to be checked; all fissures in the indigenous social system were to be kept in abeyance for the time being. It is at this point that the major difference between the two came to the fore.

A host of disclaimers are in order. The concern here is not with the Gandhian critique of civil society or modernity in general. Nor does this chapter offer a comparative appraisal of twentieth-century interpretations of the *Gita*, even though one is obliged to discuss interpretations of Gandhi and Sahajanand and refer to those of Tilak or Aurobindo occasionally. The exercise is restricted to the extent the text is crucial to understand Gandhi and Sahajanand. Similarly, like the previous chapter, an examination of the relationship between the religious language and communal (*sampradayik*) politics that had begun to produce very serious consequences for Indian polity, is beyond the purview of this work.

COLONIAL EPISTEMOLOGY

All India is full of holy men stammering gospels in strange tongues; shaken and consumed in the fires of their own zeal; dreamers, babblers, and visionaries; as it has been from the beginning and continue to the end. (Rudyard Kipling, *Kim*)

Of all the systems of false religion ever fabricated by the ingenuity of fallen man, Hinduism is surely the most stupendous. . . . There is omnipotence; but bereft of creative energy, it is limited to the power of education and fabrication. There is omniscience; but it is restricted to the brief period of wakefulness. . . . (Alexander Duff, *India and India Missions, Including Sketches of the Gigantic System of Hinduism, Both in Theory and Practice*)

How could the mind take hold of such a country? Generations of invaders have tried, but they remain in exile. The important towns they build are only retreats, their quarrels the malaise of men who cannot find their way home. India knows of their trouble. She knows of the whole world's trouble to its uttermost depth. She calls 'Come' through her hundred mouths, through objects ridiculous and august. But come to what? She has never defined. She is not a promise, only an appeal. (E.M. Forster, *A Passage to India*)

Colonial governmentality was precariously based on a system of representation. The latter taken as a system of meaning, provided colonialism with a mechanism of distancing itself from the Other whom it took upon itself to represent. In that, it assumed a moral responsibility to spread the message of Enlightenment to the 'dark corners of the non-Western world'. In other words, colonial superiority over the colonized in its material sense was a form, or outer line, of a relationship; the core of the relationship concerned itself with the processes of constructing the colonized in order to know it. Knowing was essential to rule. To rule and to legitimize the rule, it became essential to 'fix' the Other in terms congenial to the reproduction of the regime.[2] Any failure of the colonial regime at defining the Other was essentially a failure to project its paramountcy. Depending upon circumstances, i.e. the degree of its stability, the colonial regime chose its vocabulary.

When William Jones (1746–94) 'discovered' an Indo-European family of languages and found in ancient Sanskrit texts, particularly in Vedic literature, a golden age of Hinduism, he did not relinquish the task of knowing and situating the Other.[3] In discovering the European heritage in ancient Indian civilization by establishing the links between Sanskrit and Greek (and Latin), colonial epistemology did not give away the moral sanction to colonial expansion. In fact, in the process of this discovery what indeed happened was that the ancient Aryan

[2] See Homi Bhabha's insightful expansion on Frantz Fanon's original idea 1990 and 1994.

[3] Raymond Schwab 1984; Edward Said 1978; Romila Thapar 1975 and 1968; Ronald Inden 1990. Also, Martin Bernal 1991.

civilization became 'almost as a lost wing of early European culture'.[4] Before Jones, it was generally believed that Sanskrit itself was the Indo-European language. Now with the tagging of European languages to Sanskrit with a common ancestry, the German Romantic belief that humankind and the Caucasians originated in the mountains of Caucasia came full circle. Thus Friedrich Schlegel (1772–1829) could exult, 'everything, absolutely everything, is of Indian origin' (quoted in Bernal 1991, p. 230). It was a grand example of discovering one's own self through constructing the Other. However, the discovery retained for the colonials their claim of supremacy in the present. It was only in the past thousand years, that they shared something at par with the people they colonized in the present. India had failed, the explanation followed, to live up to its past glories because of the religious degeneration that enveloped it in the wake of its many foreign dominations. Ironically, this realization too could dawn upon the fallen Indians only with the help of the British.

As the Empire gained in confidence, its respect and sympathy for the lost greatness of the Indian civilization were replaced by contempt and critique of the colonized's present. William Jones and company were replaced by the likes of James Mill (1773–1836). The golden age of Hinduism gave way to the new image: ruins of a decadent civilization, an unruly culture that must be disciplined. This critique hovered around the supposedly escapist, fatalist, other-worldly nature of Hindu religion that refused to confront the problems gripping the present. The wandering sannyasis (renouncers), visionaries spending their lives in jungles, the Hatha yogis (ascetics) almost indifferent to the mundane realm, and sadhus (mendicants), provided much wanted fodder to the colonial mind in a rush to define the Other. What has refreshingly come to light in a study by William R. Pinch (1996) is that the so-called other-worldly orientation of the Indian sannyasi, defined squarely in opposition to this-worldly concerns, may well be yet another instance of a colonial construction of the subject-world. Focusing on the lives of *gosains* and *bairagis* (Shaiva and Vaishnava monks respectively) in Gangetic India, Pinch informs us about their significant political and economic influences as 'merchants, bankers, and most importantly, soldiers' (p. 24). Prior to 1800

[4] Romila Thapar (1968) brings to the fore the unstated political motives of the British.

> [P]owerful *mahants* (abbots) speculated in real estate and engaged in extensive money-lending activities in order to diversify monastic endowments in urban centers throughout the north, thus facilitating links between the increasingly regional political economies of the late Mughal era. . . . [G]osains in particular 'came the nearest of any Indian business community to the emerging bourgeoisie that European theorists from Sleeman[5] to Marx wished to see'.
>
> . . . [t]hey not only possessed excellent commercial intelligence and political connections but had access to a significant degree of independent armed force to back their profit making ventures. . . .
>
> . . . [i]n addition to protecting monastic endowments, sectarian shrines, pilgrimage routes, and commercial interests, gosain and bairagi regiments were increasingly incorporated in the armies of the major regional powers (ibid.).

The first sizeable opposition to the East India Company came from sadhus and fakirs (1760s to 1800) with interests in land who violently resented Company's excesses in fixing land revenues. The East Indian Company realized the open threat the armed sannyasis presented to its authority. As Pinch tells us:

> the phenomenon of armed monasticism certainly posed more than simply a 'law and order' challenge for newly ascendent Company officials. Armed sadhus were the very antithesis of the world the company-state [*sic*] was endeavoring to create in the eighteenth and nineteenth centuries, namely, a settled peasant society that would render forth vast agrarian revenues on a regular basis with as little resistance as possible. The modern state in India could not countenance recalcitrant sadhus wandering about the country-

[5] Colonel William Henry Sleeman, the man credited with the suppression of *thugee* (banditry) and one who ardently believed in hereditary crimes, had special dislike for the section of subject population that denied the rules of a sedentary life. Very much like the wandering *nats* and *doms* (untouchable castes) of the eighteenth century, the sannyasis too were highly suspect in Sleeman's eyes as far as the Colonial law and order situation was concerned:

> Three-fourths of these religious mendicants, whether Hindoos or Muhamadans, rob and steal, and a very great portion of them murder their victims before they rob them. . . . There is hardly any species of crime that is not throughout India perpetrated by men in the disguise; for Hindoos of any caste can become bairagis and gosains; and Muhammadans of any grade can become Fakirs. (cited in Pinch 1996, p. 8)

side armed . . . claiming to represent an alternate locus of authority. *The Company needed a modern sadhu: a priestly monk unconcerned with worldly power and given over completely to religious contemplation and prayer.* Hence Warren Hastings's proclamation of 21 January 1771 banishing 'all Biraugies and Sunnasses . . . who are travellers strangers and passengers in this country' from the provinces of Bengal and Bihar. . . . [T]hose sadhus who were 'neither vagrants nor plunderers but fixed inhabitants', could, in Hastings's view be tolerated. (pp. 25–6, emphasis added)

Without doubting the significance of Pinch's research, however, it must be remembered that the colonial construction of the other-worldly sannyasi was not absolutely baseless as the post-Shankaracharya (AD 788–820) interpretation of the *Gita* did prioritize renunciation over action. The construction was not exclusively colonial in another sense too. The native ruling segments certainly had this version of religiosity working in their favour. It is possible that the native elites might have lent a helping hand to the colonials since they were also going to benefit by the philosophy that portrayed and produced people as indifferent to worldly affairs. The point is that religion or religious practices at large were never monolithic and homogenous. The popular (which again was never given or fixed) did 'imagine' on many occasions a contradictory story of religion which suited them vis à vis the notables. The main purpose behind preferring one kind of depiction over others was primarily due to the colonial desire of fanning a difference that inevitably marked the subject population with an inherent inferiority. The Islamic religion of the rulers of Delhi further consolidated the colonial canon that over the centuries the Hindu ruling elites had become effeminate, thereby unfit to stake any claim to rule on their own. The Mughals had already lost militarily to the British. They were martial but barbaric. With this preface, the saga of the colonial legitimacy to rule appeared complete.

Early Responses

Since the imperial ideologues defined colonial relationship on the basis of civilizational superiority/inferiority, it was only befitting that the counter argument would also emerge from a similar plain. Unfortunately, studies on early Indian responses to colonial domination do not go beyond Hindu responses to the same.[6] The latter is further confined to one region, i.e. Bengal.

Bhikhu Parekh (1989) constructed a trifle tentatively, a four-fold classification of Hindu responses. The traditionalists saw nothing wrong with their society and thus were somewhat indifferent to British rule (p. 35). Those who were disturbed by the existing state of affairs were classified as: modernists, critical modernists and critical traditionalists (ibid.). For the modernists, there was no hope of salvaging Hindu society except to restructure it along the model of the master's. The critical modernists were arguing for a 'creative synthesis of the two civilizations', whereas the critical traditionalists sought to rejuvenate the traditional resources, leaving a space for borrowing from the West in order to supplement them when needed. All, in one way or another, brought forth the centrality of religious scriptures as referents to the Hindu past, good or bad Ashis Nandy (1991) takes the psychoanalytic route to trace the early attempts by the Bengali intelligentsia at re-covering the self under colonialism. His 'modernists'[7] are somewhat similar to those of Parekh though a shade more aggressive in their contempt of Hindu traditions. Reflected in nineteenth-century 'social reforms', the articulation of criticism by the modernists of Nandy 'was not merely an attempt to explain Indian culture in Indian terms, or even in Western terms, but was an attempt to explain the West in Indian terms and to incorporate it in the Indian culture as an un-avoidable experience' (p. 22).[8]

[6] Two of the most interesting accounts on the subject are Bhikhu Parekh 1989 and Ashis Nandy 1983. All references to Nandy are from the 1991 impression.

[7] Nandy does not call them so; the phrase is mine.

[8] Though one agrees with Nandy's concluding remarks in general, his illustration of early Hindu responses through the example of Michael Madhusudan Dutt's (1824–73) *Meghnadvadh Kavya* leaves much to be desired. Nandy equates *Meghnadvadh* with other similar but older works, in Jainism or in south Indian literature, which subvert the tale of *Ramayan* to the extent that the villain becomes the hero and vice versa. In that, the colonial situation fails to mark any break from the past: it becomes like any other moment in the past when Hinduism faced criticism from within. Indeed, it is the all-inclusive nature of Hinduism, developed through centuries, that 'survived' such criticism and in the process neutralized or/ and at times even Hinduized many dissenting voices. The question is, to what extent Dutt could be held as the one from within? His was a blatantly tactical

The second stream of cultural criticism too was based on the reinterpreted sacred texts, though it borrowed heavily from the colonial world-view and in order to legitimize its interpretations, accepted current Christian norms of sacredness. Bankimchandra Chatterjee (1838–94), Swami Dayanand Saraswati (1824–83) and Swami Vivekanand (1863–1902) were leading exponents of this strand, argues Nandy. Bankimchandra found in Lord Krishna a historically conscious God who could give substance to the claim of the golden age of Hinduism. His Krishna was bereft of many traditional qualities which did not stand the moral test of time. All ancient references to his playful personality with strong sexual undercurrents, his linkages to 'soft, child-like, self-contradictory, and sometimes immoral being' were carefully dropped, Nandy continues. He was made somewhat into an all-perfect non-pagan Christian God. Swami Dayanand and Swami Vivekanand took further steps to Christianize Hinduism, to turn it into an organized religion, with organized church and salaried priesthood. This model explained the cultural regression of Hinduism on the premise that it had lost its original Aryan qualities it had shared with the Western world. No surprise then, notes Nandy, that Swami Dayanand chose to call his church 'Arya Samaj' (Society of the Aryans). All the streams however, continued to speak in the language of social reform, regeneration of (Hindu) society, purging Hinduism from its present-day malpractices, etc. The political will to confront the colonial regime collectively, continued to elude the Hindu intelligentsia. It reflected in the political philosophy of the early Congress as well.

Before the Congress' articulation of political challenges to colonial rule is outlined, a word on the latter's reaction to attempts at Hindu regeneration based on a critical appraisal of their past. Even though colonial authority welcomed the Modernist reforms of Hindu society (and later of Muslim society as well) initiated by its intelligentsia, they were not oblivious to the logical limits to which the critical traditionalist could reach. That the moments of doubt about their own tradition, culture, and religion were arrived at because of the changes brought

device, unlike others in the past who posed challenges to Hinduism with counter life-philosophies. A new convert to Anglican Christianity, who cared not more than 'a pin's head for Hinduism', whether Dutt's construction could be accepted as a model of Hindu response is doubtful.

forth by colonial domination, was apparent to quite a few ideologues of the Raj. Sir Henry Maine (1822–88) noted the danger apparently inherent in a non-European society's efforts at constructing an imaginary past:

It is not to be concealed . . . that they [natives with European education] have, by the fact of their education, broken forever with much in their history, much in their customs, much in their creed. Yet I constantly read and sometimes hear, elaborate attempts on their part to persuade themselves and others, that there is a sense in which these rejected portions of Native history and usage and belief, are perfectly in harmony with the modern knowledge. . . . [T]here can be no great mistake, and, under the circumstances of this country, no more destructive mistake. . . . The only India . . . to which he [the educated native] could hope to return . . . is the India of Mahratta robbery and Mahomedan rule [which did not even need an adjective!]

I myself believe that European influences are in great measure the source of these delusions. The value attached in Europe to ancient Hindu literature, . . . for its poetical and philosophical interest, has very naturally caused the native to look back with pride and fondness on the era at which the great Sanskrit poems were composed and great philosophical system evolved.[9]

In such an uncharitable construction of the colonized where they are not in full control of even their delusions, their past could never be allowed to remain as the one imagined by the likes of William Jones. In the journey from Jones to Maine, the Hindu past in the colonial epistemology had turned, from a fount of glory and inspiration, to a misplaced fiction:

unquestionably this tendency [to romanticise the ancient Hindu past] has its chief root in this,—that the Natives of India have caught from us Europeans our modern trick of constructing by means of works of fiction, an imaginary past out of the present. . . . Now this is all very well for us Europeans. . . . [T]he activity of social life in Europe is so exuberant, that no serious or sustained disadvantage arises from our pleasing ourselves with pictures of past centuries. . . . On the educated Native of India the past

[9] 'The "Dangerous" Past', a speech delivered at University of Calcutta, in Murarisharan Manglik, *Deep-Mala or Inspirational Passages, Selected from University Convocation Addresses*, Allahabad: The Indian Press, 1934, pp. 37–40.

presses with too awful and terrible a power for it to be safe for him to play or palter with it. (pp. 41–2)

Why this is so, Sir Maine had an explanation:

the educated Native mind requires hardening. That culture of imagination, that tenderness for it, which may be necessary in the West, is out of place here; for this is a society in which, *for centuries upon centuries, the imagination has run riot*, and much of the intellectual weakness and moral evil which afflict it to this moment, may be traced to *imagination having so long usurped the place of reason*. What the Native mind requires, is stricter criteria of truth.[10]

Natives schooled in the European knowledge system were dangerous to the health of the Empire, particularly when they were allowed to nurture and develop a capacity for imagination. This was true not only for the intelligentsia, but for the kisan as well. Whenever the latter 'cooked a story', 'spread a lie' or participated collectively in a 'bazaar *gup*', a shudder passed through the imperial authorities. It was fatal for them to let the spring of fiction flow uninterruptedly. After all, who knew the latent potential of imagination better than the likes of William Jones and James Mills, not to mention the people like Maine, who meticulously manufactured the difference between the ruler and the ruled?

Gandhi, who knew no other language but of transparency, struggled to liberate the secretive elements from the 'dreams-rumoured' to the foreground. He invited people to dream collectively *and* to share their dreams even with the guardians of the Raj. Now follows a section on the Congress before Gandhi.

The Congress before Gandhi

'Ladies and Gentlemen, let us understand clearly what the Congress is: It is an assembly of educated Indians. . . .'[11] Thus welcomed the Chairperson of the Reception Committee his delegates to the All India National Congress to the 1909 session. These, however, were not the educated natives whom Maine feared. They were 'well meaning' individuals whose political vision was probably too limited to cause

[10] Maine 1907 [1871], pp. 275–6, emphasis added.

Similar sentiments were echoed by Lord Curzon in 1900 (pp. 101–2).

[11] Welcome Address by Mr. Harikishan Lal (1864–1937), in *The Congress, Conference and Conventions of 1909* [n.d.], p. 6.

much concern among the British; they petitioned the officials to redress the grievances they could see. To be fair, they did see many; however, they sincerely believed that making patient appeals was the best way to conduct politics at that time. They appealed to the Raj because they either accepted its legitimacy or did not dare challenge it openly. In any case, they were enamoured by the achievements of the British and hoped some to accrue to Indian society as well, if it maintained proximity with the Empire. The decline of British supremacy, in their scheme of things, meant disaster: 'we shall have anarchy, war, and rapine. *The Mohammedans will try to recover their lost supremacy. The Hindu races and chiefs will fight amongst themselves.*'[12]

Colonial epistemology, as articulated by Maine, had found an ardent student in Sankaran Nair (1857–1934). On his part Surendranath Banerjea (1848–1925, President, All India Congress, Ahmedabad, 1902), said:

> We live in happier times, under more fortunate circumstances, under the beneficent protection of a rule which affords the widest tolerance for the widest differences of opinion and evinces the deepest sympathy for all constitutional struggles for constitutional liberty. Yet we have our trials and our disappointments. The forces of reaction are now in the ascendant .... We bide our time in firm conviction that the turn in the tide will come and the forces which make for progress will once again assert their undisputed supremacy. (Ghose 1972, p. 14)

The reactionary forces were unleashed by imperialism (ibid., p. 15). 'The cause of progress has met with a temporary check' (ibid., p. 14). The hope that the halted Prometheus would march again sooner or later for them as well, however, remained intact. As Sankaran Nair had reminded in his Presidential address at the 1897 annual Congress, 'it should not be forgotten for a moment that the real link that binds us indissolubly to England is the hope, the well-founded hope and belief, that *with England's help* we shall, and, under her guidance alone, we can attain national unity and national freedom' (Majumdar 1937, p. 151, emphasis added). The President of the 1909 Congress, Madan Mohan Malviya (1861–1946), reiterated the sentiment when he told the delegates that 'British rule is for the good of India and we derive to the

[12] Sankaran Nair's Presidential speech at the 1897 annual session of the Congress. See J.K. Majumdar 1937, p. 151 (emphasis added).

utmost advantages which accrue from the British rule' (The Congress, Conferences and Conventions of 1909, n.d., p. 58). B.N. Dhar showed the heights the Empire had gained in its efforts at colonizing the minds of the educated natives when he remarked in his Presidential speech that 'I thank God that I am a British subject. . . . England is the only country that knows how to govern those who cannot govern themselves' (Majumdar 1937, p. 174).

In the light of such political utterances, it is not very difficult to draw conclusions about the nature of the Congress in this period. However, once in a while, beneath the thick layer of eulogies, there did appear a dim, convoluted murmur of dissent here, a faint one there:

> British Imperialism, which seeks to draw closer the bonds of union between the Mother country [*sic*] and the colonies, has literally done nothing to cement the loyalty or deepen the gratitude of the Indian people. I would welcome an Imperialism which would draw us nearer to Britain by the ties of a common citizenship and which would enhance our self-respect, by making us feel that we are participators in the priceless heritage of British freedom. (Madan Mohan Malviya in Ghose 1972, p. 15)

Shame may grip a self-respecting Indian today on hearing such utterances. It did not go un-decried in its own days as well; the militant nationalists, known as Revolutionary Terrorists, minced no words to expose the cowardice of such Congressmen. No doubt, statements of this nature underline the ideological boundaries within which the early Congress operated and the political confidence it had/lacked in itself and in its people.

However, it is possible at times to detect the double-speak, the subversive spirit of the statement that may not appear on centre-stage at first sight. For example, to desire a common citizenship for master and subject, that would celebrate the heritage of nothing less than freedom, is to deny the very basis of master-subject relationship. The phrases of loyalty and gratitude might have been covers to demand self-respect. If one agrees that the colonial system rested on mechanisms of representation hammered through incessant manufacturing of differences, then only will it be possible to appreciate the full force of such remarks which aimed at nothing less than eradicating the difference itself. What in any case remains relevant for us is the exclusion of the masses from the whole process of conceptualizing politics, which was limited primarily to petitioning the Raj and thus in the process legitimizing its constitutional authority. It is altogether a different matter that even if they had tried to involve the masses, it is unclear, whether or not the latter would have paid any heed at all to the highly Westernized language of the early Congress politics articulated in abstract terminologies like constitutionalism, parliamentarism, citizenship and democratic rights.[13] At the turn of the twentieth century a few Congress persons began to move away from such elitist and eulogist policies that had kept the party distanced from the masses for so long.

Bal Gangadhar Tilak (1856-1920) was probably the first major leader who sought to build a mass movement that stood on the ground of an imagined Hindu past. A reinterpretation of scriptures and legends provided Tilak a counter to the claims to greatness of the West, which it denied those it had colonized. However, it was Gandhi who perfected the language of religiosity in a way that was most easily comprehensible to the masses. For him every act was a religious act; politics itself was the religion of the new time. And, thus, politics divorced from religion was 'dirt'. He achieved tremendous success in winning peoples' hearts and confidence. To do that, Gandhi carefully chose his words, metaphors, and images, which struck a familiar note with the people at large. As will be demonstrated, Gandhi's choice of a particular language was not merely a strategic one, but one in which he believed, and tried to live up to. Since political activities were religious concerns for him, he could not close his eyes to the means through which a particular goal was to be attained. His way of life itself became a critic of everything that he ever chose to criticize. It became a

[13] It is not uncommon to find lower caste people in general, and kisans, in particular, welcoming British rule, or preferring the British to their immediate exploiters. In late nineteenth-century Bihar, a group of kisans demanded the zamindari to be abolished and desired to be 'directly under George *Pancham*'. Jotiba Phule (1827–90), charismatic leader of the nineteenth century, thought that 'the creator has purposely sent the English people to this country to liberate the disabled sudras from the slavery of the crafty Aryas'. Jotiba argued that the Brahmins were 'worse exploiters' than the British. This is not so surprising because it is possible that Jotiba might have taken the abolition of slave trade and, later, slavery by the English on its face value and regarded it as their highly benevolent gesture. The fact that he dedicated his book to the 'Good People Of the United States, as a token of admiration for their sublime disinterested and self sacrificing devotion in the cause of Negro slavery' shows Jotiba's sensitivity to the issue of slavery, on the one hand, and his hope on the 'civilized' British in regard to the upliftment of the shudras, on the other (Phule 1872, Preface and pp. 1–4).

political message by itself; 'my life is my message', as Gandhi so aptly used to say.

GANDHI AND THE SPIRITUALIZATION OF INDIAN POLITICS

The Hindu social reformers of nineteenth-century India turned to (Hindu) religious texts with different purposes in mind. Some sought inspiration from them; some just wanted to highlight the golden moments of Hindu civilization; others sought to revive them to look for justification for the changes they wanted to introduce in modern India. However, active political engagement was not articulated in terms of confrontations with the Empire. That is perhaps one of the conventional reasons for their being remembered as social reformers.

The beginning of the twentieth century witnessed in leaders like Tilak, Aurobindo (1872–1950), and Gandhi a departure from past practices. Religion was discovered as a bridge between the masses and the educated section of Indian society. Aurobindo recounted 'the indispensable conditions' for the political awakening of India in the following words:

> To bring in the mass of the people, to found the greatness of the future on the greatness of the past, to infuse Indian politics with Indian religious fervour and spirituality, are the indispensable conditions for a great and powerful awakening in India. Others, writers, thinkers, spiritual leaders, had seen this truth. Mr. Tilak was the first to bring it into the actual field of practical politics.[14]

It is important to note two things here. First, there is a significant difference between Gandhi and the leaders before him on the question of the public uses of religion. Pre-Gandhian leaders sought to employ religion in a purely mechanical fashion, almost as empty rhetoric, as a tactical device. It is questionable whether or not they were really convinced of the religious path they were recommending to the masses, Second, the assumption that the masses would not comprehend the intricacies or even the significance of a particular kind of politics if spoken in temporal terms, highlighted the limits of their political vision. When Tilak talked about the tactic of using religious symbols to

[14] Quoted in Robert W. Stevenson 1986, p. 46.

mobilize Hindu masses, he assumed it would be the quickest way of popularizing nationalism. Any other technique would take centuries to get the same results, he would argue.[15]

There is yet another side to this story. It was popularly and uncritically held by the early leaders of the Congress that the masses were indifferent to political affairs because of their fatalism. Due to their supposed faith in *Karma* and *Maya*, Hindus, it was believed, had a predilection for individual deliverance, were inclined to renounce the world and to turn their backs on worldly problems.[16] In other words, they had little or no empathy for things pertaining to a collective, or society in general. This was doubtless capitulation to the colonial prejudice that ridiculed Hindu religion precisely in these terms.[17] To arouse Hindu masses from their stupor with the help of religious symbols and idioms, therefore, was problematic to say the least. Gandhi's intervention had to overcome this problematic.

As early as 1915, Gandhi spoke about 'spiritualizing political life and political institutions'. He prefaced his autobiography with the declaration that it was his devotion to truth that drew him into politics,

[15] See an engaging study of Tilak and his uses of Hindu festivals and idioms by Cashman, 1975.

[16] '*Maya* denotes the unsubstantial, phenomenal character of the observed and manipulated world, as well as of the mind itself—the conscious and even subconscious stratification and powers of the personality', writes Heinrich Zimmer 1990 [Indian Edition], p. 22. Equally useful is the editorial note:

> *Maya*, from the root ma, 'to measure, to form, to build', denotes, in the first place, the power of a god or demon to produce illusory effects, to change form, and to appear under deceiving masks. Derived from this is the meaning 'magic', 'the production of an illusion'. (ibid.)

[17] For example, the following remark of Bishop Robert Caldwell (1814–92) on Vedantism captures the imperial sentiment:

> All this time the philosophy of quietism has been sound asleep, or 'with its eyes fixed on the point of its nose', according to the directions of the *Gita*, it has been thinking itself out of its wits. This philosophy has substantially been the creed of the majority of the people for upwards of two thousand years, and if it had emanated from God, the proofs of its divine origin ought long ere this to have been apparent, but it has all this time been *too much absorbed in 'contemplating self by means of self' to have had any time or thought left for endeavouring to improve the world. What could be expected of the philosophy of apathy, but that it should leave things to take their course*? (cited by Wilhelm Halbfass, 1995, p. 220, emphasis added)

that his power in the political field was derived from his spiritual engagements with himself, that swaraj was ultimately an issue of self-realization. Those who trained themselves in the Western school of secularism and talked about separating religion from politics 'do not know what religion means', Gandhi argued.[18] It becomes evident from the start that 'to spiritualize religion' was not a matter of political strategy for Gandhi, unlike many others. Religion was too important for him to allow to be dictated by political expediencies. As he said, '[M]ost religious men I have met are politicians in disguise. I, however, who wear the guise of a politician, am at heart a religious man' (*Speeches and Writings*, 2nd edn., 1918, p. xxiv). What we find in Gandhi is an entirely new meaning of both politics and religion.

Even though Gandhi seemed to have narrowly defined the meaning of politics as he held it to be an avoidable evil (*Young India*, May 1920), his broadening of the concept of religion broadened the horizon of politics. 'Power resides in the people, not in legislative assemblies', he could conclude, because

> I could not be leading a religious life unless I identified myself with the whole of mankind [*sic*] and that I could not do unless I took part in politics. The whole gamut of man's activities today constitute an indivisible whole. . . . I do not know of any religion apart from activity. It provides a moral basis to all other activities without which life would be a maze of sound and fury signifying nothing. [V.K. Jhaveri and D.G. Tendulkar (eds.), *Mahatma*, 1951–4, vol. IV, p. 53]

His religion was not the religion of beliefs and formal allegiance to dogmas around him. When he spoke of religion, he spoke of values and not beliefs which could be sectarian and inhibiting to religious experience. This literally is the distinction between dharma and religion. The former refers to the principles, moral codes which guide our conduct, and 'is nothing but morality'. Insistence on values, and rejection of beliefs and ritualized practices, automatically opened for Gandhi the doors not only of Hindu but many religions known to him: Buddhism, Jainism, Judaism, Islam, Christianity, etc., helping him rise above the prevailing ethos of sectarianism. He could find many moral codes common to many religions and thus speak to people who would

[18] See Iyer 1973; and many editions of *The Speeches and Writings of Mahatma Gandhi*, Madras.

normally have very little to share with each other as long as they put beliefs before values.

Tilak in contrast to Gandhi had an extremely narrow sense of religion. Due to his 'impatient political aspirations' (Stevenson, p. 47), religion was only to play second fiddle to his notion of nationalism:

> We must raise a nation on this soil. *Love of nation is one's first duty. Next comes religion* and the Government. Our duty to the nation will be first. . . .
> . . . [I]t is the special divine plan that we must achieve success at some time. God and our nation are not separate, on the contrary, *our nation is one of God's forms.* (quoted in Stevenson, pp. 46–7, emphasis added)

This led him to talk of 'Hindu nation' and to mobilize Hindus (defined aggressively against Muslims), a factor which is religiously underplayed in the Nationalist narrative of the Freedom Struggle,[19] and which had debilitating impact on the national movement.[20]

In Gandhi, religion reigned supreme. It was second to none, not to the nation, not even to the people.[21] However, it did become possible for him to transcend the barrier of elite, Sanskritized, Brahmanic Hindu sphere and to reach the vast vernacular world of pre-literate kisans and to an extent Untouchables—a world that was largely Hindu, but a world that was not restricted to scriptural utterances of the few who knew Sanskrit and had been close to the seat of power.

[19] See, for example, P. Sitaramayya 1946–7; R.C. Mazumdar (ed.), 1974 and 1969; Tarachand 1961-72.

[20] It reaches its logical culmination in today's Hindu communalism where to be a Hindu is a passport to patriotism, and conversely, to be a Muslim is to be anti-national.

[21] Despite the fact that Gandhi chose to serve the masses in order to serve God, notwithstanding even his liking for the metaphor *Daridranaryan* (the Lord who resides in the poor), he remained unrelenting when it came to seeing God, the Truth, in them per se. In this regard, his conception of selecting the right path to meet God was always to be decided by him. He preferred to stand alone when the final moment of judgement arrived. It suffices to recall his telegram to one Zahur Ahmad after the incident of violence at Chauri Chaura during the Non-Cooperation movement in 1922, in order to illustrate the point:

> Thank wire. Misrepresentation [of his messages by the kisans of Chauri Chaura who openly resorted to violent acts to vent their outrage] inevitable. But God with us. *Let us derive strength from Him rather than from public support.* (*Collected Works*, vol. XXII, 1967, p. 398, emphasis added)

In this respect, Gandhi's adherence to the religious grammar of the quotidian language was to some extent inherently unsettling for traditional Hindu elites, his insistence on a united front of all classes against colonialism notwithstanding. His language was religious *and* political at the same time. Though he continued to decry the 'soullessness' of everyday politics, Gandhi's solution was not to shun it. He knew that 'politics is as essential as religion'. But politics divorced from religion was 'like a corpse, fit only for burning' (*Speeches and Writings*, 4th edn., 1934, p. 315). That is the reason why he wanted to 'spiritualize' politics.[22] Iyer (1973) informs us that 'Gandhi was in accord with Indian [Hindu?] tradition in rejecting the modern dichotomy between religion and politics' (p. 47). Hindu cosmology which revolves around moral codes, specific to one's social location, does not separate the two in everyday affairs. Instead, the *Upanishads* distinguish between *shreyas* and *preyas*, what we know to be true and what we believe to be desirable. Iyer is right in suggesting that Gandhi would have agreed with Kant's essay 'On the Discordance Between Morals and Politics':

> Kant argued that there could be a conflict between morals and politics if ethics is itself regarded as a general doctrine of prudence or expediency, a view that he wholly rejected in favour of the view that it was a system of unconditionally authoritative laws in accordance with which we always ought to act. 'I can easily enough think of a moral politician as one who holds the principles of political expediency in such a way that they can co-exist with morals: but I cannot conceive of a political moralist who fashions a system of morality for himself so as to make it subordinate and subservient to the interest of the statesman.'[23]

Gandhi thus had the dilemma around 'means and end' neatly resolved for him. Politics was important, swaraj was most desirable, but

[22] The concept of 'spiritualizing politics' is accredited to Gokhale (1866–1915) by Gandhi, who held him as his 'political mentor'. However, there is a distinction between his and Gokhale's usage of the term. For Gokhale religion and politics, religious and secular, remained two separate domains. He wanted 'to tap' the sea of energy the sannyasis possessed for the 'social and political regeneration of the country'. He was vastly impressed by the reserve of self-sacrifice that Hindu sannyasis exhibited in their ascetic pursuit of para-worldly truths. At a deeper philosophical level, Gokhale retained the instrumentalist understanding of religion, championed by Tilak. For details on Gokhale, see B.R. Nanda 1977.

[23] Iyer 1973, p. 48. The quotation is from Immanuel Kant.

not through *any* means. The path we choose to reach our destination, Gandhi argued, should tell us about the validity of the entire journey and the meaning of the destination as well. A pure goal must be reached through pure paths, no matter how strenuous. Religion, in other words must not be sacrificed at the altar of political expediency. Gandhi always maintained that the politician in him had never dominated a single decision of his, that he had sacrificed no principle to gain a political advantage (Iyer 1973, p. 8). The fusion of politics and religion created a singular philosophy of life, Karma yoga, in which one must do what is expected of him/her to meet spiritual realization. No wonder that Gandhi could declare, 'I do not know of any religion apart from activity.' He could formulate the idea thus as he had reinterpreted the *Gita* in a new light. The *Gita* provided him with utmost clarity, the need to struggle incessantly for justice. Not only for oneself but for the entire humankind. By finding a religious source of energy that could be used to confront and resolve the dilemma of the present, Gandhi quietly turned the tables on the British who denounced Hinduism for its allegedly other-world orientation. And he did so without resorting to an instrumentalist application of religion. A break from the past was made.

The Gita

The rediscovery of the *Gita* in the colonial context of India reconfirmed the Nationalist claim of the glorious Hindu past illustrated in its rich Sanskrit literature. Its new interpretations with energized emphasis on action provided the Nationalist leaders with an effective retort to the colonial charge that Hindu religion made its adherents inherently escapist and inward-looking. Though attempts were made to reinterpret the *Gita* in the latter half of the nineteenth century by thinkers like Ramkrishna Paramahans (1836-86) and his disciple Swami Vivekanand, the emphasis was on underlining the cultural distinction between the colonizer and the colonized and regeneration of Hindu society on the lines of socio-cultural reform. Elite participation in the politics of direct confrontation was seen as minimal. The attempt to build a mass movement was evident only in its absence. This attitude underwent a sea-change with the advent of Gandhi.

The *Gita* is an episode in the *Mahabharata* (estimated period of composition 400 BC–AD 400). The war depicts the tussle between good and bad, between the legitimate claimants of the throne, the Pandavas, and its illegitimate occupants, the Kauravas, both branches of a single family tree. On the eve of the war, when the army and generals from both sides were facing each other on the battlefield of Kurukshetra, Arjuna, sensing that actually he would have to kill his kith and kin in order to win the war and capture the throne, developed cold feet. Shri Krishna, his charioteer, held as the incarnation of Lord Vishnu encouraged Arjuna to fight, as it was the duty he must perform in order to restore the dharma of life. *Shrimad Bhagavat Gita* (The songs of God), popularly known as the *Gita* is a dialogue between Shri Krishna and Arjuna on morality, action and dharma. Though it is not the only Hindu scripture that discusses the problematic, practical and metaphysical, of right and wrong actions, the *Gita* stands apart for reasons we now explore.

The *Ramcharitmanas* of Tulsidas, also known as *Ramayan*, was another popular religious epic available to kisans, which provided a moral reference to their existential experiences. Like any other epic, it catered to a host of social classes, including those whose interests were in direct collision with each other. Though there has been no work comparing it with the *Mahabharata* in ways they were used by kisan struggles in colonial India, some tentative remarks can be made. The *Ramcharitmanas* is linguistically more easily accessible than the *Mahabharata*, but it was more to the latter that kisans turned when articulating their protest. The reason lies in the nature of central characters of the epics, Ram and Krishna. Krishna is more human and is closer to the mundane universe. He is seen to be dealing with worldly dilemmas, intrigues, politics, deceits, fights over property, rivalry, jealousy, etc. His fight is for just *rights*. In contrast, Ram epitomizes *duty* of an ideal son and of an ideal king, not all duties, and certainly not those of an ideal husband. In the case of a fight between king and subject, zamindar and kisans, the icon of Ram was not of much help.

Krishna's playful nature was an indulgent leitmotif for Bhakti poets. He was an ideal *sakha* (friend) of Pandavas and later of all His devotees, particularly of the wronged and oppressed. This is not to suggest that Ram was never allegorized to show the inevitable victory of the pious over evil. For instance, Baba Ramchandra, a peasant leader of Oudh in the United Provinces in the 1920s and 1930s, used couplets of the *Ramcharitmanas* to further the cause of the kisans (Kapil Kumar 1984).

In Bihar too it was not very rare. A lyricist, musician and singer, Goswami Chandreshwar Bharati of Saran district wrote a booklet called *Ramji par Notice*.[24] The poet asked Ram,

पानी बिन सुख गइल देस भरके धान, ई का कइलीं भगवान!
करजा काढ़ के खेती कइलीं, मर–मर रोपलीं धान
खेत के पैदा दहल सूखल, रोअता किसान।

[The paddy of the whole country dried up without water, what did you do, lord! We took loans to cultivate, broke our backs replanting paddy. The crop is ruined, kisans are weeping.]

His wishes could be inspired by Ram-rajya though:

हम राज-किसान बनइतीं हो।
धनी–गरीब–अमीर सभी के एके राह चलइतीं हो।
हक-भर भोजन सबके दीतीं, दुखी ना कहवइतीं हो।
जेकरा घर में नइखे भोजन, चाउर से भरवइतीं हो।

[Wish I could establish the rule of kisans. The rich and poor would have the same destination. All would get their rightful share, none would be miserable. Those without a morsel of grain would get their houses filled with rice.]

Nirghin Ram too wrote a *Ramayan* in which, along with the story of Ram, he included tales of his own trauma as a kisan and a Chamar. But he felt no incongruity in addressing Krishna in his *Ramayan* (*hamani ke beria nithur bhaile banwari*).[25] He could open his heart to both with ease.

Krishna continues to be the more popular, especially among the poor and the lowly. The songs of migration discussed in Chapter 2 bring this out convincingly. The *sakhya bhava* associated with Krishna is further explored in the next chapter. However, there is yet another reason why the *Gita* has been preferred to the *Ramcharitmanas*.

The Nationalist discourse on religion as a language of political mobilization centred on the *Gita*. From Tilak and Aurobindo to Gandhi, the *Gita* was referred to as the spiritual guide of Indian nationalism, a

[24] Benaras: Bombai Press, n.d.

[25] Nirghin Ram was born in Janaidih, Shahabad (present-day Bhojpur), around late 1850s. A disenchanted Gandhian, he took to writing the *Ramayan* and often punctuated it with his own life-story. Brief extracts are available in Badrinarayan 1996.

text that could re-energize one and all. And its appeal was not confined to the Nationalists alone. The Bihar Kisan Sabha leader, Swami Sahajanand Saraswati, engaged with it to find a common cause between its central teachings and his own Communist concerns. Thus it becomes essential, in a study of political languages of kisans in Bihar, to examine how the *Gita* was being read and interpreted. To show how kisans viewed religion, it is imperative to explore the religious concerns of those who represented them. Let us turn now to the *Gita*.

To realize the self, the *Atman*, and to rise above the temporal cycle of life and death, i.e. to meet the *Brahman*,[26] the Absolute, or to attain moksha, Hindu scriptures put varying emphasis on the pursuit of three possible yogas (ways of doing): gyan (also spelt as jnyan), karma, and, bhakti (knowledge, action, and devotion respectively). Followers of each path over the centuries have developed sets of philosophical arguments in support of their cases, the details of which do not concern us here. At the risk of oversimplification, true devotion to the Supreme Being empowers one to discriminate between right and wrong, good and bad, spiritual and temporal, and thus transcend the dualities of this world. A Gyan yogi through his renunciation of worldly ties and his metaphysical power to meditate, attains this goal. The Karma yogi while retaining worldly ties attains moksha through right conduct. And the Bhakta yogi, through unquestioned surrender and devotion to the God achieves the same. These also differ in their ways of seeking communion with the God in the sense that in Bhakti yoga the Almighty is *sakar*, manifest, while in Gyan yoga He is *nirakar*, unmanifest.

[26] Nakamura 1983 tells us how the terms *Atman* and *Brahman*, changed their meanings in the course of time:

> 'Brahman' meant originally the hymns, sacrificial addresses and incantations of the Vedas and, further, the mystical power latent in them, but it finally was taken among the Brahmins who respected the Vedic rituals, as the usual term for the fundamental principle of the world. The word in time lost its original meaning in the Vedanta school to become a technical term used only for the Absolute itself.
>
> The word 'atman' originally meant 'Breath', but it was also employed derivatively in the sense of 'vital force', body, and further became a word meaning 'one's self'. As a philosophical concept, it was taken as a technical term meaning 'one's ego', 'one's self', and further 'soul'. (Nakamura, pp. 105–6)

The *Gita* primarily talks of Gyan and Karma yogas.[27] but at the turn of the twentieth century in its various readings emphasis was given to the Gyan yogi, as propagated by Shankaracharya (AD 788–820) in his early *bhashyas* (commentaries) on the text. In congruence with his philosophy, Shankaracharya emphasized the supremacy of Gyan yoga over the other two yogas, and advocated sannyas as a higher level of life than that of a householder.[28] The Karma yogi while retaining worldly ties through right conduct attains moksha and the Bhakti yogi through unquestioned surrender within. No wonder that colonial epistemology, based on the textual readings of high culture Sanskrit texts and distanced from the mentalité of the kisans, concluded that the Hindu scriptures preached individual transcendence and remained indifferent to pursuits for salvation of a collective.[29] The twentieth-century readings of the *Gita* were to alter this image quite significantly.

The *Gita* in the new scenario challenged many traditional beliefs, of which sannyas was probably the most significant. The new readings of the text now propounded that renunciation did not mean abandoning action or running away from duty. Rather, it meant renouncing desire, selfish purpose, and dependence on the fruit of an action. The

[27] Gandhi's reading of it remains somewhat unique in the sense that among all the major modern interpreters of the *Gita* he alone finds strong advocacy of bhakti in it. 'In order that knowledge may not run riot, the author of the *Gita* has insisted on devotion accompanying it and has given it the first place', Gandhi insists (see Mahadev Desai 1946, p. 129). His emphasis on devotion in order to minimize the distance between a Gyan yogi and a Bhakta yogi (to curtail the elitism of a Gyan yogi, if you wish) went a long way in shaping his relationship with the common masses.

[28] Tilak infers from the introduction to the first and third chapters of the *Shankarabhashya* that commentators before Shankara interpreted the central purport of the *Gita* to be Karma yoga (G.V. Saroja 1985, p. vii). However, since Shankara, renunciation as the route to gyan dominated the debate against those who advocated the path of karma. The trend can be said to have continued up to the late nineteenth century. Consider the following remark of Vivekanand:

> Like the difference between the biggest mountain and a mustard seed, between the sun and a glow worm, between the ocean and a streamlet, is the wide gulf between a sannyasi and a householder. (*The Complete Works of Vivekanand*, vol. III, Mayavati Memorial Edition, Calcutta: Advaita Ashram, 1964, pp. 409–10)

[29] Add to the list the desired other-worldliness of the sannyasis and fakirs as discussed above.

traditional emphasis which privileged renunciation of all actions for the sannyasi in search of right knowledge waned in favour of Nishkam karma, selfless action, actions devoid of hankering after fruit. The second chapter of the *Gita*, along with the sixth, became the central reference point. Of particular interest is verse 47, where Krishna tells Arjuna that his concern is with 'action alone, never with its fruits'. The fruit of work should not be the motive, nor should one take refuge in abstinence from action (Iyer ed. 1985, p. 81).

To Gandhi, this was the central message of the *Gita*. It is only through remaining unattached in action that one could avoid the worldly tangles that action necessarily entails.[30] This opened up a new space for the householder to make a mark on the political landscape, particularly when the fight for freedom was being preached as the most important dharma of life.

Aurobindo sought to highlight the significance of action as propounded in the *Gita* on the basis of Vedantic aspiration to transcendence. According to him, Vedanta even in its most transcendent mood, 'presupposes a preparation in life, for it is only through life that one can reach immortality' (Robert N. Minor, 'Sri Aurobindo as a *Gita-yogin*', in Minor (ed.), 1986, p. 72). He denounced Shankaracharya's devaluation of activity in the world and invited Indians to perform their *swadharma* in order to equip themselves for the political task that awaited them:

> The nineteenth century in India was imitative, self forgetful, artificial. It aimed at a successful reproduction of Europe in India, forgetting the deep saying of the *Gita*, 'Better the law of one's own being though it be badly done than an alien dharma well followed; death in one's own dharma is better, it is a dangerous thing to follow the law of another's nature'. (pp. 72–3)

The other important change introduced by the reinterpretation of the *Gita*, was its concept of *loksangraha* (interpreted differently by different leaders of the time, it generally refers to 'maintenance of the world'; 'taking the world with one'; 'universal welfare'; or 'preservation of society' Tilak saw in it the 'seeds of a dynamic social

[30] In contrast, Tilak interpreted the emphasis on action in the *Gita* as the dharma of human being, the sole way to purify one's mind. A pure mind was a prerequisite to realize the final goal of life: the salvation (see Chapter 1 of P.M. Thomas 1987).

philosophy' (Thomas 1987, p. 37). According to him, the *Gita* strictly preaches all actions to be driven by desire for the welfare of society, instead of individual salvation. The confusion that appeared to have consumed Arjuna in the battlefield was symptomatic of all humankind. The message the Lord delivered to him was similarly applicable to the entire world.

The basis of *loksangraha* could be said to lie in the old Vedantic belief, *tat twam asi* (thou art that), which holds that everyone is divine. Therefore there is no impossibly high ideal, there is oneness in all.

The focus on the welfare of the *lok* (world, society, cosmos) as opposed to individual transcendence, equipped the nationalists with an effective rebuttal to the colonial construct that had rendered Hindu religion individualist. Along with its advocacy of Karma yoga and interpretation of sannyas as renunciation of fruits rather than renunciation of actions themselves, the *Gita* provided the nationalist leaders of the twentieth century a scriptural doctrine of a sort that demanded and justified complete dedication of individuals to the cause of swaraj.

In Gandhi, the philosophies of the *Gita* touched a new height, so much so that he wanted to enlighten and liberate not only the colonized but even the colonizer who had deviated from the right path, the dharma of Christianity. It was only his moral stature that could entertain a space for the redemption of the oppressor. It is commonplace that Gandhi fought English rule and not the English. However, seldom is this conceptualized in a framework of epistemological tussle between him and the British. To desire redemption even of the 'Master' after all, was to subvert the imperial canon of 'civilizing the barbarians'. It is precisely in this sense that the Gandhian Congress imagined and discovered the 'inner' realm of India to which British material supremacy had allegedly no access, let alone control.[31]

[31] Read this argument with a thought provoking thesis of Partha Chatterjee (1986). In a limited way, many of the Indian intelligentsia before Gandhi did try to accomplish this task of overturning the colonial epistemology of domination. However, invariably, all of them located their critiques in the uniqueness of India and its universality at the same time. Once freed, India of their thoughts, thanks to its spiritual achievements, was going to save humanity. But only India could accomplish this task. Aurobindo, for example, wrote that:

> Of all the proud nations of the West there is an end determined. When their limited special work for mankind [*sic*] is done they must decay and disappear. But the

Gandhi, Gita, and Nationalist Language of Politics

Early in my childhood, I had felt the need of a scripture that would serve me as an unfailing guide through the trials and temptations of life. The Vedas could not supply that need. . . . But the *Gita* gave . . . the quintessence of all the Shastras and the Upanishads. That decided me. I learnt Sanskrit to enable me to read the *Gita*. Today, the Gita is not only my Bible or my Quran; it is more than that—it is my Mother. I lost my earthly mother who gave me birth long ago; but this Eternal Mother has completely filled her place by my side ever since. (Gandhi, *Gita—My Mother*, Bombay: Bharatiya Vidya Bhavan, 1965, pp. 1–2)

So central was the *Gita* to Gandhi's life and philosophy that the 'Mother who never let him down' became his 'spiritual dictionary', his *kamdhenu*. Ironically, despite being born in a practising Hindu family, Gandhi's first meaningful encounter with the text of the *Gita* took place when he was invited by two Theosophist friends to read with them the translation by Sir Edwin Arnold (*Song Celestial*) in 1889, during his second year in England. And, it was in 1903, ten years after his arrival in South Africa, that he took up once again studying the

---

function of India is to supply the world with a perennial source of light and renovation. Whenever the first play of energy is exhausted and earth grows old and weary, full of materialism, racked with problems she [it was customary to feminize the nation then, a practice that continues even now] cannot solve, the function of India is to restore the youth of mankind and assure it of immortality. . . . The world needs India and needs her free. The work she has to do . . . is a work she cannot do while overshadowed by a foreign power and a foreign civilization. (quoted in Karan Singh 1963, p. 81)

Gandhi's discourse was more complete and effective because (a) it was not parochial and (b) it allowed the West a moment of introspection and a chance to transform itself. He was prepared to borrow even from the West if there were people who shared his views. And there were many; Ruskin, Tolstoy, and Thoreau were probably the most influential. The following remarks of Gandhi say it all:

Jesus Christ, Daniel and Socrates represented the purest form of passive resistance or soul force. . . . Tolstoy was the best and brightest [modern] exponent of the doctrine. . . . In India, the doctrine was understood and commonly practiced long before it came into vogue in Europe. (Prabhu and Rao 1946, p. 78)

So much so that Gramsci saw in Gandhi and in India 'a form of primitive Christianity that the Catholic and Protestant world can no longer even manage to comprehend'. (Gramsci 1995, p. 119)

Gita seriously at the behest of Theosophist friends. He acquired a rudimentary know-ledge of Sanskrit but as yet there was no trace of the text playing any significant role in his life. The first major statement on the message of the *Gita* appeared in his 'Satyagraha Leaflet No. 18' of 8 May 1919 when Gandhi called for a hartal (non-violent non-cooperation) and advised people to observe a fast and read the book (p. 89).

After that he never looked back. His main thesis (*Discourses on the Gita*) appeared in the form of morning talks that he delivered at the Ashram at Ahmedabad over a period of nine months in 1926. During his stay in Yeravada jail in 1929, Gandhi wrote a Gujarati translation of the *Gita* with an introduction and commentary entitled *Anasaktiyoga*. This was later translated by Mahadev Desai as *The Gospel of Selfless Action or the Gita According to Gandhi* (Ahmedabad, Navjivan Publishing House, 1946). Gandhi also wrote weekly letters about the *Gita* to be read out at Ashram prayer meetings (Jordens 1986, p. 88).

The *Gita* is an easy text, notes Gandhi, written in 'incredibly simple Sanskrit'. The purpose of the Gujarati translation was to make it available 'for women, the commercial class, the so-called shudras and the like, who have little or no literary equipment' (Desai 1946, p. 126).[32] The need to do so was, Gandhi said, that The *Gita* 'in a short compass . . . gives a complete reasoned moral code' and provides 'in a nutshell the secret art of living' (Jordens 1986, p. 93). This quality is even more valuable than the fact that it synthesized many strands of Hinduism, was 'free from dogma' and 'excludes no Faith and no teacher' (ibid.). In Gandhi's view, if religion is not observable in quotidian form, it cannot be called religion at all. As argued by Mahadev Desai, the *Gita* 'performs the unique function of making what was an esoteric doctrine [in the *Upanishads*] a living reality for the unlettered, the lowly and the lost' (cited in Thomas 1987, pp. 15–16).

Gandhi reminded his readers on many occasions that his knowledge of Sanskrit was rudimentary. His command over Gujarati was not particulary scholarly either (Desai 1946, p. 126). The reason he felt that he was 'well qualified' to interpret it was that religion was all about

[32] In any case, it was in tune with the mood of the nation. Many vernacular commentaries of the text were being brought out. Tilak's *Gita Rahasya* itself, for example, appeared in Marathi, Hindi, and Gujarati editions, and also in Bengali, Kanarese, Telugu and Tamil (Stevenson 1986, p. 49).

action; those who did not abide by the teachings of the *Gita* in everyday life had no moral authority to interpret it. He believed that 'the correctness of [an] interpretation [would] be in proportion to [one's] success in living according to the teaching' of the *Gita* (Jordens 1986, p. 96). Gandhi felt so strongly about this that it led him to make a most un-Gandhian remark, one that verges on arrogance:

> This desire [to translate the *Gita* which could be unrivalled for its spiritual merit] does not mean any disrespect to the other renderings. They have their own place. But I am not aware of the claims made by the translators of enforcing the meaning of the *Gita* in their own lives. At the back of my rendering there is the claim of an endeavour to enforce the meaning in my own conduct for an unbroken period of forty years. (Desai 1946, p. 127)

To claim that nobody else could claim to have lived his/her life as strictly in accordance with the *Gita* as he had, was certain to have far-reaching consequences.

The *Gita* however, posed a serious challenge to non-violence, a central Gandhian category of resistance. In the *Mahabharata*, Krishna convinces Arjuna he must pick up arms and kill the forces representing evil. Also, a strand of Hinduism strongly justified violence in order to eliminate the forces of sin and evil.[33] In contemporary India as well, violence had gathered substantial momentum. Tilak's redefinition of the Ganapati festival in Maharashtra region, reinterpretation of Durga, the goddess of (also sometimes referred to as) *Shakti*, by 'terrorist'[34] of

[33] See Parekh 1989, specially Chapter 5.

[34] This was the name given by the English to the militant Indian nationalists who waged a violent war of Independence. 'Terrorists' were known for their sacrifice and appetite for bloodshed. One *Appeal* issued after the murder of a 'terrorist', Shams-ul-Islam, captures the relationship between their mood then and the use to which a particular reading of Hinduism was put: 'When God has so ordained, think ye not that at this auspicious moment it is the duty of every good son of India [it is not surprising this brand of politics attracted mostly sons and not daughters of India] to slay these white enemies? . . . . Our *Shastras* [classical religious texts] repeatedly tells us that the killing of these white fiends and their aiders and abettors is equal to a great ceremonial sacrifice (*Aswamedh Jagna*). Come, one and all. Let us offer our sacrifice before the altar in chorus, and pray that in this ceremony all white serpents may perish in its flames as the vipers perished in the serpent slaying ceremony of *Jammajog*. Keep in mind that *it is not murder but jagna*—a sacrificial rite' (Parekh 1989, p. 151).

Bengal, propitiation of Kali who apparently demanded the blood of the 'intruders'—all indicated veneration of violence, suitably wrapped with the zeal of *dharmayuddha*, a war of religion.[35] The preaching of ceaseless action by the *Gita*, its emphasis on Nishkam karma (selfless, detached action that renounced the desire of its fruit), and the exalted position it assigned to *loksangraha*, were all suited to the philosophy of 'terrorism'. In fact, it had become the most important religious text for the 'terrorists' too.

Tilak in his zest to propagate action against colonialism, called for breaking the rules:

> The laws which bind society are for the common man like yourself and myself. . . . *Great men are above the common principles of morality*. . . . Did Shivaji commit a sin in killing Afzal Khan?[36] The answer . . . can be found in *Mahabharata* itself: Krishna's advice to Arjuna to kill his Guru and kinsmen for the sake of the conquest of Dharma over evil. . . .
>
> Do not circumscribe your vision like a frog in a well: get out of the Penal Code, enter into the extremely high atmosphere of the *Bhagavad Gita*. . . . (in Parekh 1989, p. 153, emphasis added)

When Khudiram (1889–1908) was hanged he chose to have the *Gita* round his neck (ibid. p. 152). Several underground groups demanded prospective members take oaths 'with a sword and a copy of the *Gita* on their heads' (ibid.). Gandhi had no doubt met a fierce challenge in his way to propagate ahinsa.

His task became even more difficult in that he shared with the 'terrorists' many grounds: religious and moral. First, he could not totally reject their claim that violence had not only a sanction but even an encouraging audience in Hinduism, or, at least in one variety of it which was no way marginal. Second, like him the 'terrorists' too strongly believed in the Karma yoga taught by the *Gita* and decried sannyas for individual salvation. The latter reflected for both a sign of weakness and passivity. Though Gandhi disapproved of their method,

[35] As declared one of the 'terrorists': 'The Mother is thirsting after the blood of the Feranghees [a derogatory for the English] who have bled her profusely. Satisfy her thirst. Killing the Feranghee, we say, is no murder Brother, chant this verse while slaying the Feranghee white goat, for killing him is not murder' (quoted in Parekh 1989, p. 150).

[36] In the hands of twentieth-century nationalist leaders like Tilak, Shivaji and Afzal Khan became 'Hindu' and 'Muslim' rulers respectively.

he found it hard to dismiss their bravery, sacrifice, and zeal to serve. In fact, he was well aware of the double gain that a win over them would have guaranteed: defeating violent struggle and recruiting energetic satyagrahis into the fold of the Congress (Parekh 1989, p. 155).

Gandhi's general argument against the deployment of violence[37] was that an act of violence fails to change the opponent's vision of the truth. The logical culmination of violence, therefore, is always a greater amount of counter-violence. Gandhi reasoned that each one of us, a manifestation of Brahman, possesses the possibility to change, or improve, or respond to spiritual and moral persuasions. A believer in violent method runs away from the rigour, persistence, and pain and suffering which are required for inducing such change in one who might be deviant, disillusioned, and blinded by narrow self-interest at a given point of time. Finally, Gandhi rejected violent patriotism on the ground that it was not even strategically viable in the face of a more brutal and militarily better organized enemy.

The most persuasive formulation of Gandhi's answer to violence was also the simplest and the most dramatic one. He found guerilla warfare and the bravery required for 'terrorism' as symptoms of cowardice, and, in turn, defined bravery in terms of moral courage to face enemies and challenge them in the open instead of annihilating them secretly. Millions of fellow countrymen and women who were numb in their passivity for centuries were not going to take to violence.[38]

Gandhi shared the colonial construction of Hindus as effeminate, identifying the moral and cultural domination of British civilization over the Indian people as the most damaging impact of colonialism. In fact, he maintained that materialism and violence went hand in hand. The European nations, the epitomes of material superiority, engulfed in the flames of war, racism and nazism, provided ample proof of this. Gandhi, thus, argued that violence could be fought only on the moral and cultural battleground, and satyagraha[39] was the most effective weapon the people of India had in this war.

However, the importance of the *Gita*, in this moral/cultural conflict,

[37] See Iyer (1973), Parekh (1989) among others.

[38] For further elaboration see Ashis Nandy 1990; Ketu H. Katrak 1992.

[39] Gandhi writes that satyagraha 'excludes the use of violence, because man is not capable of knowing the absolute truth and therefore not competent to punish' (*Speeches and Writings*, 4th edn., p. 506).

was yet to be resolved. Contrary to the belief of many Hindus, Gandhi had refused to consider the *Mahabharata* a historical account. Conscious of the sentiment involved in the issue, Gandhi was quick to qualify:

> By ascribing to the chief actors superhuman or subhuman origins, the great Vyasa [held as the author of the text] made short work of the history of Kings and their peoples. The persons therein described *may be historical, but the author of the Mahabharata has used them merely to drive home his religious theme.* (Gandhi 1959, p. 3, emphasis added)

He painstakingly illustrated from the text to point out its allegorical nature: for example, the name of the characters, their origin, their individual prowess, etc. The allegorical device, according to Gandhi, was adopted as a literary genre only to narrate the perpetual conflict that one encountered in his/her heart. The conflict in the heart and mind of Arjuna was symptomatic of all human beings. His refusal to fight had nothing to do with violent or non-violent path of resolving crisis. Gandhi was truly at his best:

> had Arjuna's obstinate refusal to fight anything to do with non-violence? In fact, he had fought often enough in the past. On the present occasion, his reason was suddenly clouded by ignorant attachment. He did not wish to kill his kinsmen. He did not say that he would not kill anyone even if he believed that person to be wicked. (Gandhi, *Collected Works*, XXVIII, p. 319)

Krishna admonished Arjuna for running away from his duty because he was being consumed by attachment. This did not mean that he preached that all should pick up arms, Gandhi concluded. In fact, the 'magnificent ending' of the *Mahabharata* imparts an altogether different message. The disaster of the war was so colossal that the victors (left few in numbers) opted to leave the world rather than savour the fruits of their victory. To Gandhi, this was clearly an indictment of violence, and not an advocacy of it.

However, sensing that this too was to some extent vulnerable to argument that certain causes 'must be pursued irrespective of their consequences', Gandhi added yet another twist. He argued that violence appeared in the *Mahabharata* only as a 'limited discourse', in a historically specific circumstance, fit to be followed only by those who had been warriors all their lives without ever questioning the legitimacy of violence. Krishna asked Arjuna to fight without announcing a *general* justification of violence. Arjuna had no other option but to fight; it was his *swadharma.* Had it been for a selfish and unjust cause, only then his recourse to violence could have been *adharma* (contrary to prescribed duty, a mistake, a sin). He had to kill the Kauravas, who had refused to pay heed to requests and peaceful persuasions of the Pandavas. Gandhi concluded that from such a limited discourse it was unwise to derive sanction for violence in the pursuit of social re-generation and national freedom: '. . . to conclude . . . that the *Gita* teaches violence or justifies war is as unwarranted as to argue that, since violence in some form or other is inescapable for maintaining the body in existence, *dharma lies only in violence*' (ibid., emphasis added).

Even though he sounded convincing, Gandhi could not help being arbitrary in according historicity to the political message of the *Gita* (that justified violence in a certain situation) and denying the same to its social and moral message (that violence could be generalized). He chose at will when and what to dehistoricize, without giving satisfactory justification for it.[40] He denied this luxury of arbitrary historicity to the 'terrorists' for they could have then used it to validate their actions on the basis of the *Gita* beyond the boundary of any doubt. Bhikhu Parekh (1989) is far from convincing when he rather hastily concludes that 'Gandhi was right and the terrorists were wrong': 'The *Gita* was designed to answer a limited question put by a specific individual in a specific historical context. It discussed violence in the context of a major war and had little relevance for the kind of violence in which the terrorists were engaged' (ibid., p. 171).

This kind of defence of the Gandhian position can be refuted on at least four counts. The dilemma of Arjuna is less that of a particular person than symptomatic of the dilemma of humanity. Why he is a historically specific person in one instance and universal in the other, demands a methodological explanation which Parekh does not offer. Second, Gandhi himself maintained that the war is an allegorical flight, a poet's journey into fantasy, not an actual war. Third, even if Gandhi changed his position on it and began to believe that it indeed was an

[40] For example, he admitted to the universal validity of the *varnadharma* as laid out in the *Gita* which had deep repercussion on his views on the caste system, his resolve to uplift the untouchables notwithstanding.

actual war, why should the war of Indian independence not be considered a major war of the contemporary period? Parekh (pp. 71–106) does dwell at length on Gandhi's *yugadharma*, the duty most appropriate for the epoch. What, then, decides which war is major enough to sanction violence? And finally, Parekh does not tell us how/why the *Gita/Mahabharata* was irrelevant for 'the kind of violence in which the terrorists were engaged'. They too were fighting an unjust opponent who had turned deaf ears to the peaceful appeals of the Congress. Gandhi was most effective in countering violence when he hammered the arguments derived from Hinduism at large and not when he undertook arbitrary deconstruction of the *Gita*, defying consistency. His opposition to violence on grounds that (a) it amounted to deicide since everybody is a part of Brahman; (b) it rested on disbelief in people's capacity to change, hence the elimination of those who were found wanting or not up to the mark in certain respect; (c) it betrayed failure in convincing the opponent about one's conception of truth, and/or, failure in transforming opponent's conception of truth, hence the impatience to annihilate those who differed—was derived from Hinduism in general and owed little to the specific teaching of the *Gita*. Gandhi was ingenious even when he declared that the *Gita* showed the futility and not the utility of violence since the victors, struck with *shoka* (pain and repentance), decided to leave the world instead of remaining to enjoy their victory. However, the argument was convincing to many, if only because it was a novel interpretation. Summing up, it can be said that the *Gita* armed Gandhi and the nationalists in general in many ways; the issue of violence got resolved, if at all,[41] only through the course of time when it became evident that it was not a sound tactic to employ against an opponent more powerful and better organized. The 'terrorists' failed to increase their hold after a point; the people remained apprehensive of their violent and secretive nationalism even though many did admire their dedication to the cause. Gandhi clearly illustrated, though unknowingly, the convoluted positions he had been taking regarding the *Gita* and the question of violence:

[41] It is more appropriate to say that Gandhi's concept of 'non-violence' acquired tremendous popularity over overtly violent methods of the 'terrorists'; the issue was resolved in favour of neither.

I do not wish to suggest that violence has no place at all in the teaching of the *Gita*. . . . There is only one dharma. Non-violence means moksha, and moksha means realizing *Satyanarayan*. . . . But this dharma does not under any circumstances countenance running away in fear. In this world which baffles our reason, violence there will then always be. The *Gita* shows the way which will lead us out of it, but it also says that we cannot escape it simply by running away from it like cowards. (*Collected Works*, XXVIII, p. 320)

SWAMI SAHAJANAND, RELIGION, MARXISM AND THE GITA

The kisan is the real god. Whether the world believes it or not, he is my god. (*Kisan Kya Karen*, p. 146)

Religion, I think, is a completely personal matter, like intelligence, heart, eyes, nose, etc. Two people do not have same intelligence or eyes. Then how can the religion of two people be one? (*Mera Jivan Sangharsh*, p. 477)

Our task is to create a classless society, not to wipe out God or to get after Him. . . . According to the *Gita*, religion is an individualized or personal affair. . . . There is no conflict in *Gitadharma* and Marxism. (*Gita Hridaya*, pp. 100–29)

These are statements of Swami Sahajanand Saraswati, arguably the most prominent leader of the kisans in the first half of the twentieth century. Born in 1889 (as far as he could recall), eighteen year-old Naurang Rai broke familial ties to quench his spiritual thirst and took the vows of renunciation in 1907 to become Sahajanand Saraswati. Sahajanand became a Dandi sannyasi (a very high order in the Dasnami sect of Shaankar Sampradaya)[42] in 1911 (*Mera Jivan Sangharsh*, 1952, p. 135. The title literally means, 'My Life Struggle') and never discarded his *gairik vastra* (saffron robe) even when he adopted Marxism as his primary political language in 1940, ten years before his death. From 1907 to 1911, he wandered between Banaras and the Himalaya,

[42] The Dandis, properly so called, and the Tridandis of the Vaishnavas, are the only legitimate representatives of the fourth ashrama, or mendicant life. It is not necessary however for a Brahman to have previously gone through all the others (see H.H. Wilson 1958, especially pp. 108–15, for a fuller discussion on Dandis and Dasnamis).

trekking the beds of the Ganga, surviving on alms, looking for a perfect yogi who would help him have communion with God. When that did not happen, Sahajanand delved into the classics of Sanskrit. With remarkable speed and concentration, he studied many religious and semi-religious texts till the end of the year 1914 when he took on himself the responsibility of restoring Brahman status to the Bhumihars, one of the four high castes found in Bihar and the eastern United Provinces. This, his first tryst with social activities, apparently ended the individualized, solitary spiritual journey of the renouncer for ever.[43]

This may well be a partial truth. As it appears from one of his most important works, *Gita Hridaya* [The Heart of *Gita*] (1988, 2nd edn., first published in 1948), Sahajanand's spiritual quest was only interiorized, it never quite left him. What seems to be the case is that the Swami developed philosophical schizophrenia, as it were, a split in his personality between the 'private' and 'public' domains,[44] since the day he joined the Congress. In his private sphere, he thought about religious and metaphysical problems and tried to follow his religious convictions as far as possible. The public sphere was reserved for issues like the nation and the freedom movement, the peasantry and the zamindari system. He tried hard to keep his two worlds apart and he was very successful in many respects. There are only a few instances when he seems to have muddled the boundaries. His attire and overall appearance was the most obvious example of it. It probably helped him traverse freely within both worlds he had constructed for himself. 'In 1937 he was reported to have said that as religious robes had long

[43] Walter Hauser (1961) and Amrita Tulika (1986), both, in their unpublished manuscripts, maintain that Sahajanand's participation in the Bhumihar upliftment activities was revolutionary, a break of sorts in the career of a sannyasi since it entailed indulging in social roles of an individual. Hauser seems to have somewhat modified this stance in one of his recent writings (July 1991 and January 1992). Only 'somewhat', because there are moments in this essay when Hauser slips back into the 'total-rupture-framework'. In addition to Hauser and Tulika could be recalled all those scholars who have worked on the Kisan Sabha and have looked into the politics of the peasant movement in Bihar in the 1930s and 1940s and not so much into the cultural and philosophical make up of the movement and its leaders. A good example is Arvind N. Das (1983).

[44] See for example the opening pages of his autobiography. The Swami is at pains to convey that it is that part of one's life that is public which should be highlighted and not the one that is private.

exploited the country, now he would exploit those robes on behalf of the peasants' (Hauser 1961, p. 86). That he began all his letters with 'Narayan' could be another example.[45] Similarly many of his books and pamphlets appear to have been completed on holy dates like *Mahashivaratri, Basant Panchami, Nag Panchami* or *Maagh Poornima*. While being a Hindu, these dates might have come easily to him, what makes them worthy of mention is that it seems too much of a coincidence that he actually completed his writings on those dates. His *Kisan Kya Karen*, intended to be a handbook for kisans, has *saat adhyaya* (seven chapters) which may not be a coincidence. The quotidian existence bound up by the seven days, and the *saat adhyaya* of *Ramcharitmanas* clearly carry a strong religious connotation.

Though it can be argued and justifiably so, that almost all individuals have certain elements of it, in his case it was so acute that his entire 'post-sannyas' life and his formulations can be explained in terms of this split. He was simultaneously two different individuals; what was worse, he was aware of his dual persona and all his life tried to come to terms with it. If it is not evident to scholars who wrote about him,[46] it could well be due to the following reasons: (a) they fail to adequately address themselves to the numerous contradictory conceptualizations of the Swami; (b) they probably see a unity of thought in each of his supposedly distinct phases, as opposed to conflicts and tensions since most of his major writings took place late in life, in 1940–2, in Hazaribagh Central jail, hence the tendency to compress and blur the nuances of his views expressed in activities throughout his life. Instead they

[45] See Suresh Paswan in Vijay Chandra Prasad Chaudhary et al. (1990, p. 49).

[46] There are many scholars who have commented on Sahajanand's involvements with kisan politics in Bihar. Unfortunately, however, there are not many, with the notable exceptions of Hauser (1961), Tulika (1986), and Pinch (1996) who have undertaken the task of combining his political endeavours with his religious and philosophical engagements (see Vijay Chandra Prasad Chaudhary et al., 1990, for some write-ups on this theme). Our submission is that Sahajanand's political activities cannot be understood in isolation. All scholars working on the Bihar Kisan Sabha agree that it developed a distinct political language, thanks primarily to the Swami. However, there is an inexplicable silence over the factors which together produced that language. The latter can be described as an amalgam of guarded religiosity, limited class struggle, idiosyncratic understanding of Gandhism and Marxism. The decisive factor remained the political expediency of the Sabha, disallowing either a fuller appreciation or rejection of both Gandhism and Marxism.

offer a glimpse into his life from a single vantage point—1940–2—when he had already declared himself a Marxist and was through with the search for solitary liberation, Bhumihar Sabha, the Congress, Gandhi, etc.; (c) and finally it is likely that they undertake a partial and fragmented reading of Sahajanand. For example if one reads only *Kisan Kya Karen* and not *Gita Hridaya* (like Hauser 1961), it would be extremely difficult to grasp the many-hued world-views of the Swami.

Sahajanand 'entered' the realm of active politics reluctantly. As he recalls in his autobiography, it was on the insistence of some well-wishers that he decided to read English newspapers to brush up his English. His friends argued that knowledge of English was essential if one wanted to be active in the socio-political sphere of the time (*Mera Jivan Sangharsh*, pp. 178–9). He had already 'entered' the social realm by taking up the issue of restoring priestly rights to the (male) members of the Bhumihar caste. It was this habit of reading newspapers that generated a political interest in him (ibid.). He took an appointment and met Mahatma Gandhi on 5 December 1920. Sahajanand describes this meeting with the Mahatma reverently in his autobiography where it is likened to a meeting between a Guru and a new disciple.[47] Sahajanand asked many questions including the duty of a sannyasi and, content with Gandhi's answers, decided to join politics instantly. On 20 March 1921, he became a member of the Indian National Congress.

Interestingly enough, in the membership form, Sahajanand struck the column that enquired about his father's name and instead mentioned the name of his Guru through whom he had become a Dandi sannyasi.[48] In the light of the discussion that we have initiated, this does not seem to be a matter of mere detail. To the contrary, it points to the manner in which he viewed himself as an individual. It strongly suggests that though he may have resolved to carve out a socio-political role for himself, at a certain level he was not prepared to let go his

[47] 'He was eating bread with milk, sitting on a cot. There was a chair in front of it. He indicated me to sit on it. But I preferred the floor' (pp. 183–4). The reverence to Gandhi is obvious, as in the traditional upper caste Hindu culture, one does not sit on an equal level with one's superior.

[48] *Swami Sahajanand Papers*, Microfilm, NMML, Delhi. There seems to be a discrepancy, however, in the name of the Guru. The paper has it as Swami Advaitanand while in his autobiography it is Swami Achyutanand Saraswati (see Saraswati 1952, p. 136).

renunciatory resolve and embrace the identity of a typical *grihastha*. It would have been indeed too sudden to be realistic. 'After the conversation [with Gandhi] I thought that I should plunge into politics right away. Not because the nation will benefit. But, because, only then can I become a true sannyasi. Right now I am an amateur' (*Mera Jivan Sangharsh*, p. 185).

Even if it was an afterthought,[49] the conclusion remains unaltered. The yearning to be a true sannyasi did not desert him altogether. Thus the question of his rejecting sannyas for something socially (as opposed to individually) meaningful did not arise in the sense scholars would have us believe. It meant that (as per the teachings of the *Gita*) he was prepared to take up roles beneficial to people at large and underplay the 'individual' seeking his own moksha, but retaining his internal faith in moksha. He worked it out through interiorizing the quest for salvation and pure dharma, through splitting his self into two compartments. Rahul Sankrityayan, a man of many hues, a scholar of many languages, a Buddhist monk, a bohemian, communist and Sahajanand's comrade-in-arms, noted in a brief passage in his autobiography that the Swami travelled between individualism and a concern for the poor kisans continuously [*Meri Jivan Yatra* (My Life-Journey), 1950, p. 543]. Though he did not dwell on it, the sense we get is that Sankrityayan found that Sahajanand's individualism often crept into his public life and affected his political decisions and activities.

Sahajanand's stint with the Congress was not very pleasant. He was deeply disturbed by the outright violation of Gandhian principles by fellow Congress workers. So hurt and outraged was he that by the time he completed his first jail sentence in 1922, he arrived at the conclusion that it was a big mistake of the Mahatma to have opened

[49] The statement appears to be of the 'post-*Gita* phase' of Indian politics, when not only the Mahatma had popularized the teachings of the *Gita*, but the Swami himself had undertaken a close study of it. The new meaning of 'sannyas' arrived at in the light of the *Gita*'s conception of *loksangraha* is indicative of the popularity action had gained over renunciation. The Swami too accepted the new meaning of karma as it is evident not only from his commentary on the *Gita* (see the Preface, pp. 5–6, to begin with), but from his active commitment to struggle as well. However, he did seek to retain some of the traditional thoughts on the *Gita*. In any event, it seems possible that thoughts in one text were influencing his formulations on other texts as well. He probably completed *Gita Hridaya* before *Mera Jivan Sangharsh*.

the movement for everyone so soon. Instead, he thought that initially the volunteers should have been a select few, chosen very carefully after cautious deliberations (*Mera Jivan Sangharsh*, pp. 251–3). Another of his conclusions was that it was an error on the part of Gandhi to have given politics spiritual overtones. To urge for a mass movement and to spiritualize politics at the same time was faulty since the contemporary state of religion as he found in the masses was far from satisfactory. Only a few were invested with the moral strength required for moral and spiritual satyagraha, he argued.

This position regarding the religiosity of the masses surfaces in Sahajanand time and again. However, consistency was not a strong point of the Swami. His reference to Yagyavalkya's *Smriti* to conclude that there were reasons after all why the people even in ancient times maintained the distinction between rajniti (politics) and dharmaniti (ethics) suggests that his contempt was not confined to the modern days (ibid. p. 253).

It may sound strange that a person whose religious thirst was so compelling since childhood (when he snapped his familial ties, took vows of celibacy and renunciation, wandered in the foothills of the Himalayas looking for a chance to have communion with the God, went without food and shelter for days) held such strong views against Gandhi's efforts at spiritualizing politics. His perception of dharma however, may provide a clue.

The rigorous search for the Brahman rendered Sahajanand a purist. It seems that he quite often equated malpractices like Brahmanic hypocrisy and superstition in religion with religion itself. Sahajanand passionately held that religion in its quotidian and collective form was almost irreparably corrupt, hypocritical, shallow and exhibitionist. It was devoid of reason and often tended to become 'communal' (in the sense of being fundamentalist, see *Mera Jivan Sangharsh*, pp. 233-4, 446-8; *Gita Hridaya*, p. 61, etc.). At one level, he was only voicing his reaction against what he observed in the practised version of Hinduism. On the other, it was also a case of elitism on the part of one who prided himself on his meticulous learning of numerous religious texts, years of sannyas, and meditation. According to Sahajanand, the religion of the masses was primarily of the 'false consciousness' variety (see, for example, *Kisan Kya Karen*, specially, Chapter 6; *Gita Hridaya*, pp. 68, 85), something that led kisans into perpetual ideological slavery to their social elites. In such discussions Sahajanand only betrayed the Marxists' folly regarding religion.[50]

And yet the question is not to dispute his observations regarding religion but to understand the whole phenomenon with its Carnivalesque and capitulative moments. This is reflected not only in momentary 'heretic' gestures, though they too were in abundance, but in continuous redefinitions/re-interpretations of everyday religious discourse. The latter facilitated a way for temporal/secular will to selective usage of under/overplaying certain aspects of religion. In other words, while a version of religion closer to the seat of power, taught non-violence and non-possession (*aparigraha*), people managed to find religious sanctions for their 'violent' and non-legal/'criminal' activities by choosing relevant portions/aspects of religion as a means of justification for their actions (see Chapter 2, and also *Gita Hridaya*, p. 412). It was more often a tussle *inside* the largely shared religion and not outside it. Only 'insiders' had the space for selective memorizing or cultivating collective amnesia.

However, in all fairness it must be said that Sahajanand was guided by an impatient desire to alleviate the condition of the toiling millions. His reading of Marxism appears far from being straightforward, as on many occasions he appeared far from decrying religion summarily. He was hesitant and always appeared to forestall the final duel between Marxism and religion:

> Actually, it is not good nor wise to claim monopoly of knowledge. If we come to know about God or the Soul [in the future], will it then be denied only because Marxism does not believe in it? Wisdom lies in not worrying too much about the future and not foreclosing any future possibilities—be it theism or atheism. Yes, today theism is . . . obstructing the path of progress. (*Gita Hridaya*, p. 67)

[50] To them religion, as an ideology, was some kind of 'false' or 'deviant' consciousness. This falsehood (or deviance) of society was about itself. And, finally, as an ideology, it was supposed to be a 'lived' form of social consciousness/perception. To try to reconcile all three aspects of their perception of religion within a single account created the epistemological anarchy: how could a society be viewed as *living* in a state of *false consciousness* of *itself*? At the level of an individual, it was articulated as 'a product of self-alienation', an 'alienated self-consciousness'. For a fuller discussion on the theme see Erica Sherover-Marcuse (1986).

It is only at this juncture, it seems, that the Swami was averse to the idea of making a religious platform available to the masses. He endorsed the views of Lenin, Marx, and, Engels to convey that one must reflect on religion as the state of class struggle deemed it appropriate. One must not be in a hurry to arrive at the final conclusion regarding religion as if that could be true and applicable for all time to come (ibid., p. 69). He quoted Lenin extensively in support of his prioritization of class struggle:

> A Marxist must be a materialist, that is, an enemy of religion, but from the materialist and dialectical standpoint, i.e., he must conceive the fight against religion not as an abstraction, not on the basis of pure theoretical atheism, *equally applicable to all times and conditions*, but concretely, on the basis of the class struggle which is actually going on and which will train and educate the masses better than anything else. (p. 71, emphasis added)[51]

The Swami cited Lenin in support of his assertion that the need of the hour was to wage a struggle and not to get into metaphysical deliberations about the existence of God. Of particular significance was the following statement of Lenin, as it captured the dilemma of Sahajanand effectively:

> If a clergyman wishes to join us in political work, and conscientiously carries out party work, and does not infringe the party programme, then he may be accepted into the ranks of Social Democracy, for the contradiction between the spirit and principles of our programme and the religious convictions of the clergyman may, in the circumstances, remain a matter that concerns him alone. (cited in *Gita Hridaya*, p. 72)

In *Gita Hridaya* Sahajanand sought to make religion a private matter for *everyone*, thinking that this was what Lenin had argued. But this was simply an incorrect reading of Lenin. Given his stance on political morality and expediency, Lenin wanted to eschew an open battle with the Church and the clergy, while he was busy organizing workers against the State and its capitalist allies. Thus he allowed clergymen to join

[51] Sahajanand extracts Lenin's views on religion from 'The Attitude of the Workers' Party to Religion', which appeared on 13 May 1909 in *Proletary* no. 45. See the full text in his *Collected Works*, vol. 15, Moscow: Progress Publishers, 1977 (3rd print), pp. 402–13. As was typical of Sahajanand, he seldom cited the source he was borrowing from.

hands with the workers till they (the churchmen) resolved their illusions. He did not envisage the same for himself or for the Social Democrats, nor for the revolutionary proletariat and the party. Lenin quoted from Engels' *Anti-Dühring*: 'Social Democrats regard religion as a private matter *in relation to the state*,[52] but not in relation to themselves, not in relation to Marxism, and not in relation to the workers' party' (p. 404, emphasis added). What is worse is that Lenin pre-empted Sahajanand's distortion:

> The party of the proletariat demands that *the state* should declare religion a private matter, but does not regard the fight against the opium of the people, the fight against religious superstitions, etc., as a 'private matter'. The opportunists distort the question to mean that the *Social Democratic party regards* religion as a private matter! (p. 410, emphasis in original)

Sahajanand, the opportunist in Lenin's view, allowed a fluid space for himself by not defining/identifying himself in strict Marxian categories. Even though he was aware that Marxism was persistent about declaring religion as a private matter *only* in relation to the State and its separation from the Church, he did not take a rigorous stand on Marxism and religion. The separation between the State and the Church, as advocated by Engels and Lenin, was grossly misconceived by him. He usesd it as a shield as he wanted to follow Marxism while he was yet to get rid of his deep-seated religious yearnings. Could it be because he viewed himself not as a Marxist, nor as a Social Democrat, nor as a leader of a workers' party, but as a clergyman? He certainly was not a man of a church or *matha*, in the sense that he never associated himself with any form of institutionalized Hinduism.[53] Perhaps he identified with the clergy only to the extent that the latter was willing to work

[52] In an essay written with the purpose to decry 'Spiritual Communism' in India in general and of Aurobindo in particular, M.N. Roy (the leading figure of the Communist movement in India and a then tireless critic of Mahatma Gandhi) took a similar line: 'Had this complex of spiritualism been an individual idiosyncracy, we could leave it alone' (Roy 1923). This is partially reproduced in G. Adhikari (1974, pp. 216–20).

[53] Despite the fact that he was a Dandi sannyasi of the Dasnami sect, the Swami never confined himself to its *parampara*. He had no hesitation in visiting and learning from a rival camp or guru. Despite being a Shaiva he was visibly influenced by the Vaishnavite beliefs in reform. His faith in the concept of *Daridranarayan* and *loksangraha* was symptomatic of his crossing the barrier set by Hindu *sect*ional orthodoxies.

with the Social Democratic party without renouncing its faith in God. Perhaps he could feel a certain degree of affinity with a believer who was willing to work with and for the working masses without being in a rush to pass the verdict against a faith he held so dear to his heart for so long. One can never know for sure what inspired the Swami's sloppy reading of a simple twelve-page text.

However, it does go one step further in denying any sharp ruptures in the intellectual life of the Swami. Perhaps the text of Lenin carried elements of certain fundamental metaphysical affinities with a text at large, i.e. Sahajanand's life and philosophy. In Lenin's formulation, that a clergyman's religious orientation is his private concern, the Swami misread an escape, a way out of his own dilemma.[54]

In his autobiography, Sahajanand remarked that an unfree India

[54] Perhaps it can be argued with some degree of justification that had nineteenth-century Young-Hegelian philosophical discourses, in general, and Marxism of Young Marx, in particular, been available to him directly, the relationship between his religious beliefs and his Marxian predilection might have taken a fascinating course. As we know, for a large part, people in India came to know Marxism from the writings of Lenin. The thoughts of Young Marx were not available to the English-speaking world in the first half of the twentieth century. G. Adhikari (1972) lists nine books published in India (1917–22) celebrating the Revolution in Russia of which six were eulogies-cum-biographical sketches of Lenin (p. 268).

Though there was a crucial difference between Sahajanand and Young Hegelians on the question of religion (in the sense that his conception of social welfare and *Daridranarayan* did not negate the existence of God while the Young Hegelians did reject God in order to elevate the human being as the supreme expression of divinity), the similarity is no less exciting. The notion of 'man's self-realization' continuously appears in Hegel and Young Hegelians like David Strauss, Ludwig Feuerbach, Bruno Bauer, and Marx. The Hegelian 'theme of man's soaring into the unlimited' attracted Marx, who reached a similar truth, however, not via the religious path of Hegel but through 'atheism'. To Young Marx, 'atheism' was an aggressive way of articulating the fact that 'God is man'. Robert C. Tucker holds that

> The religious essence of Marxism is superficially obscured by Marx's rejection of the traditional religions. This took the form of a repudiation of 'religion' as such and an espousal of 'atheism'. Marx's atheism . . . meant only a negation of the transmundane God of traditional Western religion. It did not mean the denial of a supreme being . . . denial of the transmundane God was merely a negative way of asserting that 'man' should be regarded as the supreme being or object of ultimate concern. Thus his atheism was a positive religious proposition. (1972, 2nd edn., p. 22)

could not have appetite for spiritualism, religion, or God in general, 'just as a sick body is left with no desire for food' (*Mera Jivan Sangharsh*, p. 447). He seemed to support postponement of a final verdict on the ontological state of religion and God. He was, somewhat like Gandhi, prepared to find his God in the peoples he served and fought for (*Kisan Kya Karen*, p. 146). The transference was symptomatic of his growing affection for Marxism and concern for the kisans on the one hand, and his studied deferral of the question of religion and God on the other.[55]

At the same time Sahajanand would not critique religion per se. Only those qualified to speak on religion and perceived by people as such, should undertake it, that too extremely cautiously and on the basis of logic and arguments alone, the Swami argued (*Mera Jivan Sangharsh*, p. 448). Not everybody who abhorred religion was fit to denounce it. In other words, in this framework the accessibility of

---

What, however, speaks directly to Sahajanand is Tucker's summary of Feuerbach's *Kleine Phiosophische Schriften*:

> Instead of fixing his gaze upon God as his object of adoration, man is to lavish his love upon man. By the love of man is to be understood not love of self but love of the *other* man: 'The true dialectic is not a monologue of a lone thinker with himself, but a dialogue between the I and the Thou'. Feuerbach's underlying idea here is that religious man, and his spokesmen the theologian and speculative philosopher, are fundamentally self-centered, concerned with the self in the form of the divine *alter ego*, whereas what man should have before him is not an illusory 'other' in God but a real and living 'other' in the other human being. So Feuerbach writes: 'The being of man is given only in communion, in the unity of man with man, a unity resting on the reality of the distinction between the I and the Thou. . . . Man for himself is man in the ordinary sense; man in the communion with man, the unity of the I and the Thou, is God.' (pp. 90–1, emphasis added)

One can clearly see the proximity of such arguments with that of the Swami while the latter was putting forward his arguments against self-fulfilling sannyas as opposed to detached karma in order to avail moksha.

[55] At least once, in a deep moment of 'raising consciousness' of the kisans, the Swami speaks disrespectfully of God:

> We hear of an Almighty that He is also kind to the poor. Is He asleep? Or dead? Or has He also accepted the bribe from zamindars? Why else, otherwise, He allows such things? Is He afraid of zamindars and the Police? Aren't poor and miserable kisans worthy of His empathy? (*Kisan Kaise Ladate Hain*?, p. 34)

'true' religion was to be mediated only by the learning of a few. If the egoist sannyasi appears to be getting the better of the Marxist activist, it only goes to confirm our hypothesis: that the sannyasi did not die even when Sahajanand took up active political life. Rather his newer avocations had to actively engage with his sannyas-dharma (which was continuously going through the processes of redefinition) and vice versa. Hardly anything reveals this interplay more clearly and forcefully than the occasion when the self-styled Marxist took upon himself the task of commenting extensively on the *Gita*.

Swami Sahajanand was not only familiar with the *Gita* right from his early days of sannyas, he used to 'exercise' it regularly.[56] In March 1922, he discovered a new light, a new meaning in it when he was forced to read the text in original because *tikas* (commentaries) were not available in the Faizabad prison. For the first time he realized why the text had such a strong hold over the people. His earlier notion was that it was the spiritualism and strong philosophical current in the text that made it incomprehensible to the common folk (*Mera Jivan Sangharsh*, pp. 233–5). The Swami claimed to have found the peace that had eluded him all these years despite his arduous engagements with Vedanta and other philosophical strands of Hinduism. The *Gita* became his favourite text and as long as he lived he always had a copy with him. 'The *Gita* and I have become inseparable from each other. I can tolerate separation from other thoughts and books, but not from hers. Can the soul be separated [from the body]? My thoughts about her have grown in my heart for a score of years. They indeed have been nurtured on my blood' (*Gita Hridaya*, p. 6).[57] Like Gandhi, Sahajanand too repeatedly reminded his readers about his 'forty years of association' with it (*Gita Hridaya*, Preface, p. 5). He acknowledged many

[56] It is not easy to translate what Sahajanand says about his interaction with the *Gita*: '*Gita ka abhyas to barabar karate the*' (*Mera Jivan Sangharsh*, p. 55). Literally, it would read as: I used to practice the *Gita* regularly, as one would practice a yoga. The expression usually connotes giving regular time to something. It is very common among believing Hindus even today to read the *Gita*, or for that matter any religious text, as the part of everyday meditation and/or worship. The reference implies Sahajanand's early faith in the text.

[57] In Hindu tradition it is fairly common to address a book, a text as a feminine figure, as a mother, to be precise. In Sanskrit and Hindi languages, book is feminine gender. Gandhi, Aurobindo, and others furthered this tradition along with Sahajanand.

changes that he went through in his religious and political career but the *Gita* stayed with him like a life-long companion.

Sahajanand's initial interactions with the *Gita* were 'only religious' in nature when he sought a narrow, selfish way towards salvation and found what was actually an action-less Vedantism in it (ibid.). Though the interaction never ceased to be religious per se, it became religious in a much broader sense of the term, as now it was universal and totally committed to social action. 'There was a phase—that lasted right till six years from now—when I used to believe that for an admirer of the *Gita* like me, there is no place in Marxism, that *Gitadharma* and Marxism do not meet, they contradict each other' (ibid.).[58] This marked yet another shift in his understanding of the text. Interestingly, like the previous one, this too happened in a Jail.

Very much in accordance with what had already gained currency, the Swami underlined detached action (Nishkam karma) and social welfare (*loksangraha*) as the central messages of the *Gita*. Like Tilak and Gandhi, he realized the importance of emphasizing selfless action directed towards the salvation of the entire society and not just of an individual. However, unlike Tilak and Gandhi, Sahajanand did not underplay Gyan yoga in order to highlight Karma yoga. As if to provide more evidence of his reluctance to renounce his *sannyas-dharma*, the Swami maintained that people like Tilak had erred in their allegations that Shankaracharya (the earliest known commentator) was against Karma yoga, or that he privileged *sankhya* or Gyan yoga over it (*Mera Jivan Sangharsh*, pp. 245–6). Instead, the Swami found equal and equitable space for both the yogas in the *Gita*.

The main difference seems to be the way karma was to be understood. Those who favoured active social life and decried selfish escapism of the sannyasi argued that action was desirable for everyone who happens to be travelling through the life-process. According to them, it was incorrect that actions per se got humans into temporal tangles, and thus hampered drives for superior knowledge, or were obstacles in the path of the realization of the Brahman. The crucial

[58] He finished writing the Preface of *Gita Hridaya* on 1 January 1942. Six Years back would be the phase when the Swami was gradually, cautiously, moving towards the demand for abolition of the zamindari without compensation. His honeymoon with the Congress and the Mahatma was soon to be over (see *Mera Jivan Sangharsh*, pp. 423–45).

thing was to do one's duty without being obsessed with its reward, they added. Sahajanand seems to have resorted to the traditional wisdom that had a hierarchy of sorts among knowledge, action, and devotion (gyan, karma, and bhakti, in that order) as three paths of salvation. He did not consider the actions of Karma yogis as karma at all (*gyaninam karma tu karmeva na bhavati*, p. 245). In *Gita Hridaya*, he illustrated a typology of karma that ranged from attending to bodily functions, to performing acts needed for others' welfare, and undertaking metaphysical and philosophical exercises (pp. 6–12). Just like the Gyan yoga of the Gyan yogis, tending to the bare minimum requirements of the human body too was not a karma. From here the next step was to describe the Gyan yogi whose mental state was to be so advanced that he was supposedly oblivious of and unperturbed by the mundane realities around him; he perpetually lived in a zone of trance as it were, intoxicated with the bliss of his knowledge (pp. 14–15). This path was open only to a few; not all were equipped to reach the state of a Gyan yogi and renounce all their duties. For those not endowed with similar intellect were prescribed the other two ways. He concluded that the *Gita* was thus opposed to forcing karma for everybody (p. 31); it concerned only the householder.

Once again, as in relation to other issues, there are moments when the Swami does not appear to hold a consistent position on this. Reminiscing about one *grihastha* he had met during the days when he was a wandering sannyasi, Sahajanand regretted that he did not understand the true nature of Vedantism then, and that the householder was a better and more mature practitioner of Vedanta than him (*Mera Jivan Sangharsh*, pp. 83–4). Sahajanand admitted to his intellectual inferiority and rooted for the commonsensical wisdom of the *grihastha* who, despite performing his worldly duties, managed to rise above the renouncer who did nothing for others. The householder in his capacity never missed a chance to serve fellow human beings. While this position is not altogether missing even from *Gita Hridaya*, it does get diluted with his view that the *Gita* does not essentially underplay Gyan yoga.[59]

What separates Sahajanand most clearly from contemporary commentators was his view that the *Gita* not only did not oppose some

[59] See, for example, *Pooja Ke Bhed* (Types of Worship), pp. 20–3, where Sahajanand holds that our duties themselves become forms of worships.

of the central concerns of Marxism, it in fact had certain things in common with Marxism. The Swami thought that though it was true that the *Gita* talked of God, it had no aversion to atheism either, and that was what made it a great text (*Gita Hridaya*, p. 54). Its belief that 'karma is dharma and vice versa' obliterated the distinction and distance if any, between a believer and a non-believer. Sahajanand held that the basic tenet of Marxism, that elicited the end of exploitation, was perfectly in tandem with what the *Gita* taught: *Sarvabhutatmbhutatma* and *Sarvabhuthiteratah* (p. 5).[60] 'Only the Marxists desire the total transformation of the entire society; they are the ones who wish that not a single soul be unhappy, unfree, deprived of means to grow and develop' (ibid.). He counts all the instances in the *Gita* where the words *sam, samatva, samya, sam-drishti* appear to underline similarities with Marxism that too has 'equal', 'equitability', 'equality' and 'egalitarianism' (literal translation of the terms) as some of its key concepts (p. 125).

In fact, one finds a range of Sahajanand's intellectual concerns converging and being re-emphasized at this juncture. His incessant attacks on the superfluous and superstitious religious practices; his belief that Gyan yoga was not accessible to everyone to attain salvation, that a true sannyasi must work for social welfare (*loksangraha*); that actions are unavoidable for everyone who has undertaken the journey of life; etc., led him inevitably towards Marxism. He envisaged Marxism as the most suitable yoga for the common folk who could not guide themselves onto the path of Gyan yoga (p. 99). For them the best way of meeting the Brahman was through the battlefields of everyday life. Marx's famous quote that many have tried to understand the world, the need is to change it, fitted perfectly with what the *Gita* so strongly advocated about karma.

To sum up, the *Gita* helped Swami Sahajanand in a way which was very different from that in which it helped Gandhi or Tilak. Even though the emphasis on action is common to all of them, the deeper philosophical meanings are discovered differently. As an example of a reciprocal interaction, their individualities produced different readings of the same text which shaped (and at the same time got shaped by) their political, religious and moral contours. In a way, it was most

[60] 'Be engrossed in doing good to all created beings, as one is in all and all is in one'

crucial to Sahajanand since it helped him overcome the apparent dichotomy between Marxism and religious belief. Even though the Swami did not take his inner dilemma to a public forum, it was extremely important for a conscientious individual like him to resolve the same at some level. In other words, the *Gita* provided him with an epistemological basis without which his intellectual life would have been nothing but a repository of confusions and contradictions. This period also coincided with his engagements with the *khet mazdoors* (agricultural labourers, also the title of his book which he wrote in 1941); a clear sign of departure from his otherwise well-known association with the struggles of tenants.[61] It was both an influence of Marxism and the philosophy of the *Gita* with its advocacy for *loksangraha* and *sam*, *samya*, and *samatva* that impelled him to speak for those at the actual bottom of the social ladder. Like a true Vedantist as it were, the Swami saw in every human being a part of the God and chose to spend his life in the service of this *Daridranarayan* (the God who resides in the poor).

The coming together of religion and the language of radical politics was nothing new for the subcontinent. Throughout the medieval period if not before, we have many seers and saints, poets and reformers who voiced their concern in rich religious metaphors against social evils as they perceived them. What was novel in subcontinental history was the coming together of religion and a strand of radical politics that defined itself as Marxism.

Liberation Theology

We could interpret Sahajanand's effort as a precursor of what came to be known as 'liberation theology' in Chile, Colombia and Peru in the 1960s and 1970s. The radical bishops of South America began their struggle against the imperialism of multi-national corporations and the institutionalized violence of capitalist society in an increasingly Marxist rhetoric, confirming their faith in active political intervention. They appealed to the Church to express its solidarity with the poor and the marginalized not only in prayer but concretely by criticizing injustice and oppression. They perceived the new theology

[61] The monograph has been reproduced with a translation and useful editorial notes by Walter Hauser (1994).

coming not from received spiritual knowledge, but 'from the Marxian concept of *praxis*' (Norman, p. 53).[62] Theologians must engage themselves, they vowed, 'where nations, social classes, people struggle to free themselves from dominations and oppression' since 'salvation is not some "other-worldly" condition: it is the practical construction of social justice in the existing world' (Gutiérrez, pp. 13, 151). Without proclaiming the 'death of God' or doubting the divinity of Christ, they had reason to believe that the scriptural texts contained a political message. In this scheme of things, Christ himself became a political liberator, the John the Baptist of Marx (Norman, p. 54). Yet some maintained that though salvation and political freedom are not identical, they must not be separated. Thus Camilo Torres (1929–66), the Columbian priest who died as a guerrilla, remarked, 'The Catholic who is not a revolutionary is living in mortal sin' (quoted in John Gerassi 1973, p. 9). However, in the less euphoric moments of the mid-1970s, the radical bishops of South America placed more emphasis on the spiritual dimensions of human emancipation and the value of folk religion, its conservatism notwithstanding (pp. 54–5).

To this can be added the experience in Burma where Buddhist monks quite imaginatively used radical vocabulary to further their agenda of liberation.[63] The strategic redefinition of the Holy Week pasyon play which was originally intended to inculcate loyalty among the Tagalog population to their Catholic Spanish masters presents us with yet another instance in which the figure of Christ and the message of Christianity were turned against colonial domination by the subject Tagalog population.[64] The poor strata of the Philippines imagined an unlettered Christ who had 'lowly people without worth on earth' (Ileto 1979, p. 23) as his lieutenants. In the idiom of pasyon the Tagalog peasants articulated their dreams and ideas of nationalism and liberation. Reading religion not in order to underline their subservience, though that has historically been always in abundance, but to upset the

[62] Our understanding on the present theme is confined to our limited readings, some of which are: Edward Norman 1979; Gustavo Gutiérrez 1974; Sergio Torres and John Eagelson 1976; John Gerassi (ed.), 1973.

[63] See Michael Adas 1982 and 1979.

[64] Reynaldo Ileto's *Pasyon and Revolution: Popular Movements in the Philippines* (1979), is a superb study on this subject.

existing structure can be found in plenty of resistance movements in many African societies.[65]

The purpose behind mentioning these ex-periences is to suggest that the construction of a language of politics often derives its epistemological energies from more than one source, often from sources which look hostile to each other at first glance. So often the sources are indeed hostile, but in the process of struggle for change, people redefine them, construct them afresh, deconstruct the older/traditional meanings, confirming that human struggles are about the struggle for definition of things that determine our lives.

Let us now see what religion as a language of politics meant to kisans in Bihar.

[65] See Catherine Coquery-Vidrovitch (1988) for a useful summary of such cases in the south of the Saharan Africa.

CHAPTER 5

Unhappy Consciousness: Dialogues and Denials

The religiosity of kisans in colonial Bihar is often taken as an anthropological axiom, eternal, oblivious to the dictates of time as it were; hence without need of elaboration as to how exactly their religious views and beliefs were translated into quotidian experiences of survival. A repetition of the traditional wisdom according to which a religious person always stands in total surrender to the one she/he worships, is inherently vulnerable to the Marxian charge of 'self-estrangement' of the believer. This happens since the idiom of 'total, unquestioned and devotional' surrender to God is often worked out as the very basic ideology of status-quoism in the society by the powers that be. In other words, the latter uses religion to assume and propagate a divine basis of its authority. Religion in such discourses can no longer be relied upon as a possible force of *transformation*; it inevitably becomes a mechanism that actualizes *trance-formation*, as it were.[1] Instead, we will have to employ those skills that enable historians to detect diachronic punctuations in the register of everyday religion. These diachronic moments may express themselves in an extra-religious or secular language.

This chapter proposes to examine such issues without losing sight of the fact that religious language was preferred by many leaders and

[1] However, as we have argued, a dream, an illusion, or a fictive real may not always be unreal. Fictionalization may well be very much a part of confronting the real.

thinkers of freedom movements, rightly assuming that it had a better receptivity among the masses. The receptivity of Gandhian language is said to be better than that of the Nationalists before or after him, precisely because he did not have to 'employ' a religious language as a tactic or out of political expediency. His religion was his politics; he did nothing that his dharma did not beckon him to.

All the more, this requires us to show the exact nature of the relationship between the religiosity of the leader and that of the follower. The complex interplay of the sacred and the so-called secular, may tell us about the complex evolution of a language in a highly tumultuous time. Social scientists must actively engage in demonstrating as much as possible the influences of one over the other, instead of juxtaposing one against the other and/or assuming a particular kind of trait or behaviour 'given' to them. A brief enquiry into the dialogues between the two would throw valuable light on the subject.

SHRADDHA AND *SHIKAYAT*?

The fact that dharma and *dharati* (the earth) both originate from the same etymological source *dhri* (which means, 'to hold'), enforces the general belief that dharma played a crucial role in constituting the world-view of the kisan, who continues to be referred to as *dharati-putra* (son of the soil; the gender bias is apparent) in popular parlance. The literal meaning of both words, 'one that holds', opens up for social scientists the vast and complex philosophical and cultural cosmology of the kisan.

The following examples seem to suggest that early twentieth-century Bihar negated the fact that a religious person was one who held the Almighty as the repository of all right strength and wisdom in the world, one who was blindly devoted to Him (and/or Her in many non-Semitic instances), who surrendered completely to God without questioning His total supremacy. As kisan assertions began to take a more coherent shape and direction from the late 1920s, we find strong hints of a different tone in their religiosity. It was a religiosity which did not always exhibit total supplication or unqualified surrender to the God. Yet it was not a war against the superiority of the Almighty, unlike say the post-Hegelians in Western Europe who had embarked on a new agenda of Secularism, increasingly pitching their arguments against God and the believers.[2] It was probably akin to the religiosity of South American liberation theologists. It was a relationship that demanded reciprocity; a relationship in which the devotees insisted on seeing the fruits of their devotion *in this very world*. An assumption about the unconditional faith of the kisan in Providence appears to be an uncritical moment of scholarship—betraying a bias in favour of the powers that be who indeed wanted the kisan to become a being of their assumption: fatalist, other-worldly, uncomplaining, and, thus, devoid of any diachronic social consciousness. However, evidence suggests a sign of a religious matrix which was woven with dual threads of reverence and 'complaints', *shraddha* and *shikayat*.

हे भोला बाबा केहन कयलों दीन।
खेती पथारी भोला सेहो लेल छीन
भाई सहोदर सेहो भे गेल भीन।
घर में न खरची बाहर न मिले रीन
गांव के मालीक न परई दैया नीन।

[O Bhola! What times are these? You snatched the little land I had. My own brother has turned on me. Not a morsel of grain in the house and no hope for loans. The Master of the village lets me no peace.] (Sankrityayan 1960, p. 30)

In this Maithili song, the kisan holds Bhola Baba (Shiva) responsible for his destitute situation. The religious language is employed to emphasize the political economy of the time: the cruelty of the master of the village (the zamindar), the difficulty in obtaining loans, the state of perpetual hunger, and so on. A similar moment of belief and reverence inseparably attached with ridicule, can be seen in a Bhojpuri song:

सुनीला अनाथन के दीनानाथ साथ देले
तोर साथ काहे नहीं देसु हो किसनऊ।[3]

[2] The idea of the uninterrupted unilinear development of secularist thinking cannot be held even in the case of Europe. In a way secularism had a long history. Some take it back to the French Revolution of 1789, some insist it began from the days of the Renaissance. Even after Hegel, there was no smooth sailing, as we saw young Marx not totally bereft of an idea of divinity.

[3] Composed by one Kavi Kailash in the 1930s, this is a part of a rather long poem against zamindari exploitation in contemporary Bihar. See Yamuna Prasad Upadhyay

[I hear, Deenanath (literally, the Lord of the Poor) helps the lordless. Why then are you not being blessed, O, kisan?].

It is difficult to miss the moment that underlines the critical consciousness of kisans about their conflictual positioning vis à vis God in this formulation. Nirghin Ram, a Chamar (an Untouchable) who had joined the Congress in 1918 thinking that it would bring him some respect in society, composed the following song after leaving the Congress, a totally shattered man:

हमनी के बेरिआ निठुर भइले बनवारी।
ऐहि चरन से अहिला के तरल, सेहु गौतम के नारी
विप्र सुदामा के दरिद्र हटवल
मड़ई से कइल अटारी।
हमनी के बेरिआ निठुर भइले बनवारी।

[When it comes to (helping) us, Banwari (Lord Krishna) becomes unkind. You redeemed Ahilya, the wife of Gautam with a mere touch of your feet; removed the poverty of Brahmin Sudama, turned his hut into a palace. (But) when it comes to us, Banwari becomes unkind.]

Banwari also becomes a third person in this beautiful Bhojpuri song whenever Nirghin Ram begins to speak about himself (and about those who are like him). This is a rather interesting device for accentuating the distance between oneself and the God who is indifferent to one's misery. It was reverence indeed but the note and voice of protest are too clear to be missed. It may not be coincidental that Nirghin Ram underlines the fact that Sudama was a Brahmin ('Vipra Sudama') upon whom God bestowed magnanimity. In fact, none of the legendary figures he mentions, Ahilya or Gautam, was lower caste. Clearly, this formulation tended to implicate Banwari on the ground of being indifferent to the people of 'lower births'. At the same time, the collectivity, 'hamani' ('we'), on behalf of whom he was speaking, was also inclusive

n.d., p. 34. Kavi Kailash, a man of modest means and education, had a small nursery near Arrah. He came into active politics after the great massacre at Jallianwala Bagh, in Amritsar (1919); took formal membership of the Congress in 1926; and by 1936 had begun to see and detest the hypocritical elements within the Congress leadership who, he thought, were not really committed to the upliftment of the kisan.

of the poor kisans in general. To infer this we need not exercise our sociological commonsense; Nirghịn Ram makes it clear in another couplet:

मालीक का खेत, अंगरेज का प्रेत
चेत, चेत, चेत, चेत ने मना चेत।

[The land of the lord, the ghost of the British. Beware, beware, beware, O man, beware].

'*Bhukhe bhajan na hoye Gopala, lehun apan kanthi-mala*' (Take your beads and the amulet, it's not possible to sing in the praise of Gopala—I am hungry)—is a popular saying in which the hungry disciple tells his Guru about his refusal to pray to God. Sahajanand himself was very fond of: *Bhookh sansar mein sabse badi hai, yahan tak ki bhagwan se bhi.*[4] As we observed earlier, the kisan could recall Maharshi Vishwamitra who defied all codes of dharma by stealing from his untouchable master a dead dog's leg to satisfy his hunger.

In contrast, high-culture Brahmanic religiosity of the elite (which social scientists often mistakenly assume to be all-pervasive) demands nothing less than total subservience to God. As can be easily imagined, this notion is then discursively deployed (and in the process, religiously

[4] It is rather difficult to translate this pithy sentence. Literally, it would read something like this: 'Hunger is the greatest thing in the world, it is even greater than God'. The implied meaning becomes clearer in his next sentences: 'No body undertakes thieving [used in a generic sense; the implied connotation is, to commit crime, in general] to have communion with God or to go to heaven. But everybody does so to kill hunger' (*Kisan Kaise Ladate Hain*, p. 35).

This seems to be the logical culmination of his increasing radicalization. Consider the following remark he made in 1936: 'The right of the toiling masses to bread is greater than all laws and zamindars put together' (*All India Kisan Bulletin*, 11 July 1936). The difference from his position in 1927, when he was 'forced to open up the Bihar Provincial Kisan Sabha' stands out. The Swami began his kisan-politics as a 'class-collaborator' who wanted to sort out kisan grievances with the local zamindars through compromise and peaceful persuasion (See Swami Sahajanand Papers, 'The Origin and Growth of the Kisan Movement in India', Microfilm, NMML, Delhi; *Mera Jivan Sangharsh*, pp. 320, 408). This complexity gets totally lost in the unilinear and hagiologic narrative of Hauser (1961 and 1992). By the time the Swami gave the call for the abolition of the zamindari system (1936), to live, to fight against hunger, had become greater than not only law and order but God himself.

defended) in all arenas of social relationship. Polemically speaking, the desire is to deny subalterns the language with which to articulate a critical consciousness of the society in which they live and of the social relations they are forced to shoulder. The same desire is shared, though often unknowingly, by a brand of scholarship that insists on seeing nothing but obscurantism and fatalism in the deep religious outlook of the kisans. This brief note of caution is not to suggest that the religious beliefs and practices of the kisans of Bihar and that of Nationalist leaders were two distinct streams that never met. The popularity of the Nationalist rhetoric, to the extent that it became successful, was significantly derived from its acceptance among the masses in general and the kisan in particular.

However, what this caveat does achieve is that it problematizes the relationship between the kisan and the principal teaching of the *Gita* according to Gandhi. As we noted in the previous chapter, for Gandhi, Anasakti yoga was the main message of the *Gita*. However, the conscious moments of kisan religiosity that we have just noted, were anything but anasakti. These songs advocated instead a strong desire on the part of the kisan to see the fruit of his action in this very world. Promises of better life-chances in another world had lost their charm in the stormy days of struggle. In any event, to expect kisans to launch a huge struggle for swaraj without making any serious intervention in their day-to-day drudgery was not a realistic move.[5] This was especially so since the kisan and the Kisan Sabha had already begun in a concerted way to question the Gandhian strategy of not taking on the fight to eliminate the zamindari system on which the imperial

[5] Rahul Sankrityayan coined a laconic phrase for this version of swaraj-politics. He called it: 'nirakar swaraj', the unmanifest self-rule (*Meri Jivan Yatra*, 1950, p. 497). Talking about Karyanand Sharma, a noted Kisan Sabha leader, Sankrityayan says:

> To him, swaraj meant eradication of poverty and humiliation; gradually his experiences convinced him that *nirakar swaraj* would not do; the *sakar* [the manifest] miseries of the kisan will have to be removed. (ibid., emphasis added)

A similar sentiment is expressed by Kavi Kailash:

> *Aye Baba Gandhi, kahiya le mili Ajadi*
> *Atana din ho gail, pahirat Khadi.*
>
> [When shall we have freedom, O Baba Gandhi. It's been ages wearing your Khadi.]

edifice rested. The distinct tone of kisan religiosity, driven by the desire to voice mundane grievances, exposed the precarious balance of the Nationalist paradigm in the realm of socio-economic conflict. To kisans, the principle of detached action became just another name for avoiding 'the real issue'. From the people who found it difficult to make both ends meet, trapped in the viciousness of poverty and debt, whose dignity and self-respect were trampled upon everyday, Gandhi was expecting too big a sacrifice by asking them to contribute selflessly to Nation building. This can be further demonstrated by contrasting the ways in which Gandhi and Sahajanand chose to interpret the battlefield, Kurukshetra, of the *Mahabharata*.

For Gandhi the great battle between the Pandavas and the Kauravas was actually an allegory of the war between good and evil that goes on in the heart of the human being all the time. The *Gita* in general was a great spiritual guide for Gandhi, telling him about the most appropriate path to be followed in every situation of moral crisis and dilemma. Though we do not know if Sahajanand was actually familiar with Gandhi's interpretation of the *Gita*, it may not be a coincidence that the Swami moved away from this formulation, which could have been too abstract for the kisans to appreciate. Instead, he likened the discourse between Krishna and Arjuna as a prime example of *chakhchukh* (a colloquial term connoting heated discussion, altercation).[6] Similar

[6] *Gita Hridaya*, p. 277. Though Sahajanand did not dwell on this point for long, it can be safely speculated that an altercation does not ideally take place between unequals. The authority of the superior does not allow space for discussion, let alone altercation. If the Swami allowed that space to the kisan, he was only echoing the age-old Vaishnavite belief that allowed the devotee to even be angry with the God. Unlike the Shaiva tradition that focusses on individual salvation through renunciation and right knowledge, the Vaishnava tradition, of which the *Gita* and (in the medieval period) Bhakti poetry are parts, permits the devotee to imagine God in many forms. The Bhakti genre of poetry is particularly known for inculcating *sakhya bhava* (the feeling of friendship) between devotees and deity. In this tradition the Lord is a friend, a lover, a son, and so on. In any form, he is very much within the reach of all human emotions, including *shikayat*. Under the smokescreen of Western epistemology, when people like Bankim began to invoke the image of Krishna, the latter was heavily sanitized in order to justify the Victorian code of morality. Bankim could not deal with a 'God' who was in the habit of stealing curd and butter, courting more than one woman and went on to have 'sixteen thousand and eight queens'. Gandhi's Krishna is also a sanitized-one. In contrast, the people's Krishna remained colourful, master of many tricks, and human. It is

moments can be found once again in the Swami when he chose to illustrate the discussion on body and soul (*Gita*, Chapter XIII) through the imagery of *khet* and *khetihar*, the agricultural field and the kisan (pp. 563–72).

It was fairly common to depict Kurukshetra as the *khet* of the kisans, where the zamindar was the evil party like the Kauravas, and the poor kisan represented the Pandavas, victimized, cheated, tricked, but eventually victorious.[7] In this portrayal, the *Mahabharata* war was a real one; it could by no means be a case of peaceful persuasion, which Gandhi was advocating in the case of sectional conflicts. Kaurava refusal to grant even five villages to the Pandavas was taken as a sure sign of the impossibility of a peaceful resolution in such matters. At the same time, the violent language of the zamindar, particularly when he perceived danger to his authority, was also commonsensical wisdom in the world of kisans. By their everyday experience, kisans knew that they stood very little chance when it came to matching the brutality with which the zamindar defended his privilege and domination. It is this historical specificity that compelled kisans to innovate a language of politics that would thrive on open defiance, the idiom of the time, with minimum chance of bloody retaliation on the part of zamindars.

It is in this context that we must analyse the radicalization of Gandhian politics by the kisan. It is in this context that we must understand why the kisan and the Sabha never made non-violence a creed as Gandhi did. The open condemnation of hinsa by Gandhi suited kisans because it put zamindars on the defensive. The advocacy of sacrifice and satyagraha empowered the kisans with a unique sense of fearlessness, willing even to die for a cause they thought was right along with a strong denial of the existing power hierarchy in society. In Gramscian vocabulary, it denied the very existence of a power relationship (Gramsci 1971).

Before we discuss the reworking of some of the central Gandhian categories by the kisans of Bihar in the process of their struggle against the excesses of zamindars, it is important to clarify another point

---

this difference between the popular and the Sanskritized version of devotion that came into play when kisans aired their grievances against the God without.

[7] The 'revolutionary terrorists' used to portray the English as the incarnations of evil.

related to the religious language of their politics. Some may prefer to read the songs cited in this chapter as not essentially articulations of grievances against God, but as a critical commentary on the existing state of socio-political affairs. The growing disenchantment within the ranks of the oppressed vis á vis the Congress and the rise of radical forces (within and outside the fold of the Congress party) may seem to provide further support to such understanding. Indeed it is difficult, at least in case of some folksongs to ascertain whether or not they were targeted against the Congress leadership in general and Gandhi in particular. People like Nirghin Ram who had left the Congress dejected, were likely to voice their wrath and despair against Gandhi. The apotheosis of Gandhi as 'Mahatma', and the Congress' compliance in the use of such construction (expressed through its near-total refusal to demystify his deification),[8] make this argument even more compelling. The given state of research does not permit us to pass a decisive judgment against such a view. However, a clarificatory note in favour of our position that contemporary folksongs portray a different religiosity among kisans is in order.

Acceptance of the premise that Gandhi indeed had acquired a godly aura in kisan mentalité and these articulations were indeed against him and not so much against God, needs an explanation as to how kisans rose against their earthly God, the Mahatma. The answer lies in the perpetuation of the age-old tradition of Bhakti. It was specific to the tumultuous moments of the first half of the twentieth century that this space was used to air mundane grievances of/by the devotees. A sanitized formulation of Krishna, the most important God in Bhakti tradition, for example, could not have imagined, let alone allowed such space for manouvre.[9] This strategic moment was available only to those who preferred a non-classical stream of religiosity. Let us now turn to the radicalization of Gandhian politics by the kisan.

It would be futile to suggest that kisans reworked Gandhian methods

[8] In one of the rare moments of demystification of the godly aura around himself, Gandhi wrote in reply to an English lady's confession [on 16 January 1922]:

> This woman sees the hand of Christ in all my work. A devout Hindu may see the hand of Ram or Krishna and a Muslim that of Khuda [Allah] and the prophet. For myself, I shall be satisfied if it has the hand of Truth. (*Collected Works*, vol. XXII, p. 209)

[9] Recall, for instance, the Krishna of Bankim in Nandy 1983, pp. 23–4.

or radicalized them as a sheer matter of tactic, i.e. without actually believing in them. They chose his ways because they were familiar with them in the first place. Of course, Gandhi's reformulation of the age-old ideas of non-violence and satyagraha were also better suited to them than the path of 'revolutionary terrorists'. This is not to suggest that by definition kisans were non-violent. If anything, the issue of violence was never a creed with the kisan and the Kisan Sabha, as the Sabhaites so pointedly brought out in their struggles in the late 1930s against the zamindars who were overtly or covertly taking advantage of the good offices of the Congress.[10] Indeed violence in general was not an effective tactic for those who were historically wronged. It can be said that to a large extent, kisans' radicalization of Gandhian politics was implicit in the spirit of the latter itself. A controlled mass movement, which the Gandhian Congress desired to construct, was a contradiction in terms. Gandhi's aim to instil fearlessness of the colonial regime among the masses, and defer inter-class conflict till swaraj was achieved, did not have an unassailable moral basis. Small wonder, we see kisans radicalizing Gandhian methods of politics once they internalized the fearlessness it taught and had their faith in themselves reconfirmed by the same. In other words, the apparent failure of Gandhian politics (to control and monitor mass movements) was at the same time its success, since the masses learned the political lesson in non-violent satyagraha very well. Only, they took it beyond the boundaries drawn by Gandhi.

[10] When kisan hopes for favourable legislation were dashed by the compromising attitude of those at the higher realm of affairs running the Ministry (1937–9), the Sabha was forced to undertake a series of militant struggles throughout Bihar. Since the Sabha had actively campaigned for the Congress candidates in the elections, it was a matter of extreme embarrassment for the Congress. To dissipate the movement, the Congress began to attack the Sabha, in general, and the Swami, in particular, for instigating violence and class hatred. The Swami, being a Dandi, always carried a bamboo staff, which soon became a symbol of kisan militancy. Slogans like 'मालगुज़ारी लोगे कैंसे, डंडा हमारा ज़िंदाबाद' [how will you collect the rent, long live our bamboo staff] initiated a heated debate between the Swami and the Congress, including Rajendra Prasad. The Swami took the position that the Sabha never preached violence, however, ahinsa was not its creed either. He recalled Gandhi's statement that violence was not only justified in order to protect oneself, it was preferred to cowardice. The difference could be seen in their reading of the *Gita* where the Mahatma was at pains to emphasize the non-violent essence of the text while the Swami had no such task before him.

II

Twenty five Bhumihar women came out of their homes with *tiranga* [tricolor flag] in their hands, went to Gram Devi's Sthan [the site of the village Goddess] first and then to the fields which were deserted by their male folks. (*Navshakti*, Hindi weekly from Bihar, 28 June 1936)

It could have been a story from any village of Bihar in the mid-thirties. Kisans had begun to challenge the atrocities of zamindars on a fairly regular basis. The prime struggle revolved around the issue of *bakasht* (tenancy) as zamindars continued to refuse receipts to kisans for rents paid. More often than not, the receipt was the only proof of the kisan's claims for settled tenancy.[11] The whimsical rack-renting by the zamindar was another thorny issue. Kisan's indebtedness made him further vulnerable to the rapacity of zamindar, whose hunger for land remained insatiable. The barbarity of zamindars touched its nadir when kisans were allowed to work all through the season only to learn that the zamindar had claimed the ownership of land (and thus of the standing crop as well) in court just before the harvest.[12] That any protest would have invited zamindar wrath is a mild statement.[13] What was probably most shocking to the kisans was that this lowest point in kisan-zamindar relationship was arrived at during the ministry of the Congress

[11] The bewilderment of the kisan and the irony of the legal paraphernalia is well captured in the following saying, brought to my notice by Indrajit Singh: '*Panch hath ke har na, char angur ke kagaje badaka saboot ho gayail!*' [A four-finger long piece of paper has become a bigger proof than the five-hand long plough!]. Swami Sahajanand mentions a slightly different version of this in his *Kisan Kaise Ladate Hain* [How Do Peasants Fight?], 1940, p. 28.

[12] The phenomenon is referred to as 'Distraint'. Technically speaking, the provision for it already existed, but due to the lengthy judicial processes involved, it was seldom used. What the Congress ministry did in connivance with the zamindar, was to over-simplify it. Now it was made easy to be abused by the zamindar; the right to execute the order of Distraint was shifted from the civil court to the revenue court. The Minister of Congress Kisan Department, Shri B. Narain, admitted in no uncertain terms the public hue and cry against the change. In his repeated letters to Rajendra Prasad, Shri Narain reported the simmering dissatisfaction and tension even among the ranks of the trusted volunteers of the Congress, let alone the Sabhaites or the kisan in general, regarding this provision (*Rajendra Prasad Papers*, Letter from Shri B. Narainji to Rajendra Prasad, 16 July 1938, [in Hindi] Microfilm, NMML, Delhi).

[13] The cited text of Swami Sahajanand, for example, carries many instances of bloody repression on kisans by the zamindars.

(1937–9) in the province.[14] Instead of enacting pro-kisan laws (as was expected because the Kisan Sabha was not only with the Congress but was instrumental in its electoral success and the formation of the Ministry), the Congress ministry chose to placate the landlords demonstrating the unabashed class bias of its leadership.[15]

What is truly remarkable about the time is that zamindars had not only begun to notice the mass awakening among the kisans, they, particularly the owner of huge zamindaris, but already started looking for alternative ways to retain their dominance. Kisans realized their mistake in electing candidates:

कांगरेस से हमनी के बहुत उमेद रहे,
इहे दुख अब दूर करी रे किसनवा।
बनी-बनी कंगरेसवा के ओटवा के लइके,
कौंसिल में गइले जमींदरवा रे किसनवा।

[We had great expectations from the Congress. This was the one that was going to alleviate all our pain. But it was zamindars who became representatives in the Council in the name of the Congress.] (Chaudhary and Shrikant 1988, p. 13)

It was thus that the kisans of Bihar chose to radicalize Gandhian notions of satyagraha and ahinsa. The process can be best viewed by examining instances of rural women taking the onslaught of zamindars head on. From 1936 to 1939, fierce struggles were waged in almost all districts of Bihar. Some of the better known movements took place in the villages of the Barahiya Tal in Munghyr; Reoda, Majhiyawan, Anuwan, Agada, Majhwe, Sandha in Gaya; Badgaon, Darigaon in Shahabad; Amwari, Parsadi, Chhitauli in Saran; Raghopur, Dekuli, Pandaul, Padari in Darbhanga; Darampura, Ankuri, Jalpura, Tarpura, Beldarichak in Patna.[16] To defy the provisions of Distraint, the kisans

[14] The Bihar special branch reports, in F/n. 331/1938 (BSA, Patna), go a step further than the usual belief about the Congress trying to *instigate* inter-class rivalry, and establishes clearly that it had begun acting *against* kisans in connivance with the zamindars. The first major anthology on this theme is D.A. Low (ed.) 1977.

[15] The speech by the Maharaja of Darbhanga which captures landlords' anxiety, on the one hand, and their political awareness, on the other, is reproduced in Appendix 2.

[16] Swami Sahajanand Saraswati, *Mera Jivan Sangharsh* (pp. 511–24). Details for background information and of struggles in these and different other areas can be found in Home Political F/n. 29/1939; F/n. 331/1938; F/n. 15/1936–7; F/n. 6(a)/1936 (BSA, Patna).

would *gherao* the standing crop and thus prevent the *lathaits* (toughs) of the zamindar from harvesting and taking away the crop. They would turn a deaf ear to provocative remarks by zamindars' men and avoid violent confrontations. Of course the zamindar and his men were not bound by the Gandhian preaching of ahinsa. As a result, instances of violent repression of kisans were many.[17] Often, kisans would run from the field on anticipating violence.

At this moment the women of kisan families would take the mantle from the male-kisans.[18] Take the case of Dharampura in Patna district (*Kisan Kaise Ladate Hain*, pp. 25–31). When the paddy grown by kisans was ready, the zamindar ordered his people to harvest the standing crop. Kisans objected to this and the zamindar obtaind a Distraint Order from the local court. When kisans defying the order went on a sit-in round the fields, the police arrested all male members, facilitating the way for the zamindar, to harvest the crop and pile it up at his *khalihan* (threshing floor). Following this, women and children left their homes and surrounded the *khalihan* of the zamindar, made tents out of the hay, began pilfering paddy from the *khalihan*, and making rice, cooking, eating and staying out there, braving the cold winter day and night. It went on like this for a while until the zamindar called the police again. The duty-bound police acted promptly and, in order to enhance the ordeal of the women and children, destroyed all the pots and earthenware used for cooking and eating. The activists of the Kisan Sabha then started bringing them some cooked food. When the police learned of this, they threatened to take 'appropriate' action against anyone who assisted the recalcitrant women in any way. For some time the activists continued to smuggle in food under the cover of darkness. As if the man-made ordeal was not enough, it started to rain. Sensing

[17] *Janata*, a Hindi weekly from Patna (edited by Ramvriksha Benipuri, a Kisan Sabhaite), brought out detailed reports of kisan struggle in Bihar through the year.

[18] The awkward expression is a result of the gendered usage of the term 'kisan'. If not specified, it generally refers only to the male peasant. However, agricultural processes are such in the province that without participation of women they cannot be completed. Be it managing the fodder for cattle, or sowing, harvesting, threshing and winnowing, women play a crucial role in agriculture. The only major thing religiously/culturally not prescribed for them is ploughing. No wonder the plough has historically acquired so much ritualistic and material importance in rural annals. Added to all these are the responsibilities of the home and the hearth, which they shoulder without any help from the male members of the family.

the opportune moment, the police destroyed the tents. Rain in *Magh* (month of Hindu calendar falling between December and January) without proper clothing meant suffering beyond imagination.[19] But the women continued their satyagraha. The zamindar was dumbfounded; so were his men. Finally, on the pretext of working out a solution before the Magistrate, the police took them to Biharsharif and tricked them again. The children were separated from the adults; the latter were put behind bars. The children were sent to a *dharmashala* while those who were a little older, insisted on joining the adult members in the jail. A moment of crisis can mature a child overnight; they suppressed their tears as onlookers thronged at the *dharmashala*, writes Sahajanand. Ultimately the police had to relent; children were allowed to join the adults in prison.

The incarceration failed to break the resolve of the women also because for them it was not merely a question of being inside or outside a prison. It was a question of life and death and if the latter was inevitable it was better to welcome it fighting, and while warm. The cells must have been more comfortable than staying day and night around the *khalihan* of the zamindar.

On their release, the women and children once again captured the field. The zamindar was now left with only one option: to run away. And that is precisely what he did. As if to put a decisive signature of people's victory over zamindari atrocities, the activists of the Kisan Sabha unfurled their red flag on top of his *kachahari* and established the Sabha's local centre there.

In yet another incident that took place in Sandha village of Gaya district, where the zamindar had managed to oust kisans from thousand acres of land they used to cultivate, we see the militant struggle of women redefining Gandhian concepts of satyagraha and civil disobedience (*Kisan Kaise Ladate Hain*, pp. 32–42). Even though the zamindar had successfully cornered most of the land, he needed the local kisans to work on them because touching the plough was ritually polluting for him. When the Kisan Sabha became popular in the area,

[19] How much Magh is feared can be imagined from the following saying: गइल माघ दिन उन्तीस बाकी [The month of *Magh* is almost gone, only twenty-nine days remain], says one who survives the first day of *Magh*. माघ के लइका बाघ [The infants born in Magh (if survives) shall be like a tiger] also probably carries the same connotation.

the zamindar feared that once the cultivators began work they would refuse to relinquish possession. He therefore, first tried to use *pahi* kisans (unsettled raiyat, who had not worked any piece of land in one village for twelve consecutive years unlike *dehi* kisan, the settled raiyat) to work the land. When that did not succeed, due to the strong mobilization by local kisans, he hired outside help, rented a few ploughs, and obtained a Restraint Order (*Dhara 144*, IPC Section 144, as it is called) from the court against eighty men of the village, and, escorted by hundreds of policemen, reached the field. Due to the Restraint Order, the male kisans could not have offered their satyagraha without risking imprisonment; as a result, the women took over. They asked the men to take care of the household and not come near the field. Breaking the cordon of the police, the women reached where ploughing had begun and lay down on the ground. The hired men did not know what to do. The *lathaits* of the zamindar could have dealt with male kisans, but it did not behove 'men' to physically attack women in public. Sahajanand himself was unable to hide his bewilderment upon seeing 'the sarees and bangles getting better of dhoti and moustache' (p. 37).[20] As a result, the men of the zamindar had to run away. When the policemen also began to leave, the women, to the surprise of many, surrounded the lorry and insisted on being taken to jail. They did not allow the lorry to move until the villagers somehow managed to dissuade them.

It is interesting to note the dwindling authority of the prison in the popular psyche. The decision that male kisans must not defy the Restraint Order, it seems, had little to do with their fear of jail. It was perhaps more of a strategy to keep off the field and avoid violent confrontation with the goons of the zamindar—for they would certainly have been at the receiving end in such a duel. Also it would then have been much easier for the police to intervene, round them up, and frame various charges against them. Prison as a disciplining institution had lost its teeth in the time of such upheaval. The credit must go to the Gandhian vision of equipping people with fearlessness.

[20] On one of the rare occasions when the Swami chose to highlight the struggle of the lower-caste and untouchable kisans, he recalled how in Barahiya Tal (1936–9) when one of the Sabha activists was being beaten up by the *lathaits* of the zamindar, it was a '*raiyan*' (a derogatory to the lower caste) woman who laid herself over the wounded activist and saved his life. Women continued to use this culture of machismo in their favour with more or less regular success.

Since the 1920s, going to jail became a badge of honour, a matter of pride, a mark of involvement in the freedom struggle. Phrases like 'a pilgrimage to Swaraj Ashram', 'Royal Hotels' and 'His Majesty Hotel' were enthusiastically employed. Cautious efforts were undertaken to destroy the traditional belief that jails were only for criminals. Gandhi earnestly mentioned the lead taken by Bengal in the '*jail bharo abhiyan*' ('Fill the Prison' Campaign) during the days of the Non-cooperation Movement, and wanted Gujarat and other provinces to catch up.[21] In brief, the jail, from a symbol of British rule and terror, became a site where nationalist forces routinely mocked the imperial insignia and demonstrated their increasing influence in day-to-day life.[22] Kisans used this Gandhian lesson too in their anti-zamindari struggle. No wonder that women of Barahiya Tal were singing at the peak of their movement, 'चलु चलु माता! जेहल के जवैयारे' (Let's go, O Mother! It's jail-going time).[23]

Another interesting aspect of this struggle is the refusal of women to enter into a compromise with zamindars. The activists of the Kisan Sabha wanted the kisans to agree to the zamindar's offer of conceding 50 *bighas* of land. The women resisted the proposal vehemently but to no avail. Sahajanand tried to defend the compromise formula of the Sabha on the point that it was the only wise thing to do in a situation when 'we are weak'. However, he admitted in the same breath that compromises had only multiplied the agony of kisans since zamindars

[21] See the many entries to this effect in *Collected Works*, vol. XXII.

[22] The contrast in our reading of the prison as an institution with Michel Foucault's is obvious. Foucault (1979) seldom concerned himself with a colonial reality. His prison is a European prison that exists only in 'normal' times. It is all powerful, allowing very little space for counter-hegemonic resistance. However, he is right in the sense that the prison does carry those elements which demand total subservience from the subject in order to maintain a rule and order. Gandhi himself was never in favour of a chaotic disruption of the authority that the prison represented: 'We are not out to abolish *jails as an institution*. Even under Swaraj we would have our jails. Our civil disobedience therefore, must not be carried beyond the point of breaking the unmoral laws of the country', (*Collected Works*, vol. XXII, p. 19, emphasis added).

The hegemonic hue of British rule was not to be completely replaced by the Nationalist government, when it came to maintaining order among the masses.

[23] In Reoda (Gaya), it was चलु चलु, सखिया, जेल के जवैया गे (Let's go, O friend! It's jail-going time), Sankrityayan 1950, pp. 504–5.

often broke their promises. [Once again, we should remember that the Swami's defence could well be an after-thought, because he was narrating this after the gap of a couple of years since the actual incidence. In 1940, he was of the view that 'now we are powerful and, normally, will not engage in any compromise' (*Kisan Kaise Ladate Hain*, p. 42).]

The struggle at Majhiyawan (1939–40) in Gaya district, took the radicalization of Gandhian methods of struggle to yet another height. Majhiyawan, a big village under the huge zamindari of Amawan Tekari, was also the village of a famous Kisan Sabha leader, Yadunandan Sharma. Historically, the village had been very loyal and subservient to the zamindar (pp. 75–80). As a result, it was difficult for the activists of the Sabha to find men who could rise against the excesses of the zamindar and his men. The mantle once again fell on the women. What was remarkable about this struggle was that it became witness to the withering away of a century-old custom. As mentioned earlier, ploughing is prohibited to women of all castes along with men of upper castes. In Majhiyawan, the fight for forcibly cultivating the land then in the possession of the zamindar began on the eve of the paddy season. The men of the village were not to break the Restraint Order passed against them, but it was time to plough. It was on this occasion that upper-caste women held the plough. Later they were joined by lower-caste women from the surrounding villages. Soon reports of women of Ghosrawan, Patna, ploughing the field appeared in *Janata* (24 August 1939).

Even though the custom was ruptured only momentarily (today the same age-old practice is still thriving), its significance cannot be denied. To take up ploughing, a task held as ritually polluting, tells us about the mood of the time which held nothing sacrosanct, nothing unassailable, nothing beyond the reach of human intervention. If they could declare Bhola Baba to be responsible for their misery, if they could admonish Banwari and/or Gandhi for being partial, it was only befitting that they cared little for a custom that came in their way.[24]

[24] A word of caution is in order. The militant participation of women in these struggles to secure tenancy did not begin to break all stereotypical patriarchal values of rural Bihar. Particularly, the male-leadership of the Sabha and the intelligentsia were at a loss for a language to articulate and express women's radicalization. For example, *Janata* (22 June 1939) in its front-page story on women participating

However, there could well be another angle to this defiance of custom. The majority of the tenants who had lost lands since the induction of the Permanent Settlement Acts were from the lower castes. Official reports categorically maintain that illegally enhanced rents were collected in full from the kisans of lower castes while it was very difficult to do so in the case of upper caste kisans. The reason is attributed to their relative strength to resist.[25] The upper castes constituted a little over 13 per cent of the entire population and the overwhelming majority of the zamindars in Bihar belonged to this group.[26] That caste indeed played a crucial role becomes even more clear from the following note of a government official about the upper caste in rural Bihar:

---

in huge number in the kisan demonstration at Gaya, did not omit to report that the women came along with their children. The headline summed it up even better: विद्रोह की प्रतिमायें—जो घरों की देवियां और मैदान की रणचंडी हैं [Icons of Revolt—who are goddesses of households and Ranchandi of the field]. That they had become like Ranachandi (a goddess of power and strength) was not to be expressed without reminding them that they were also the ones upon whom rested the responsibility of running the house and the hearth. They appeared nowhere when it came to taking decisions, forming policies or chalking out strategies. Even Sahajanand who was extremely impressed by their determination to fight, was so deeply moved by their sacrifice and suffering that 'tears blinded [my] vision' (*Presidential Address*, All India Kisan Sabha, 3rd Session, 1938, Comilla Conference), could articulate their courage and resolve only in terms of an exalted motherhood (*Kisan Kaise Ladate Hain*, p. 39).

[25] For example, *Proceedings of the Government of Bengal, Revenue Department* (*Land Revenue Branch*), January–March 1910, acknowledges the overall increase in illegal rents throughout north Bihar and remarks, '(B)ut owing to the low caste of the tenants and their inability to resist exactions, these illegal rents had frequently been recovered in full' (p. 485). Stevenson Moore, the Settlement Officer (Muzaffarpur), reiterates this view:

> The general impression is that the tenantry of Bihar are a down-trodden body of men, in complete subservience to their landlords who evict and enhance their rents at pleasure. The impression, however, is only partially true. Like most things in India, it is largely a question of caste. I believe this impression to convey a correct idea of low caste raiyats such as Dusadh, Kurmi, etc., but cultivators of higher caste, like Babhans, are usually quite prepared to fight their landlord if he attempts to oppress them. (*BDG: Muzaffarpur*, Patna: The Superintendent Secretariat Press, 1958, p. 192)

[26] Tabulated from the *Census of 1931* (Lacey 1931), it comes to 13.31 per cent to be precise.

'[As landlords they] lose no opportunity to rack-renting their tenants, while as tenants they observe the excellent principle of never paying any rent' (*BDG: Monghyr*, Patna, p. 176).

III

In the volatile moments of the 1930s, attempts to 'make use' of their strategic location in the caste hierarchy had begun on part of the lower caste kisans. They began to use the fact that the very nucleus of agricultural production depended on them, as a weapon in the struggle for secured tenancy and other land rights. This is not to suggest that the 'realization' of this fact dawned on them in the thirties. We have no reason to believe that earlier they were unaware of their social position. What was new for the decade was the fact that the political assertion became much more generalized. Studies on the emergence of numerous caste movements in this period note this factor, some more obliquely than others. The refusal to do *begari* (forced labour), instantly invited the wrath of upper caste landlords. The emergence of the Triveni Sangha[27] (literally, three streams; an association started by members of Yadavas, Kurmis and Koeris) in this period could be countered by upper caste zamindars only with the help of landless labourers from the untouchable castes who were yet to organize themselves into a united bloc and were still with the Congress by and large. Often untouchable castes performed agricultural services refused by lower castes and thus dissipated whatever pressure was built up by the latter. In the following song we can hear the lower castes' ridicule of and assertion against the upper caste:

अइसन आवता समइया हरवा जोते के परी।
बिन हर जोते फसल ना होइहें
ना ही उपजी धान
बाबूलोग सब हरवा जोतिहें
बबुनी रोपिहें धान।
हरवा जोते के परी।[28]

[27] The Triveni Sangha, on the other hand, went to the other extreme and focused primarily on issues related to socio-cultural identity and dignity and left the struggle for land rights to the Sabha, as it were. See along with Chaudhari and Shrikant 1998, K.K. Verma 1979; Mukherji and Yadav 1980.

[28] I am thankful to Ram Talika Singh who not only recalled this song in his

[The time is coming when everybody will have to plough. Without ploughing, no paddy, no crop would grow. The upper caste men will have to plough their land and their women will have to sow.]

What is even more striking about this song is that it shows the realization on part of lower castes to take the untouchable along in the struggle against upper caste dominance; it had already acquired the political acumen which for certain reasons always eluded the Kisan Sabha and its (upper caste) strategists:

अइसन आवता समइया खेतवा बांटे के परी।
दस रोपेया मजुरा लिहें
खाये और जलपान
भंगी होके कुरसी बइठी
बाबूलोग झुक-झुक करिहें सलाम।
खेतवा बांटे के परी।

[The land will have to be distributed. Laborers will charge ten Rupees, over and above a meal and snacks. The *Bhangi* (untouchable) will sit in the chair and the upper caste men will bow and salute him.]

As is well known, the Sabha and the Swami did not pay attention to caste-based exploitation in their effort to mobilize kisans against the zamindari system. Despite ample evidence (noted in the following section) of the fact that the reproduction of cultural and economic subordination substantially rested on the ritualized repression of lower castes and untouchables, the Sabha (and, the Congress) refused to acknowledge the phenomenon. The total inversion of the caste hierarchy that is reflected in this song, failed to make a mark on even those who had embarked on the path of bringing a real swaraj, a '*sakar* swaraj' to the people. This invariably resulted in a poor economism in the name of developing an understanding about how social relations were structured, maintained, and reproduced.

There is indeed a great deal of truth in the assertion that 'caste' emerged in the late nineteenth century as the defining characteristic of South Asian people, especially Hindus, thanks to the imperial need and

---

interview with me (31 January 1996) but also informed me that it was written by one Bhajanik Yadav from Patna 'around 1938'

logic of governance. As a distinct marker of difference, agelessness, inertness and 'a lack', the caste system was reformulated afresh; and it is in this sense that it was a colonial invention.[29] It provided the imperial think-tanks with an ideal locus to orchestrate their superiority over the subject-race they had 'dutifully' decided to govern, and to civilize in the process. However, it would be a grave error to assume that the caste system was a misnomer, a non-entity before the British 'invented' it, especially through their late nineteenth-century censuses (the first census was conducted in 1871). We must not forget that it indeed provided an ideal base from where the imperial imagination about Indian society could take off. True, it was one of the many ideologies available to the Indian ruling strata from which they drew, determined, and defended the line of social and cultural control. But it was an important one. It was probably as central as religion itself, since the religious map of South Asia would be incomplete without the lines of the caste system.

In any event, the colonial census operations, unknowingly, opened up a vast terrain where fresh assertions could be made by the lower castes and untouchables of their social locations. They vied with each other to prove Brahmin, Kshatriya, or Vaishya status in the past.[30] Almost every caste wanted to 'be placed higher in the order of precedence' (*Census 1931*, p. 440): the Nais/Hajjams (barbers) wanted to be recorded as a sub-caste of Brahmin; the Tambulis/Panwaris wanted to be recognized as Nagbansi Kshatriyas; the Kurmis wished to be identified as a sub-caste of the Kurmi-Kshatriya; the Rajbansis re-presented to be returned as Kshatriyas; the Bhatts/Bhants desired Brahmin status; the Dosadhs/Dusadhs claimed themselves to be of Rajput origin, and so on. The desire to scale up the social ladder was not confined to the lower and untouchable castes. The Bhumihars/Babhans were trying 'to obtain recognition as full Brahmins'. As a result there was a sudden drop in the population of Babhans and increase in the number of Brahmins (p. 237).

Once a new space to rethink one's identity became available, the existing socio-cultural structure became ever more vulnerable. Numerous caste associations/assemblies began to mushroom in the

[29] See Dirks 1992 and Inden 1986.

[30] The past itself acquired a new urgency, indeed, a new meaning, but that is another story.

period, primarily with twin perspectives: to initiate large-scale social reform movements and to politically organize themselves under one umbrella to assert various economic and political demands. The Ahirs/ Gwalas/Gops/Yadavas (different names of one single caste), who had chosen to claim Kshatriya status for themselves, refused to do *begari* (forced unpaid labour), began to wear the sacred thread customarily allowed only to the upper castes, ceased to drink liquor, and avoided child-marriage. Numerically the most powerful caste in Bihar, the Yadavas formed their Gope Jatiya Maha Sabha (The Great Association of the Gope Caste) in 1912 and in true 'Pan-Ahir movement' style stretched its hold from Punjab to Bengal, from Bihar to the United Provinces. They also began to bring out a monthly journal called *Ahir Samachar.* The Doms, Mehtars, and Dusadhs, almost every caste, began to organize itself in some form or the other.[31] No doubt, the signs were ominous for the ruling members of the upper castes.

The following incident captures this changing language of social relations. The Gwalas of Khagri, Pakaura and other adjoining villages of Jahanabad Police Station in Gaya district decided in a meeting that they would no more consent to *begari.* They also took a decision against an age-old practice of carrying milk on their heads to supply it to the upper caste people at their doorsteps.[32] The zamindars who demanded *begari* from these Gwalas were Bhumihars and Muslim, in one instance. On the morning of 19 June 1921, they were summoned by the zamindar and asked to continue *begari*. On refusal, their hands were tied behind their backs and they were beaten by the Rajput *lathaits* of the zamindar. In the afternoon of the same day, when they met again to discuss the steps to be taken against the high-handedness of the zamindar, 'a mob' attacked them. Many were injured; one Jagan Gope of Koin Khanda village was severely wounded and was brought to the police station on a *charpoy* by fellow caste-men. He later died in the hospital and apparently left no 'dying declaration'.

Gopi Goala (Gwala), a kisan of Khagri, filed a petition the next morning before the Sub-Divisional Officer, Jahanabad, charging some

[31] The model of Sanskritization, à la M.N. Srinivas (1962), does not take into account the element of conflict between castes. The so-called 'upward mobility' never goes uncontested by those who are higher up the ladder.

[32] Details have been drawn from F/n. 244/1921, Pol. Spl. (Special Report I & II, Case no. 29), BSA, Patna.

of the *lathaits* of Behari Babu (the zamindar) with calling at his and other Gwalas' houses of Khagri and asking them to explain why they were not giving the *muthia* (literally, a hand full). The Congress used to take/request a handful of grain, *muthia*, from the poor kisans who could otherwise not contribute to its fund, as a symbol of support 'according to the orders of Mahatma Gandhi'. The kisans of Khagri refused to give *muthia*, and as a consequence they were beaten and taken to the bungalow of Behari Babu, and beaten up again.

This episode gives significant clues on the changing script of the rural/agrarian drama. The connection the Gwala kisans made between the demand for *begari* and *muthia* is significant. It tells us about their apprehension that those who were asking for *muthia* in the name of Mahatma Gandhi would certainly not stop the practice of *begari* because the local-level representatives of the Congress and the champions of feudal traditions were actually two faces of the same people. In other words, it gives us an early glimpse of the way the class and caste alliances were to unfold vis à vis the Congress of the province in the coming years.[33] Though it is true that there are not many (written, recorded) instances of this nature from such early dates, the incident indicates the direction in which kisan consciousness was moving before the forum of the Kisan Sabha became available.

This brief but unavoidable detour was in order to draw a quick sketch of prevailing socio-cultural moods of the kisans around the time the Bihar Kisan Sabha began its activities. The sketch is drawn also to suggest that the Sabha was aware of the increasing caste consciousness among the kisans of the province. A quick look at the list of kisan grievances recorded by the Enquiry Committee of the Sabha, 1933 confirms the fact.

After much prodding by the Kisan Sabha, the Congress in Bihar conducted an enquiry into the plight of the kisans in Gaya and Patna districts, but never made its report public.[34] As a result the Sabha con-

[33] Gyan Pandey (1978) has shown in his study of the Congress in the United Provinces how by the 1930s the Congress consolidated itself as an organization while its 'social base' among the poor peasantry was gradually eroded.

[34] Awadheshwar Prasad Singh 1935; Saraswati, *Mera Jivan Sangharsh*, pp. 403–4. Both observe that the Congress deliberately suppressed the report on the pretext that during the Civil Disobedience Movement in 1932, the police destroyed many papers including the enquiry details.

ducted its own detailed enquiry in 1933 and published its findings.[35] The outstanding feature of the enquiry was the detail of illegal cesses (*abwabs*) exacted from the kisans by their respective zamindars. These exactions find their way into works on Kisan Sabha movement, albeit obliquely or in the form of details of an extra-economic burden on the kisan. More than merely economic extractions, I submit, these illegal cesses constituted the mechanism through which power relations in rural Bihar were culturally reproduced.

The following is a very short list of some of those cesses against which the kisans of Gaya spoke with Sabha activists during the enquiry:

(a) A Dusadh or a Barahil is forced to sit on the door of the kisan. As a result, the kisan or any member of the family cannot come out of the house, because Dusadhs and Barahils are untouchable; any physical contact with them is considered ritually polluting. The inconvenience was greater particularly because houses did not have toilets (Singh 1935, p. 25).

(b) For the daily consumption of the zamindar and his family, the Gwala had to supply *ghee* (refined butter), milk, curd, yogurt, cow-dung for fuel almost at no cost; during festival times the demand would increase. All this was in addition to *begari* which was by definition unpaid labour.

(c) The Chamar had to supply leather-shoes; the Koeri vegetables. Both for no remuneration.

(d) The Kumhar had to supply baked-earthen tiles for a fraction of the cost; for the roofing of the *kachahari* and on special occasions like marriage of any member of the zamindar family; no money was paid at all.

(e) The Teli was supposed to supply oil at half the market price; for *kachahari*, it was free.

(f) The Gaderi (shepherd) had to give blankets and *asanis* (small squarish woven cloth-piece of cotton and wool) for no money whatever; the iron-smith supplied kitchen-ware free.

[35] Saraswati, *Gaya Ke Kisanon Ki Karun Kahani* [A Story of the Mĭserable Plight of the Kisans of Gaya], Patna, n.d. A good detail of illegal exactions is reprinted in Awadheshwar Prasad Singh (1935). All references to Gaya in this section is from that source. In addition to Gaya, Singh also mentions reports from Patna, Purnea and Darbhanga.

(g) The Dhobi had to wash the clothes of the zamindar and all his family without asking for any money.
(h) The Nai would cut hair, shave and massage as the duty of his caste, for free.

The list is very long; every non-upper caste person (i.e. the untouchable and the lower castes) had to offer some service or commodity to the zamindar, who was invariably from the upper caste, for negligible or no remuneration at all. Reports from other districts, like Patna, Purnea, and Darbhanga, repeat most of the above-mentioned *abwabs* with very little variation (Singh 1935, pp. 25–43).

Such *abwabs* were quotidian reminders of the kisans' place in caste-ridden Hindu society. Though their economic relevance cannot be denied, they played a crucial role in reproducing power relations. The following example illustrates our point. A Nai (barber) used to visit an agent of the local zamindar every night 'to give massage' (also a euphemism for homosexuality). Upon learning that the agent was going to be away one night, the Nai did not go. When the agent returned next morning and found this out, he was furious. The Nai pleaded that since the agent was away, he had found no reason to make the visit. To that, the agent retorted, 'you should have come and given massage to the pillar (of the bungalow). At least, the habit would have been intact' (*Mera Jivan Sangharsh*, p. 406).

Enquiries also brought out many details of bodily tortures inflicted on kisans; some of the forms of tortures it seems, were reserved for the lower caste. Consider the following Bhojpuri song:

ऊ दिन परेला इयाद नयन भर आवेला रे भाई।
हाथ गोड़ में बान्हल रसरिया
लाठिन देह थुराई।
नयन भर आवेला रे भाई।

[O brother, when I remember those days, my eyes fill up. Hands and feet used to be tied up in a rope and the body would be crushed with a *lathi* (a bamboo staff). My eyes fill up.][36]

[36] Source: Ram Talika Singh. Indrajit Singh, Mahatwaniyan, however, recalled a slightly different version of this song. Instead of *hath gode mein banhal rasariya*, he thought, the correct version was *hathe hathkariya pair mein beriya lage* [hands were hand-cuffed and there were shackles in the feet]. The latter version, if taken literally, I think, refers to the British Government, to the colonial state with a prison and not to the zamindar. The zamindar, being a civilian, did not have/use hand-cuffs.

We may also recall 'stories' of rape and molestation of lower caste women by zamindars and the notorious *dola* system in the region. They all strongly suggest the crucial place of the caste hierarchy in the life of kisans.

Despite the enquiry and the explicit nature of the findings, the Kisan Sabha and the Swami continued with their efforts to construct a kisan who was purely *homo-economicus*. The Swami, who had taken up the cause of restoring pride to the community he hailed from as his first 'social'/post-sannyas assignment, however, failed to appreciate the significance of the caste system in the overall structure of society. That not even a single person from lower castes figured in the leadership of the Sabha, despite the fact that the overwhelming majority of the kisans came from this section, could not become a problematic worthy of his attention. At best, his concerns were confined to sporadic rhetorical utterances when, at the peak of kisan struggles during the 1930s, he told peasants to produce their own leaders just as they produced wheat or *ghee* (*Kisan Kaise Ladate Hain*, p. 6). In any event, he chose to overlook the socio-cultural distance between the upper and the lower castes kisans which empowered the former, irrespective of its economic position in the society. Or perhaps, he did not wish to see any socio-cultural differences between the two. When he was accused of being casteist[37] for running the Sitaram Ashram at Bihta (Patna) which imparted education (since 1927) exclusively to the children of Bhumihars, and was asked why he did not do the same for the children of other castes, his defence said it all:

> the reasons which existed in the former case [for setting up the Ashram for Bhumihar children], did not exist [in the case of any other castes]. If a similar question of self-respect were involved here, and reading Ved-vedang were required, I might have done it. But that's not the case. Why should I then get involved in this? It also should be kept in mind that for others there are thousands places . . . but all the doors were closed for Bhumihars when I started the Ashram. (*Mera Jivan Sangharsh*, p. 292)

Coming from a sharp observer like him, this statement was nothing less than a distortion of facts. If a space did not exist for Bhumihars, who were next only to the Brahmans in the caste hierarchy, there was

[37] The term 'caste-ist' is used in the South Asian context to denote an explicit or implicit bias of a person in favour of fellow caste members and against the members of other castes. Often the one subsumes the other.

simply no question of it being available to lower and untouchable castes. The question is, how does one explain the persistent denial of a reality as vivid as the phenomenon of caste-based exploitations?

Historians of the Kisan Sabha and biographers of the Swami try to get around the issue by saying that Sahajanand was not a casteist person and a leader because if he was a Bhumihar, so were most of the zamindars he was fighting against.[38] The same defence is made for the Sabha whose leadership mostly came from the Bhumihar caste (Hauser 1961, p. 77). It is true that Sahajanand consistently conceptualized kisan problems in the context of kisan-zamindar relationship, irrespective of the caste of the kisan and the zamindar. He certainly was not a casteist in this sense. However, this may not touch upon the real issue in its entirety. One could be casteist by commission or by omission. Sahajanand overlooked caste-based exploitation all around him.

What needs to be considered is the fact that both the Swami and the Sabha failed to evolve a political language that would be sensitive not only to the economic reasons behind the kisans' plight, but the whole environment of exploitation, including the one in which economic 'reasons' were defined and reproduced. After all, economic exploitations too are systematized into social *relations* in a specific socio-cultural context (Gramsci 1971; Thompson 1991). If this does not occur they can never evolve as a system or as a net of social relations. Then they will be akin to episodic plunder. And the more brutal and episodic an act of plunder is, the more vulnerable it will be to defiance, resistance, and rejection. The Sabha and the Swami knew very well that zamindari exploitation was not episodic.

It may be recalled that the Sabha and the Swami had formulated their ideological distance from the Congress and Gandhi on the premise that the latter did not aspire for 'true swaraj'. The 'true swaraj' in the scheme of the Sabha, did not merely mean freedom from British rule, but freedom from the zamindari system as well. So convinced were they of this insight that they rejected the Gandhian idea that the anti-zamindari struggle could be postponed until political independence was achieved. The concept of a total struggle that they applied in their fight for true independence was intriguingly missing from their struggles against zamindari. The latter could never have been total without

[38] Hauser 1961, pp. 77–8; D.N. Dhanagare 1983, p. 141; Rakesh Gupta 1982, pp. 51–2, etc.

a consistent attack on the caste system—the cultural cosmology that held the kisan–zamindar relationship. My assertion is amply supported by the fact that once the abolition of the zamindari was legally announced in 1950, the Sabha as a movement died a premature death. Premature, because the stroke of legislative justice failed in reality to sound the death-knell for the zamindari system. Kisan struggles in post-Independence India for more or less the same 'economic' justice continued without respite in sight.

Thus the real issue is not whether the Swami or, the Sabha, was overtly casteist or not. The real issue is that none had (and, not unknowingly) contributed to the evolution of a political language that would have been informed by the system of exploitation. Possibly, it required greater political acumen and courage than what was available to either of them. The consistent denial of casteism was certainly a paradigmatic failure. It took many years, probably three decades, if not more, for a language of politics based on the recognition of caste-based exploitation to be accepted in Indian political life.[39]

[39] A polity sensitive to the caste system cannot be said to have evolved in Bihar before the 1980s, when mobilizations of intermediate castes by Lohiaites and of landless labourers and marginal kisans, who were largely Dalits, by the Naxalites began.

Conclusion

Pointing out the relationship between poverty and caste system of the gendered Indian society, Ram Manohar Lohia, a prominent Socialist thinker, remarked in 1953 that 'all war on poverty is a sham, unless it is, at the same time, a conscious and sustained war on these two segregations [of caste and sex]' (Lohia 1964) Lohia himself (or the Socialist Party to which he belonged), never carried any consistent campaign against these twin evils during kisan struggles before Independence in 1947. In 1950, when the Bihar Government announced the abolition of zamindari, the Kisan Sabha collapsed as a movement. Its most important demand was 'fulfilled' by a mere stroke of legislation.

Though the disintegration of the movement had already begun, as struggles launched by the Sabha were few and far between in the 1940s, now it was left with no issue to 'mobilize' and agitate over. The Sabha lived on in the capacity of an organization since the task of ensuring a systematic implementation of the provisions of the legislation was still unaccomplished.

Twenty years later, the kisans were as harassed as before; tenancy was yet not secured for them as Wolf Ladejinsky noted:

> The provisions for security of tenure are crucial to the whole scheme of land legislation and it has been the experience all over India that the right to resume land for self-cultivation by the landlord has tended to defeat the provisions for security of tenure. Resumption is all the more damaging in the case of small landlords who have made up viable units of cultivation by leasing an additional acre or two of the land. (1970, p. 336)

Of course, Ladejinsky, as an agent of the World Bank, was primarily interested in land reforms as mechanisms for enhancing the 'purchasing power of the peasants'. It was not his intention to advocate the 'socialization of the means of production'. Ironically, those who swore by the latter (the Socialists, the Communists) had apparently no clue as to how to proceed. A favourable legislation had been passed and yet the redistribution of power in the rural milieu remained a distant dream. Those who had lands above the allowed ceiling continued to keep them. It indeed was a sardonic *deja vu*, a repeat of the Raj syndrome where laws were routinely passed to orchestrate sympathy with the kisans, while in reality, the ruling elite remained reluctant to enforce them.

The Naxalite movements of the late 1960s and early 1970s began around the issue of *izzat* (dignity) of labouring men and women, and *later* re-articulated demands like 'minimum wages' and 'land to the tiller' (Mukherjee and Yadav 1980). For the kisans who 'went underground' and those who supported them from 'outside', the foremost concern was to re-write the script of power in the countryside of Bihar. Little wonder, they began to locate the locus of their struggle in the caste system that ritually reproduced a set of hierarchized power relations in the rural Bihar. Though the thrust was in the right direction this time, probably it was its intensity, an epochal wrath, as it were, that lured the kisan onto the path of extreme violence. A peaceful democratic movement was perhaps not available in the first place. Whatever be the justification for their violent method, the state quickly moved in to reclaim its monopoly over violence and crushed the movement.

Despite its apparent failure, the Naxalite movement achieved what none of the kisan movements had managed before. It brought the self of the lowly and the labouring to the very centre of the political pursuits. It was an irony of a historic proportion that those who sought to celebrate human dignity were forced to pick up arms while the contemporary practitioners of Gandhian non-violence, like Vinoba Bhave, once again refused to refocus their vision of social reconstruction and continued to cajole the dominant for charity. As it was not to be, history denied Gandhi a rebirth; Vinoba Bhave failed miserably.

In the coming years, the political language formulated around caste-based repressions gained unprecedented currency. Many political parties adopted into their electoral rhetoric, the issue of job reservation for candidates of 'backward classes'. In 1989, when V.P. Singh as Prime Minister, announced the implementation of the Mandal

Commission recommendations which enforced affirmative action, the political language hitherto denied became *the language* of politics.[1] Irrespective of its 'actual intentions', no political party can today hope to win an election by ignoring this language. Not that there are enough jobs to economically uplift the downtrodden, the provisions of Mandal Commission principally seek to redistribute power to those who have been kept on the margins so far.

II

The book has sought to examine the cultural cosmologies of kisans in colonial Bihar. Instead of focussing merely on open resistance and revolt, where the given power relations are openly challenged, I have argued for more comprehensive ways of studying kisan political culture through unravelling both its religious and temporal worlds. And to study political culture and consciousness of kisans, I have prioritized examination of languages in which dissent is articulated. Since language, by definition, gives vent to its users' cultural, religious, philosophical beliefs and experiences, the trope of 'language of politics' invites us to explore the deeper meanings of politics at any given point of time. Finally, since a language can function only in a collectivity, to examine kisan expressions of discontent and dissent is to effectively explore their political consciousness.

Expressions of political consciousness are often couched in the language of 'rights' and 'wrongs'. Rarely do they appear outrightly political. Migration, 'agrarian crimes', cattle-thefts in particular, or rumours as expressions of kisan consciousness may not be immediately apparent to the students of kisan politics. However, the link between these and the political domain is undeniable. And precisely because the

[1] The Commission (1979–80) has recommended the reservation of roughly one-third government jobs for 'Other Backward Classes', or the OBCs. The Commission also has an exhaustive list of castes and sub-castes in all states of India, which are identified as OBCs. In a number of states, the list includes certain sections of Muslims as well. The OBC category includes almost the entire population minus the upper castes and Scheduled Castes and Tribes. The category of Scheduled Castes and Tribes enjoys 22 per cent of government job reservations. Though primarily an affirmative provision, the majority of the upper caste populace views the Mandal Commission recommendations as sectarian and threatening to its well-being.

linkages are not immediately obvious, these expressions are more likely to be enormously potent. As illustrated, for these languages to succeed, a collectivity that participated in a common belief-system was necessary. A '*chor gaon*' could not survive for a day without it. Nor would a rumour travel very far unless the political properties in it were perceived as a common good. I have shown that rumours provided a way to articulate and vent political desires in a period when open political actions were rare. Indeed, they sought to build a *janmat* and prepared the ground on which Gandhian politics could be launched.

Religion and caste-based sensitivities were further proofs of kisan desire to construct a collectivity where a political act could acquire social meaning. Kisans did not 'use' religion to propagate their concerns, they did not have to. Their politics was merely an extension of what they thought their religious vocations rendered 'right'. The separation of religion from politics, the sacred from the temporal, was too alien to be real and meaningful. This is what distinguished them from a Congress leader like Tilak. This is what they shared with Gandhi. And yet there was a difference between how Gandhi and kisans perceived religion in relation to quotidian drudgery and discontent.

Kisans had both *shraddha* and *shikayat*, veneration and complaints, as integral parts of their religiosities. Being a *dharmik* did not necessitate surrendering one's critical and temporal consciousness. As a result, kisans could send a notice to Ram or admonish Banwari for ruined crops, increased land rent, or general misery. Gandhi recast his language of politics after the *Gita*. (In fact, that a language is a repository of action is richly illustrated in various interpretations of the *Gita* by Tilak, Aurobindo, Gandhi and Sahajanand, and others.) Kisans radicalized Gandhian language of politics to further their struggles against the zamindar and the agrarian policies of the British. Their apprehension about postponing the fight against the zamindari system was vindicated by what followed in free India. History confirmed the misgivings kisans had that the Congress leadership, largely constituted of landed gentry, would not defy its own class interests.

There was yet another factor responsible for overall disenchantment: the overlap between class and caste. The Congress and the Kisan Sabha, the Mahatma and the Swami, were in unison in denying caste as a viable language of politics. Kisans who had to survive exploitation legitimized by caste practices, were, however, convinced otherwise.

Today caste has not only emerged as the most potent language of politics, it is threatening even to altogether obfuscate class.

The book has tried to situate its narrative as much in archival sources as in folklore. Much history writing misses the latter, while a conventional social anthropology seldom takes cognisance of the former. We have argued for not merely a juxtaposition of the two, but a more critical and dialectical reading of both to gain fuller access to the world of kisans. 'Voices of the subalterns' cannot be retrieved just by upending the notes of colonial scribes. Folksongs and sayings, stories and proverbs, abound. Just as one is expected to be critical of an archival notation, caution is required in gleaning out the folklore from the 'fakelore'.

The trope of 'language of politics' is a new area of historical enquiry. Peasant historicity has been largely confined to moments of ruptures in history. On the other hand Social Anthropologists in India have rarely engaged with historical processes, underlining the disciplinary divisions which have hitherto yielded fragmented knowledges. Relatively unexplored has been the trope of language of politics to write a history of specific political expressions used by kisans.

To study the latter is to examine the emergence and evolution of kisan political idioms in a specific geographical milieu within a delimited time-span. As politics gets articulated in many languages, which may not necessarily be overtly political, this approach opens up many entry points to the understanding of peasant political culture. It also has the potential of highlighting all the political choices made by kisans, and not simply those which apparently make histories.

Appendix I

THE POPULATION OF 15 MAJOR CASTES IN THE 1931 CENSUS

Caste	*Population*	*Percentage of the total Bihar Population*
Ahir	34,55,141	11.02
Brahman	15,40,306	4.91
Rajput	13,70,338	4.37
Kurmi	13,57,302	4.33
Koeri	13,01,473	4.15
Dusadh	12,84,398	4.10
Chamar	12,55,689	4.00
Bhumihar	8,94,657	2.87
Dhanuk	5,47,308	1.75
Kahar	5,24,030	1.67
Kandu	5,06,384	1.61
Mallah	4,59,560	1.46
Hajjam	4,56,779	1.45
Kayasth	3,68,431	1.18
Pasi	1,72,061	0.55
Total Population	1,54,93,857	

SOURCE: Girish Mishra and Braj Kumar Pandey, *Sociology and Economics of Casteism in India: A Study of Bihar*, Delhi: Pragati Publications, 1996.

Appendix II

SPEECH BY THE MAHARAJA OF DARBHANGA

The time has come when the landlords themselves have to change their outlook . . . if they are to exist as a class.

The world itself is shaking today with the struggles of the forces between the 'haves' and the 'havenots'. Germany, Italy and Japan are making frantic efforts to find an outlet of their population and trade. Great Britain, France, America, not to speak of other world-powers . . . are struggling hard to consolidate their position and keep what they possess. The war clouds are rumbling, weaker states are trembling and nobody knows what the world-situation will be tomorrow.

'Why should the capitalist rule Great Britain, France or America? Have the working classes who toil to produce national wealth no place under the sun?'

We should not be dismayed if the echo of this world-wide jargon is heard even in India. This is not an industrial country. . . . It is predominantly an agricultural country and has been for centuries systematised by the introduction of landlordism. Naturally the eyes of all who want to destroy capitalism have turned first to the landlords. . . . Landlordism is only a buffer—and I should think a strong buffer—in this country for the capitalist class and once that is gone the avowed enemies of this class will in one full swoop take away the rest.

We must, however, recognize that we cannot stand aloof from the factors governing the tendencies of the new world in which we find ourselves. The wave of democracy is too powerful for that, specially as we are aspiring for national solidarity and . . . freedom. We must think how best we can fit ourselves in the general scheme of national regeneration. . . . Today a boldchallenge has been thrown to us; it is a challenge to our leadership of the rural India. . . . I would ask you to re-establish your contacts with the villagers, think in terms of their welfare and make them feel that your interest is not antagonistic to theirs.

After all, what do we take from our tenants? A fraction of the yield which they get from our land. Are we then their exploiters, or are their exploiters those numerous middlemen who undervalue their commodity, bind them with shackles of debt. . . ? [n]ot only our tenants but we ourselves have been victims of this economic exploitation and it is high time that we co-operate with them and attempt to check the enormous drain of our resources. . . .

Most of those who are in power in the Congress organization which runs the government of seven provinces want adjustment and peace. We may have our differences with them in matters of detail, but so far as the general policy is concerned we cannot have any disagreement. We want adjustment because therein lies our security. . . . For a minority interest like ours it is only desperation that can drive us to fight and I have reasons to believe that so long as the group following the directions of Mahatma Gandhi rules in the Congress and the socialists and communists are kept in check we shall not have to take the extreme step. . . . Forcible possession of zamindar's land, loot, terrorism and murder are matters of almost every day occurrence. These atrocities are misnamed 'Kisan Satyagraha' ('The All India Landlords' Conference', Lucknow, 8–9 April 1939, cited in *The Indian Annual Register, January–June 1939*, Calcutta: The Annual Register Office, n.d.).

Bibliography

PRIMARY SOURCES

1. Government of India
National Archives of India, New Delhi.
Home Political (*inclusive of the Fortnightly Reports* for Bihar and Orissa; after 1936—only for Bihar).

2. Bihar and Orissa Government (up to 1936 and for only Bihar after that)
Bihar State Archives, Patna.
Annual Administration Reports.
Home Political Special.
Revenue (*Land Revenue Branch*).
Patna Commissioner Records.
Political Proceedings.

3. Published (Government) Reports
Final Report on the Survey and Settlement Operation—
Saran (*1893–1901*), J.H. Kerr, Calcutta, 1903;
Maksudpur Estate, Gaya (*1900–4*), E. Lister, Calcutta, 1907;
Bhagalpur (*1902–10*), P.W. Murphy, Calcutta, 1912;
Monghyr South (*1905–12*), P.W. Murphy, Patna, 1914;
Monghyr North (*1905–12*), H. Coupland, Calcutta, 1914;
Patna (*1907–12*), J.F.W. James, Patna, 1914;
Muzaffarpur (*1892–99*), C.J. Stephenson-Moore, Patna, 1922;
Darbhanga (*1896–1903*), J.H. Kerr, Patna, 1926;
Kosi Diara Area in Purnea (*1923–6*), N.L. Bose, Patna, 1927;
Shahabad (*1907*), J.A. Hubback, Patna, 1928;
Kosi Diara Area in Bhagalpur and Purnea (*1926–31*), Ray H. Prasad, Patna, 1932.

Report of the Indian Police Commission 1902–3, Simla, 1903.

Report of the Agriculture Department, Bihar and Orissa, 1st April 1931 to 31st March 1932, Patna, 1932.

Report on the Administration of Bihar and Orissa, 1929–40.

Report on the Land Revenue Administration of Bihar and Orissa, 1929–40.

Report of the Indian Industrial Commission, 1916-18, Calcutta, 1917–18

Report of the Indian Factory Labour Commission of 1908, 2 vols., London, 1909,

A Note on the General Measures Taken to Deal with the Movement. The Civil Disobedience Movement, 1930–4, Confidential, 99, Delhi, 1942.

R.A.E. Williams Final Report on the Rent Settlement Operations Under Section 112 of Bihar Tenancy Act in 11 Subdivisions of Patna, Gaya, Shahabad, and Monghyr, 1937–41, Patna, 1943.

Report on Budhuk Alias Bagree Dacoits and Other Gang Robbers by Hereditary Profession, Calcutta, 1849.

Report of the U.P. Criminal Tribes Enquiry Committee, 1948.

Report of the Royal Commission on Labour in India, Calcutta, 1931.

Report, Corruption Enquiry Committee, Bihar, 30 November 1938, Patna.

4. Series

Bengal District Gazetteers (up to 1912).

Bihar (and Orissa) District Gazetteers (many editions/vols.).

The Indian Annual Registers (many editions).

5. Miscellaneous

Bihar 1946–51: A Brief Review, Patna: Director of Public Relations, Bihar Government Press, n.d.

Selected Speeches from University Convocation Addresses, Allahabad, 1934.

Replies of the British Indian Association to the Questionnaire Issued by the Land Revenue Commission, Bengal, Calcutta, 1939.

Fraser Report: Report of the Indian Police Commission 1902–3, Karachi: National Institute of Public Administration [1965].

Datta, K.K., *History of Freedom Movement in Bihar*, 3 vols., Patna: Government of Bihar, 1957.

6. *Census of India* (1871–1941)

7. Private Papers

Swami Sahajanand Papers, Microfilm, Nehru Memorial Museum & Library, Delhi.

Rajendra Prasad Papers, Microfilm, Nehru Memorial Museum & Library, Delhi.

8. Newspapers/Periodicals

All India Kisan Bulletin

Bihar Bandhu

Congress Socialist

Janata
Navshakti
Reis and Rayyet
Searchlight
Yogi

9. 'Interviews'

The following is the list of only those villagers who are cited in the text. Our conversations took place in between 1 October 1995 and 31 January 1996, except in the case of Ram Talika Singh and Indrajit Singh, whom I have known since my childhood.

Places in square brackets indicate the name of the districts during the period of our study, which do not always correspond to the existing district divisions.

Mahabir *alias* 'Azad Baba', Age 70, Amain, Jahanabad [Gaya].
Debi Dayal Singh, 60, Bhangawatipur, Bhojpur [Shahabad].
Indrajit Singh, 44, Mahatwaniyan, Bhojpur [Shahabad].
'Kariwaa', 62, Shahpur [Patna].
Ram Charan Sharma, 65–70, Baheri [Darbhanga].
Ram Talika Singh, 72, Garahani Tola, Bhojpur [Shahabad].
Saraju Yadav, 65, Ramgarh, Bhojpur [Shahabad].
'Sambhua' *alias* Sambhu Nath Singh Yadav, Demhan, Bhojpur [Shahabad].

SECONDARY SOURCES

Adas, Michael, *Prophets of Rebellion: Millenarian Protest Against the European Colonial Order*, Chapel Hill: University of North Carolina Press, 1979.

———, '"Moral Economy" or "Contest State"?: Elite Demands and the Origin of Peasant Protest in Southeast Asia', *Journal of Social History*, vol. 13, 1980.

———, 'From Avoidance to Confrontation: Peasant Protest in Pre-Colonial and Colonial Southeast Asia', *Comparative Studies in Society and History*, no. 23, 1981.

———, 'Bandits, Monks, and Pretender Kings: Patterns of Peasant Resistance and Protest in Colonial Burma, 1826-1941', in Robert Weller and Scott E. Guggenheim (eds.), *Power and Protest in the Countryside*, Durham: Duke University Press, 1989.

Adhikari, G. (ed.), *Documents of the History of the Communist Party of India*, vol. I, *1917–1922*, Delhi: People's Publishing House, 1972.

———(ed.), *Documents of the History of the Communist Party of India*, vol. II, *1923–1925*, Delhi: People's Publishing House, 1974.

Alavi, Hamza, 'Peasant Classes and Primordial Loyalties', *Journal of Peasant Studies*, vol. I, no. 1, October 1973.

Allport, Gordon W. and Leo Postman, *The Psychology of Rumor*, New York: Russell & Russell, 1965.

Amin, Samir et al., *Transforming the Revolution: Social Movements and the World-Systems*, New York: Monthly Review Press, 1990.

Amin, Shahid, 'Gandhi as Mahatma', in Ranajit Guha (ed.), *Subaltern Studies III*, Delhi: Oxford University Press, 1984.

———, 'Agrarian Bases of Nationalist Agitations in India: An Historiographical Survey', in D.A. Low (ed.), *The Indian National Congress: Centenary Hindsights*, Delhi: Oxford University Press, 1988.

———, *Event, Metaphor, Memory: Chauri Chaura 1922–1992*, Delhi: Oxford University Press, 1996.

Amin, Shahid and Dipesh Chakrabarty (eds.), *Subaltern Studies IX*, Delhi: Oxford University Press, 1996.

Anderson, Benedict, *Imagined Communities: Reflections on the Origin and Spread of Nationalism*, London: Verso, 1983.

Appadurai, Arjuna, *Worship and Conflict under Colonial Rule*, Cambridge: Cambridge University Press, 1981.

Arnold, David, 'Dacoity and Rural Crime in Madras, 1860–1940', *Journal of Peasant Studies*, vol. 6, no. 2, January 1979.

———, 'Looting, Grain Riots and Government Policy in South India 1918', *Past and Present*, no. 84, August 1979.

———, *Police, Power and Colonial Rule, Madras 1859–1947*, Delhi: Oxford University Press, 1986.

Arnold, David and David Hardiman (eds.), *Subaltern Studies VIII*, Delhi: Oxford University Press, 1996.

Arrighi, Giovanni, 'Labor Supplies in Historical Perspective: A Study of the Proletarianization of the African Peasantry in Rhodesia', *Journal of Development Studies*, vol. 6, 1970.

Arrighi, Giovanni and John S. Saul, *Essays on the Political Economy of Africa*, New York: Monthly Review Press, 1973.

Asad, Talal, *Anthropology and the Colonial Encounter*, Atlantic Highlands: Humanities, 1973.

———, *Genealogies of Religion*, Baltimore: Johns Hopkins University Press, 1993.

Asiwaju, A.I., 'Migrations as Revolt: The Example of the Ivory Coast and Upper Volta before 1945', *Journal of African History*, vol. 17, 1976.

Baden-Powell, *The Land Systems of British India*, vol. I, Delhi: Oriental Publishers, 1974 [1892].

Badrinarayan, *Lok-Sanskriti Mein Rashtravad* [Hindi, 'Nationalism in Popular Culture'], Delhi: Radhakrishna Prakashan, 1996.

Balibar, Etienne, 'Racism as Universalism', *New Political Science*, vol. 16/17, 1989.

Banerjee, Anil Chandra, *The Agrarian System of Bengal*, vol. II: *1793–1955*, Calcutta: K.P. Bagchi and Company, 1981.

Barrett, Michele, *The Politics of Truth: From Marx to Foucault*, California: Stanford University Press, 1991.

Barthes, Roland, *Image-Music-Text*, trans. Stephen Heath, London: Fontana Press, 1977.

Bartlett, F.C., *Remembering*, Cambridge: Cambridge University Press, 1967.

Basham, A.L., 'Traditional Influence on the Thought of Mahatma Gandhi', in Ravinder Kumar (ed.), *Essays on Gandhian Politics*, Oxford: Clarendon Press, 1971.

Baxi, Upendra and Bhikhu Parekh (eds.), *Crisis and Change in Contemporary India*, Delhi: Sage, 1995.

Bayly, C.A., *Rulers, Townsmen and Bazars: North Indian Society in the Age of British Expansion, 1770–1870*, Cambridge: Cambridge University Press, 1983.

———, *Empire & Information: Intelligence Gathering and Social Communication in India, 1780–1870*, Cambridge: Cambridge University Press, 1996.

Bayly, Susan, '"Caste" and "Race" in Colonial Ethnography of India', in Peter Robb (ed.), *The Concept of Race in South Asia*, Delhi: Oxford University Press, 1995.

Behal, Rana Pratap, 'The Emergence of a Plantation Economy: Assam Tea Industry in the Nineteenth Century', *Occasional Papers*, NMML, vol. XXI, 1985.

Becker, G.S., 'Crime and Punishment: An Economic Approach', *Journal of Political Economy*, vol. 76, no. 2, 1968.

Benedict, Ruth, 'Myth', entry in *Encyclopedia of the Social Sciences*, Edwin R.A. Seligman (ed.), New York, 1948.

Benipuri, Ramvriksha, *Mujhe Yad Hai* [Hindi, 'I Still Remember'], Allahabad: Lok Bharati Prakashan, 1979.

Bentham, J., *Theory of Legislation*, London: Kegan Paul, 1896.

Berger, John, *A Seventh Man: The Story of a Migrant Worker*, London: Penguin, 1975.

Bernal, Martin, *Black Athena: Afroasiatic Roots of Classical Civilization*, London: Vintage, 1991.

Béteille, A., *Studies in Agrarian Social Structures*, Delhi: Oxford University Press, 1974.

———, 'Caste and Family in Representation of Indian Society', *Anthropology Today*, vol. 8/1, 1992.

Bhabha, Homi K. (ed.), *Nation and Narration*, New York: Routledge, 1990.

———, *The Location of Culture*, New York: Routledge, 1994.

Bhalla, Alok and Peter J. Bunke (eds.), *Images of Rural India in the Twentieth Century*, Delhi: Sterling Publishers, 1992.

Bharati, Goswami Chandreshwar, *Ramji par Notice* [Hindi], Benaras: Bombai Press, n.d.

Blackburn, Robin (ed.), *Ideology in Social Science: Readings in Critical Social Theory*, New York: Pantheon Books, 1972.

Blaut, J.M., *The Colonizer's Model of the World: Geographical Diffusionism and Eurocentric History,* New York/London: Guilford Press, 1993.

Bloch, Marc, *The Historian's Craft*, Manchester, London, 1963 [1953].

Blum, Jereome, *Lord and Peasant in Russia: From the Ninth to the Nineteenth Century*, Princeton: Princeton University Press, 1971 [1961].

Bohannan, Paul and George Dalton (eds.), *Markets in Africa*, Northwestern University Press, 1968.

Bottomore, Tom (ed.), *A Dictionary of Marxist Thought*, Delhi: Oxford University Press, 1987.

Bourdieu, Pierre, *Outline of a Theory of a Practice*, Cambridge: Cambridge University Press, 1977.

Brückner, Heiden et al. (eds.), *Flags of Flame: Studies in South Asian Folk Culture*, Delhi: Manohar, 1993.

Calhoun, Craig (ed.), *Habermas and the Public Sphere*, Massachusetts: MIT Press, 1992.

Callinicos, Alex, *Making History: Agency, Structure And Change in Social Theory*, London: Polity Press, 1987.

Cashman, Richard I., *Myth of the Lokmanya: Tilak and Mass Politics in Maharashtra,* Berkeley: University of California Press, 1975.

Cassirer, Ernst, *Language and Myth*, tr. K. Langer, Harper, 1946.

Césaire, Aimé, *Discourse on Colonialism*, tr. Joan Pinkham, New York and London: Monthly Review Press, 1972.

Chafe, Wallace, *Discourse, Consciousness, and Time: The Flow and Displacement of Conscious Experience in Speaking and Writing*, Chicago: University of Chicago Press, 1994.

Chakrabarty, Dipesh, 'Invitation to A Dialogue', in Ranajit Guha (ed.), *Subaltern Studies IV*, Delhi: Oxford University Press, 1996 [1985].

———, 'Postcoloniality and the Artifice of History: Who Speaks for "Indian" Past?', *Representations*, vol. 37, Winter 1992.

———, 'Radical Histories and the Question of Enlightenment Rationalism: Some Recent Critiques of Subaltern Studies', *Economic and Political Weekly,* 8 April 1995.

Chandra, Bipan, *Indian National Movement: Long-term Dynamics*, New Delhi, 1988.

———, *Communalism in Modern India*, Delhi: Vikas Publisher, 1984.

Chandra, Sudhir, 'The Cultural Component of Economic Nationalism: R.C. Dutt's "The Lake of Palms"', *Indian Historical Review*, XII, 1–2, 1985-6.

Charlesworth, Neil, 'The Myth of the Deccan Riots of 1875', *Modern Asian Studies*, vol. 6, 1972.

———, 'The Middle Peasant Thesis and the Roots of Rural Agitation in India 1917–1947', *Journal of Peasant Studies*, 8/3, 1981.

Chartier, Roger, *Cultural History: Between Practices and Representations*, tr. Lydia G. Cochrane, New York: Cornell University Press, 1988.

Chatterjee, Partha, *Nationalist Thought and the Colonial World: A Derivative Discourse?*, London: Zed Books, 1986.

———, 'Their Own Words? An Essay for Edward Said', in Michael Sprinker (ed.), *Edward Said: A Critical Reader*, Oxford: Blackwell, 1992.

———, *The Nation and its Fragments: Colonial and Postcolonial Histories*, Princeton: Princeton University Press, 1993.

Chaudhary, Vijay Chandra Prasad et al., *Swami Sahajanand Saraswati: Onkar Se Hunkar Tak* (Hindi, 'From Religious Contemplation to Militant Political Elan'), Patna: Rahul Press, 1990.

Chaudhuri, B.B., 'Agrarian Movements in Bengal and Bihar, 1919–1939', Seminar on *Socialism in India, 1919–1939*, 28-30 November 1968, Organized by NMML, Delhi.

———, 'The Proces of De-peasantization in Bengal and Bihar 1885-1947', *Indian Historical Review*, vol. II, no. 1, 1975.

Chesneaux, Jean (ed.), *Popular Movements and Secret Societies in China 1840–1950*, Stanford: Stanford University Press, 1972.

———, *Peasant Revolts in China*, London: Thames and Hudson, 1973.

Cohen, Robin et al. (eds.), *Pesants and Proletarians: The Struggles of Third World Workers*, New York: Monthly Review Press, 1979.

Cohn, Bernard S., 'Society and Change Under the Raj', *South Asian Review*, 4, 1970.

———, 'Representing Authority in Victorian India', in Eric Hobsbawm and Terence Ranger (eds.), *The Invention of Tradition*, Cambridge: Cambridge University Press, 1983.

———, *An Anthropologist Among the Historians and Other Essays*, Delhi: Oxford University Press, 1990.

Cohn, Bernard S. and M. Singer (eds.), *Structure and Change in Indian Society*, 1968.

Cole, John W. and Eric Wolf, *The Hidden Frontier*, New York: Academic Press, 1974.

Colls, Robert and Philip Dodd, *Englishness: Politics and Culture 1880–1920*, Beckenham: Croom Helm, 1987.

Comaroff, Jean, *Body of Power, Spirit of Resistance: The Culture and History of a South African People*, Chicago: University of Chicago Press, 1985.

Comaroff, John and Jean Comaroff, 'The Colonization of Consciousness in South Africa', *Economy and Society*, vol. 18/3, 1989.

———, *Of Revelation and Revolution: Christianity, Colonialism, and Consciousness in South Africa*, Chicago: University of Chicago Press, 1991.

Comninel, George C., *Rethinking the French Revolution: Marxism and the Revisionist Challenge*, New York: Verso, 1987.

A Collection of the Presidential and Inaugural Speeches, Madras: G.A. Nateson, n.d.

Conquergood, Dwight, 'Ethnography, Rhetoric, and Performance', *Quarterly Journal of Speeech*, vol. 78, 1992.

Cook, S.B, *Imperial Affinities: Nineteenth Century Analogies and Exchanges Between India and Ireland*, Delhi: Sage, 1993.

Cooper, Fredrick et al. (eds.), *Confronting Historical Paradigms: Peasants, Labor, and the Capitalist World System in Africa and Latin America*, Madison: University of Wisconsin Press, 1993.

———, 'Conflict and Connection: Rethinking Colonial African History', *The American Historical Review*, vol. 99/5, 1994.

Coplan, David, 'Eloquent Knowledge: Lesotho Migrants' Songs and the Anthropology of Experience', *American Ethnologist*, vol. 14/3, 1987.

Coquery-Vidrovitch, C., *Africa: Endurance and Change*, California: University of California Press, 1988.

Cornforth, M. (ed.), *Rebels and Their Causes*, London: Lawrence and Wishart, 1978.

Crooke, W., *The Popular Religion and Folklore of Northern India*, vol. I, Delhi: Munshiram Manoharlal, 1968 [1893].

Dalmia, Vasudha and Heinrich Von Stietencron (eds.), *Representing Hinduism: The Construction of Religious Traditions and National Identity*, New Delhi: Sage, 1995.

Damodaran, Vinita, *Broken Promises: Popular Protest, Indian Nationalism and the Congress Party in Bihar, 1935-1946*, Delhi: Oxford University Press, 1992.

Darnton, Robert, *The Great Cat Massacre And Other Episodes in French Cultural History*, Harmondsworth: Penguin, 1984.

Das, Arvind N., *Agrarian Unrests and Socio-Economic Change in Bihar, 1900–1980*, Delhi: Manohar, 1983.

Davis, Natalie Zemon, *Society and Culture in Early Modern France*, Stanford, California: Stanford University Press, 1975 [1965].

de Certeau, Michel, *The Practice of Everyday Life*, tr. Steven Rendall, Berkeley: University of California Press, 1984.

———, *Heterologies: Discourse on the Other*, Minneapolis: Minnesota University Press, 1986.

Desai, A.R., *Social Background of Indian Nationalism*, Bombay: Popular Prakashan, 1976 [1948].

Desai, Mahadev, *The Gospel of Selfless Action or the Gita According to Gandhi*, Ahmedabad: Navjeevan Publishing House, 1946.

Deva, Indra, *Folk Culture and Peasant Society in India*, Jaipur: Rawat Publications, 1989.

Dhanagare, D.N., *Peasant Movements in India, 1920–50*, Delhi: Oxford University Press, 1986.

Dharampal, *Civil Disobedience and Indian Tradition: With Some Early Nineteenth Century Documents*, Varanasi: Sarva Seva Sangh Prakashan, 1971.

Dirks, Nicholas, *The Hollow Crown: Ethnohistory of an Indian Kingdom*, Cambridge: Cambridge University Press, 1987

———, 'The Invention of Caste: Civil Society in Colonial India', *Social Analysis*, 25, 1989.

———, 'Castes of Mind', *Representations*, vol. 37, 1992.

Dirks, Nicholas, et al. (eds.) *Culture/Power/History*, Princeton: Princeton University Press, 1994.

Diwakar, R.R., *Bihar Through the Ages*, Calcutta: Orient Longman, 1959.

Doongaji, Damayanti, *Crime and Punishment in Ancient Hindu Society*, Delhi: Ajanta, 1986.

Dorson, Richard M., *Folklore and Fakelore: Essays Toward a Discipline of Folk Studies*, Cambridge: Havard University Press, 1976.

Doyle, Brian, *English and Englishness*, London: Routledge, 1989.

Draper, Hal, *Karl Marx's Theory of Revolution*, vol. II, New York: Monthly Review Press, 1978.

———, 'The Principle of Self-Emancipation in Marx and Engels', in R. Miliband and J. Saville (eds.), *The Socialist Register 1971*, London, 1971.

Dube, Leela, 'On the Applicability of the Concept of Sanskritization: Comment on Hetukar Jha', *Indian Economic and Social History Review*, vol. XV, no. 4, 1977.

Duff, Alexander, *India and India Missions: Including Sketches of the Gigantic System of Hinduism Both in Theory and Practice*, Delhi: Swati Publications, 1988 [1830].

Duggett, Michael, 'Marx on Peasants', *Journal of Peasant Studies*, vol. 2, no. 2, 1975.

Dumont, L., 'World Renunciations in Indian Religions', *Contributions to Indian Sociology*, vol. 4, 1960.

———, *Homo Hierarchicus: The Caste System and Its Implications*, Chicago: Chicago University Press, 1966.

Dundes, Alan, *Essays in Folklore Theory and Method*, Madras: Cre-A, 1990.

Eisenstadt, S.N., R. Kahane and David Shulman (eds.), *Orthodoxy, Heterodoxy and Dissent in India*, Berlin: Mouton Publishers, 1984.

Eley, Geoff, 'Nations, Publics, and Political Culture: Placing Habermas in the Nineteenth Century', in Craig Calhoun (ed.), *Habermas and the Public Sphere*, Massachusetts: MIT Press, 1992.

Engels, Ḍagmar and Shula Marks (eds.), *Contesting Colonial Hegemony: State and Society in Africa and India*, London: British Academic Press, 1994.

Engels, Frederick, *The Condition of the Working Class in England in 1844*, 1892.

Erikson, H., 'On the Nature of Psychohistorical Evidence: In Search of Gandhi', *Daedalus*, no. 3, 1968.

———, *Gandhi's Truth: On the Origins of Militant Nonviolence*, New York: W. W. Norton & Company, 1969.

Fabian, Johannes, *Time and the Other: How Anthropology Makes its Objects*, New York: University of Columbia Press, 1983.

———, *Language and Colonial Power*, Cambridge: Cambridge University Press, 1986.

Fanon, Frantz, *The Wretched of the Earth*, New York: Grove Press, 1963.

———, *Black Skin, White Masks*, New York: Grove Press, 1967.

Faruquee, Ashrufa, 'Conceiving the Colonial Woman: Indentured Labour, Indian Women and Colonial Discourse', *South Asia Research*, vol. 16, no. 1, Spring 1996.

Fields, Karen, *Revival and Rebellion in Colonial Central Africa*, Princeton: Princeton University Press, 1985.

Fisher, F.E., *Journal of the Royal Asiatic Society, Bengal*, Part I, 1883.

Fleisher, B.M., 'The Effect of Unemployment on Juvenile Delinquency', *Journal of Political Economy*, vol. 71, no. 6, 1963.

Forman, Shepard, *The Brazilian Peasantry*, New York: Columbia University Press, 1975.

Forster, E.M., *A Passage to India*, New York: Harcourt, Brace & World, 1952 [1924].

Foucault, Michel, *The Archaeology of Knowledge*, New York: Pantheon Books, 1972.

———, *The Order of Things*, New York: Vintage Books, 1973.

———, *Power/Knowledge*, New York: Pantheon Books, 1980.

———, 'The Subject and Power', Dreyfus, Hubert L. and Paul Rabinow, *Michel Foucault: Beyond Structuralism and Hermeneutics*, Chicago: University of Chicago Press, 1980.

———, 'What is Enlightenment?', in Paul Rabinow (ed.), *The Foucault Reader*, New York: Pantheon Books, 1984.

———, *Discipline and Punish: The Birth of the Prison*, tr. Alan Sheridan, New York: Vintage Books, 1979.

Fox, Richard, *Lions of the Punjab: Culture in the Making*, Berkeley and Los Angeles: University of California Press, 1985.

Frietag, S., 'Sacred Symbols as Mobilising Ideology: The North Indian Search for a "Hindu" Community', *Comparative Studies in Society and History*, vol. 22, no. 4, 1980.

Frykenberg, Robert Eric (ed.), *Land Control and Social Structure in Indian History*, Madison: University of Wisconsin Press, 1969.

Furet, François, *Interpreting the French Revolution*, Cambridge: Cambridge University Press, 1981.

———, *Marx and the French Revolution*, tr. Deborah Kan Furet, Chicago: University of Chicago Press, 1988.

Gandhi, M.K., *Hind Swaraj*, Ahmedabad: Navjivan Trust, 1938.

———, *Collected Works of Mahatma Gandhi*, Delhi: Publications Division, Ministry of Information and Broadcasting, GOI.

———, *Speeches and Writings of Mahatma Gandhi*, Madras: G.A. Nateson (many editions).

———, *The Message of the Gita*, Ahmedabad: Navjivan Trust, 1959.

———, *Gita—My Mother*, Bombay: Bharatiya Vidya Bhavan, 1965.

Gandhi, Rajmohan (ed.), *Language, Tradition and Modern Civilization*, Poona: I.P.Q. Publication, no. 5, 1983.

Gardner, Katy, *Global Migrants, Local Lives: Travel and Transformation in Rural Bangladesh*, Oxford: Clarendon Press, 1995.

Gaur, Albertine, *A History of Writing*, London: The British Library, 1987.

Gellner, Ernest, *Nation and Nationalism*, Oxford: Basil Blackwell, 1983.

Gender and History, Special Issue on Gender, Nationalisms and Identities, vol. 5, no. 2, 1993.

Geras, Norman, *Literature of Revolution: Essays on Marxism*, London: Verso, 1986.

———, 'Louis Althusser', in Tom Bottomore (ed.), *A Dictionary of Marxist Thought*, Delhi: Oxford Univesity Press, 1987.

Gerassi, John (ed.), *Camilo Torres: Revolutionary Priest*, Harmondsworth: Penguin, 1973.

Ghose, Sankar, *Congress Presidential Speeches: A Selection*, Delhi: All India Congress Committee, 1972.

Ghosh, Aurobindo, *Essays on the Gita*, Pondicherry: Sri Aurobindo Ashram, 1987 [1916–20].

Gidley, Mick (ed.), *Representing Others: White Views of Indigenous Peoples*, The University of Exeter Press for AMCAS, 1992.

Gilroy, Paul, *The Black Atlantic: Modernity and Double Consciousness*, Cambridge: Harvard University Press, 1993.

Gluckman, Max, *Order and Rebellion in Africa*, Illinois: Glencoe, 1963.

Goffman, Erving, *Presentation of Self in Everyday Life*, New York: Anchor Books, 1959.

Goody, J.R. (ed.), *Literacy in Traditional Societies*, Cambridge: Cambridge University Press, 1968.

———, *The Logic of Writing and the Organization of Society*, Cambridge: Cambridge University Press, 1986.

Gordon, R.L., *Mines, Masters and Migrants: Life in a Namibian Compound*, Johannesburg, 1977.

Gramsci, A., *Selections from the Prison Notebooks of Antonio Gramsci*, ed. and tr. Quintin Hoare and G. Nowell Smith, London: Lawrence and Wishart, 1971.

———, *Further Selections from Prison Notebooks*, ed. and tr. Derek Bootham, Minneapolis: University of Minnesota Press, 1995.

Greenfeld, Liah, *Nationalism: Five Roads to Modernity*, Cambridge: Harvard University Press, 1993.

Grierson, G.A., *Behar Peasant Life*, Calcutta, 1885 [1975].

———, *Notes on the District of Gaya*, Calcutta, 1893 [Microfilm: NMML, Delhi].

———(ed. and coll.), *Linguistic Survey of India*, vol.V, Part II, *Specimens of the Bihari and Oriya Languages*, Calcutta: Government Printing, India, 1903.

Guha, Ranajit, *Rule of Property for Bengal: An Essay on the Idea of Permanent Settlement*, Paris: Mouton, 1963.

———, *Elementary Aspects of Peasant Insurgency in Colonial India*, Delhi: Oxford University Press, 1983.

———(ed.), *Subaltern Studies I-VI*, Delhi: Oxford University Press, 1982–90.

———, 'On Some Aspects of the Historiography in Colonial India', in Ranajit Guha (ed.), *Subaltern Studies I*, Delhi: Oxford University Press, 1982.

———, 'The Prose of Counter-Insurgency', in Ranajit Guha (ed.), *Subaltern Studies II*, Delhi: Oxford University Press, 1982.

———, 'Chandra's Death', in Ranajit Guha (ed.), *Subaltern Studies V*, Delhi: Oxford University Press, 1987.

Guha, Ranajit and Gayatri Chakravorty Spivak (eds.), *Selected Subaltern Studies*, New York: Oxford University Press, 1988.

Gupta, Rakesh, *Bihar Peasantry and the Kisan Sabha*, Delhi: People's Publishing House, 1982.

Gwassa, G.C.K. and J. Iliffe (eds.), *Records of the Maji-Maji Rising*, Part I, Nairobi: East African Publishing House, 1968.

Gutierrez, Gustavo, *A Theology of Liberation: History, Politics and Salvation*, London, 1974.

Habermas, J., *Structural Transformation of the Public Sphere*, Cambridge: Cambridge University Press, 1989.

———, 'The Public Sphere', *New German Critique*, vol. 3/49, 1974.

Habib, Irfan, *The Agrarian System of Mughal India, 1556–1707*, London: Asia Publishing House, 1963.

Halbfass, Wilhelm, 'Practical Vedanta', in Dalmia and Stietencron (eds.), *Representing Hinduism: The Construction of Religious Traditions and National Identity*, Delhi: Sage, 1995.

Hamp, Eric P. et al., *Readings in Linguistics II*, Chicago, 1966.

Hanagan, Michael and Charles Stephenson (eds.), *Proletarians and Protest: The Roots of Class Formation in an Industrializing World*, Greenwood Press, 1986.

Harasym, Sarah (ed.), *Gayatri Chakravorty Spivak: The Post-Colonial Critic, Interviews, Strategies, Dialogues*, New York: Routledge, 1990.

Hardiman, David, *The Coming of the Devi: Adivasi Assertion in Western India*, Delhi: Oxford University Press, 1987.

Hasan, Mushirul, *Nationalism and Communal Politics in India, 1916–1929*, Delhi: Manohar, 1979.

Hauser, Walter, 'The Bihar Provincial Kisan Sabha, 1929–1942: A Study on Indian Peasant Movement', Ph.D. Dissertation, Department of History, University of Chicago, 1961.

———, *Sahajanand on Agricultural Labour and the Rural Poor*, Delhi: Manohar, 1994.

———, 'Swami Sahajanand and the Politics of Social Reform, 1907–50', *Indian Historical Review*, vol. XVIII, nos. 1–2, July 1991 and January 1992.

Hay, Douglas, Peter Linebaugh, E.P. Thompson, *Albion's Fatal Tree: Crime and Society in Eighteenth-Century England*, London, 1975.

Haynes, Douglas E., *Rhetoric and Ritual in Colonial India: The Shaping of Public Culture in Surat City, 1852–1928*, Berkeley: University of California Press, 1991.

Haynes, Douglas E. and Gyan Prakash (eds.), *Contesting Power: Resistance and Everyday Social Relations in South Asia*, Delhi: Oxford University Press, 1991.

Heesterman, J.C., 'Householder and Wanderer', *Contributions to Indian Sociology*, vol. 15, 1981.

———, *The Inner Conflict of Tradition: Essays in Indian Ritual, Kingship, and Society*, Chicago: University of Chicago Press, 1985.

Henningham, Stephen, *Peasant Movements in India: North Bihar, 1917–1942*, Canberra, 1982.

———, *A Great Estate and Its Landlords in Colonial India: Darbhanga 1869–1942*, Delhi: Oxford University Press, 1990.

Hilton, Rodney, *Bond Men Made Free: Medieval Peasant Movements and the English Rising of 1381*, London: Maurice Temple Smith, 1971.

———, *The English Peasantry in the Later Middle Ages*, Oxford: Oxford University Press, 1975.

History Workshop, Special Feature. Cultures of Conflict: The French Revolution, Issue 28, Autumn 1989.

Hobsbawm, E., 'The Machine Breakers', *Past and Present*, no. 1, February 1952.

———, *Primitive Rebels: Studies in Archaic Forms of Social Movements in the 19th and the 20th Centuries*, Manchester, 1959.

———, *Labouring Man*, London: Weidenfield and Nicolsan, 1968.

———, *Bandits*, New York: Delacorte Press, 1969.

———, 'Class Consciousness in History', in I. Meszaros (ed.), *Aspects of History and Class Consciousness*, London: Routledge & Kegan Paul, 1971.

———, 'Peasants and Politics', *Journal of Peasant Studies*, vol. 1, no. 1, 1973.

———, 'The Historians' Group of the Communist Party', in M. Cornforth (ed.), *Rebels and Their Causes*, London: Lawrance and Wishart, 1978.

Hobsbawm, E. and Terence Ranger (eds.), *The Invention of Tradition*, Cambridge: Cambridge University Press, 1983.

Hulme, Peter, *Colonial Encounters*, Cambridge: Cambridge University Press, 1987.

Hunt, Lynn, 'Hercules and the Radical Image in the French Revolution', *Representations*, vol. 1, no. 2, Spring 1983.

———, *Politics, Culture, and Class in the French Revolution*, Berkeley: University of California Press, 1984.

Hunter, W.W., *A Statistical Account of Bengal*, vols. XI, XII, XIII, XV, Delhi: Concept Publishing Company, 1976 [1877].

———, *Annals of Rural Bengal*, London, 1897.

Huyssen, Andreas, *After the Great Divide: Modernism, Mass Culture, Postmodernism*, Bloomington: Indiana University Press, 1986.

Hyam, Ronald, *Britain's Imperial Century 1815–1914: A Study of Empire and Expansion*, New York: Barnes and Noble, 1976.

Ileto, Reynaldo, *Pasyon and Revolution: Popular Movements in the Phillipines, 1840–1910*, Quezon City: Ateno de Manila University Press, 1979.

Inden, Ronald, 'Orientalist Constructions of India', *Modern Asian Studies*, vol. 20, 1986.

———, *Imagining India*, Oxford: Basil Blackwell, 1990.

Isaacman, Allen, 'Peasants and Rural Social Protest in Africa', *African Studies Review*, vol. 23, no. 2, 1990.

———, *The Tradition of Resistance in Mozambique: Anti-Colonial Activity in the Zambesi Valley*, Berkeley: University of California Press, 1976.

Islam, Dr. Mazharul, *A History of Folktale: Collection in India and Pakistan*, Dacca: Bengali Academy, 1970.

———, *Folklore: The Pulse of the People*, Delhi: Concept Publishing Company, 1985.

Islam, Shamsul, *Chronicles of the Raj: A Study of Literary Reaction to the Imperial Idea Towards the End of the Raj*, Delhi: Macmillan, 1979.

Iyer, Raghavan N., *The Moral and Political Thought of Mahatma Gandhi*, Delhi: Oxford University Press, 1973.

——— (ed.), *The Bhagavad Gita with the Uttar Gita*, New York: Concord Groove Press, 1985.

Jannuzi, F. Tomasson, *Agrarian Crisis in India: The Case of Bihar*, Austin: University of Texas Press, 1974.

Jayakar, M.R., *Talking of Gandhiji*, Delhi: Orient Longman, 1957.

Jha, Hetukar, 'Lower Caste Peasants and Upper Caste Zamindars in Bihar: An Analysis of Sanskritization and Contradiction between the two Groups', *Indian Economic and Social History Review*, vol. XIV, no. 4, October-December 1977.

Jha, J.C., 'Political Consciousness in Bihar before the Formation of Indian National Congress', in P.N. Ojha (ed.) *History of the Indian National Congress in Bihar*, Patna: K.P. Jayaswal Research Institute, 1985.

Jha, S., *Political Elites in Bihar*, Delhi, 1972.

Jha, Sudhir Kumar, *Raj to Swaraj: Changing Contours of Police*, Delhi: Lancer Publishers, 1995.

Jordens, J.T.F., 'Gandhi and the Bhagvadgita', in Robert Minor (ed.), *Modern Indian Interpreters of the Bhagavadgita*, Albany: State University Press, 1986.

Joshi, Pushpa, *Formations of Nations and Peoples*, London: Routledge, 1984.

———, *Gandhi on Women: Collection of Mahatma Gandhi's Writings and Speeches on Women*, Ahmedabad: Navajivan Publishing House, and Delhi: Centre for Women's Development Studies, 1988.

Kant, Immanuel, *Eternal Peace*, tr. W. Hastie, Boston: World Peace Foundation, 1914.

Katrak, Ketu H., 'Indian Nationalism, Gandhian Satyagraha and Representations of Female Sexualities', in Andrew Parker et al. (eds.), *Nationalism and Sexualities*, New York and London: Routeldge, 1992.

Katznelson, Ira and Aristide R. Zoleberg (eds.), *Working Class Formation: Nineteenth Century Patterns in Western Europe and the United States*, Princeton: Princeton University Press, 1986.

Kaviraj, Sudipta, *The Unhappy Consciousness: Bankimchandra Chattopadhyay and the Formation of Nationalist Discourse in India*, Delhi: Oxford University Press, 1995.

Kaye, Harvey J., *The British Marxist Historians: An Introductory Analysis*, Oxford: Polity Press, 1984.

———, *The Face of the Crowd: Studies in Revolution, Ideology and Popular Protest*, New Jersey: Humanities Press, 1988.

Kaye, Harvey J. and Keith McClelland (eds.), *E.P. Thompson: Critical Perspectives*, Oxford: Polity Press, 1990.

———, *The Education of Desire: Marxists and the Writing of History*, New York and London: Routledge, 1992.

Kay, John, *History of Indian Mutiny*, ed. G.B. Malleson, London: W.H. Allen & Co., 1888.

Keith, A.B. (ed.), *Speeches and Documents on Indian Policy*, Oxford: Oxford University Press, I, 1922.

Kipling, Rudyard, *Kim*, London: Macmillan, 1943.

Kishwar, Madhu, 'Gandhi on Women', *Economic and Political Weekly of India*, 5 and 12 October 1985.

Kolenda, P., *Caste In Contemporary India: Beyond Organic Solidarity*, London: Benjamin, 1978.

Koselleck, Reinhart, *Critique and Crisis: Enlightenment and the Pathogenesis of Modern Society*, Cambridge, Mass.: MIT Press, 1959.

Kruger, B. and P. Mariani (eds.), *Remaking History*, Seattle: Bay Press, 1989.

Kubayanda, Josaphat, *On Colonial/Imperial Discourse and Contemporary Critical Theory*, Lecture Series, Working Papers 10, University of Maryland, 1992.

Kumar, Arun, 'Vartman Sampradayikta Ka Atit' [Hindi, 'A History of the Present Day Communalism'], *Saancha*, Dec. 1989–Jan. 1990.

———, 'Review of Anand Yang, The Limited Raj: Agrarian Relations in Colonial India, Saran District, 1793–1920', *Indian Economic and Social History Review*, vol. 33, no. 4, 1996.

———, 'Beyond Muffled Murmurs of Dissent? Kisan Rumour in Colonial Bihar' *Journal of Peasant Studies*, vol. 28, no. 1, 2000.

Kumar, Kapil, 'Congress-Peasant Relationship in the late 1930s', in Shive Kumar, *Peasantry and the Indian National Movement 1919-1933*, Meerut: Anu Prakashan, 1979–80.

———, *Peasants in Revolt: Tenants, Landlords, Congress and the Raj in Oudh, 1886–1922*, Delhi: Manohar, 1984.

Kumar, Ravinder, *Essays on Gandhian Politics*, Oxford: Clarendon Press, 1971.

———, *Essays in the Social History of Modern India*, Calcutta: Oxford University Press, 1986 [1983].

Laclau, Ernesto, and Chantal Mouffe, *Hegemony and Socialist Strategy: Towards A Radical Democratic Politics*, tr. Winston Moore and Paul Cammack, London: Verso, 1985.

Landes, Joan B., *Women and the Public Sphere in the Age of the French Revolution*, Ithaca and London: Cornell University Press, 1988.

———, 'Representing the Body Politic: The Paradox of Gender in the Graphic Politics of the French Revolution', in Melzer and Rabine (eds.), *Rebel Daughters: Women and the French Revolution*, New York: Oxford University Press, 1992.

Lang, K. and G.E. Lang, *Collective Dynamics*, New York: Crowell, 1963.

Langbein, John H., 'Albion's Fatal Flaws', *Past and Present*, no. 98, February 1983.

Landsberger, Henry A. (ed.), *Latin American Peasant Movements*, Ithaca and London: Cornell University Press, 1969.

Lefebvre, Georges, *The Great Fear*, London, 1973.

Lenin, V.I., *The Development of Capitalism in Russia*, Moscow: Foreign Languages Publishing House, 1956.

———, *Collected Works*, vol. 15, Moscow: Progress Publishers, 3rd print, 1977.

———, 'Socialism and Religion', in *Collected Works*, vol. 10, Moscow: Progress Publishers, 4th print, 1978.

Le Roy Ladurie, Emmanuel, *The Peasants of Languedoc*, Urbana: University of Illinois Press, 1974.

——— *Carnival in Romans*, tr. Mary Feeney, New York: George Braziller, Inc., 1979.

Lentrichhia, Frank and Thomas McLaughlin (eds.), *Critical Terms of Literary Study*, Chicago and London, 1990.

Lewin, Linda, 'The Oligarchical Limitations of Social Banditry in Brazil: The Case of the "Good" Thief Antonio Silvino', *Past and Present*, no. 82, February 1979.

Lewis, John Wilson (ed.), *Peasant Rebellion and Communist Revolution in Asia*, California: Stanford University Press, 1974.

Liebman, Marcel, *Leninism Under Lenin*, tr. Brian Pearce, London: Jonathan Cape, 1979.

Lohia, Rammanohar, *Swaraj: Kya Aur Kaise* [Hindi, Swaraj: What and How], Essay based on his speech at Bihar Provincial Communist Party, 5 December 1936, n.d.

———, *Marx, Gandhi and Socialism*, Hyderabad: Samta Vidyalaya Nyas, 1963 [1943].

———, *The Caste System*, Hyderabad: Navahind, 1964.

Lovett, Sir Verney, *A History of the Indian Nationalist Movement*, London: John Murray, 1920.

Low, D.A. (ed.), *Congress and the Raj: Facets of the Indian Struggle 1917–1947*, London: Arnold-Heinemann, 1977.

———(ed.), *The Indian National Congress: Centenary Hindsights*, Delhi: Oxford University Press, 1988.

Low, Gail Ching-Liang, *White Skins/Black Masks: Representation and Colonialism*, London and New York: Routledge, 1996.

Ludden, David (ed.), *Making India Hindu: Religion, Community, and the Politics of Democracy in India*, Delhi: Oxford University Press, 1996.

Lukacs, G., *History and Class Consciousness: Studies in Marxist Dialectics*, tr. R. Livingstone, Boston: MIT Press, 1971.

Mackerras, Colin and Nick Knight, *Marxism in Asia*, London: Croom Helm, 1985.

Macmunn, George, *The Indian Social System: Castes, Tribes, Religions and Crime*, Delhi: Discovery Publishing House, 1984 [1933?].

McLane, John R., *Indian Nationalism and the Early Congress*, Princeton: Princeton University Press, 1977.

———, 'Bengali Bandits, Police and Landords After the Permanent Settlement', in Yang (ed.), *Crime and Criminality in British India*, Tucson: University of Arizona Press, 1985.

Madan, T.N., *Non-Renunciation: Themes and Interpretations of Hindu Culture*, Delhi: Oxford University Press, 1987.

Maine, Sir Henry, *Village Communities in the East and West: Six Lectures Delivered at Oxford with Additional Addresses*, London: John Murry, 1907 [1871].

Majumdar, J.K., *Indian Speeches and Documents on British Rule: 1821–1918*, London: Longman, 1937.

Mallon, Florencia, 'The Promise and Dilemmas of Subaltern Studies: Perspective From Latin American History', *The American Historical Review*, vol. 99/5, 1994.

Manglik, Murarisharan, *Deep-Mala or Inspirational Passages, Selected from University Convocation Address*, Allahabad: The Indian Press, 1934.

Mannheim, H. (ed.), *Pioneers in Criminology*, London: Stevens, 1960.
Mannoni, O., 'Psychoanalysis and the Decolonization of Mankind', in J. Miller (ed.), *Freud*, London: Weidenfield & Nicolson, 1972.
Marriot, M. and Ronald Inden, 'Social Stratification: Caste', entry in *Encyclopedia Britannica*, 15th edn, vol. 27, 1985 [1974].
Marx, Karl, *The Civil War in France*, New York: International Publishers, 1940.
———, *The Eighteenth Brumaire of Louis Bonaparte*, New York: International Publishers, 1964.
———, *The Class Struggles in France 1848–50*, New York: International Publishers, 1976.
———, *Capital*, vol. I, London Penguin Classics, 1990.
———, *Grundrisse*, London Penguin Classics, 1993.
Marx, Karl and Fredric Engels, *The Communist Manifesto*, London: Oxford University Press, 1992.
———, *The German Ideology*, London: Lawrence & Wishart, 1965.
Masson, J.M., 'Psychology of the Ascetic', *Journal of Asian Studies*, vol. 35, no. 4, 1976.
Mazumdar, R.C., *Struggle for Freedom*, Bombay, 1969.
———, *British Paramountcy and Indian Renaissance*, Bombay, 1974.
McLellan, David, *The Thought of Karl Marx*, London and Basingstoke: Macmillan, 1972.
Melzer, Sara E. and Leslie W. Rabine (eds.), *Rebel Daughters: Women and the French Revolution*, New York: Oxford University Press, 1992.
Memmi, Albert, *The Colonizer and the Colonized*, tr. Howfard Greenfield, New York: Beacon, 1967.
Meszaros, I. (ed.), *Aspects of History and Class Consciousness*, London: Routledge & Kegan Paul, 1971.
Metcalf, Thomas R., 'Laissez Fair and Tenant Right in Mid-Nineteenth Century India', *Indian Economic and Social History Review*, vol. I, 1963.
———, 'Struggle Over Land Tenure in India 1860–1868', *Journal of Asian Studies*, vol. XXI, 3, May 1962.
Migdal, Joel S., *Peasants, Politics, and Revolution: Pressures Toward Political and Social Change in the Third World*, Princeton: Princeton University Press, 1974.
Miliband, R. and J. Saville (eds.), *The Socialist Register 1971*, London, 1971.
Millar, Joseph (ed.), *The African Past Speaks: Essays on Oral Tradition and History*, Kent Dawson Archon, 1980.
Miller, J. (ed.), *Freud*, London: Weidenfield & Nicolson, 1972.
Minor, Robert N., 'Sri Aurobindo as a *Gita-yogin*', in Minor (ed.), *Modern Indian Interpreters of the Bhagavadgita*, Albany: SUNY Press, 1986.
——— (ed.), *Modern Indian Interpreters of the Bhagavadgita*, Albany: SUNY Press, 1986.
Mishra, Girish, *Agrarian Problems of Permanent Settlement: A Case Study of Champaran*, Delhi: People's Publishing House, 1978.

Mishra, Kuber, *Mauritius ke Bhojpuri Lokgiton ka Vivechanatmak Adhyayan* [Hindi, 'An Analytical Study of Bhojpuri Folksongs of Mauritius'], Varanasi: Sanjay Prakashan, 1981.

Mishra, Pandit Ramnandan, *Kisanon ki Samasyayen* [Hindi, 'Problems of the Peasantry'], Sabhapati, Prantiya Kisan Sabha, 1947.

Mitchel, W.J.T., 'Representation', in Frank Lentrichhia and Thomas McLaughlin (eds.), *Critical Terms of Literary Study*, Chicago and London, 1990.

Mitrany, D., *Marx Against the Peasant: A Study in Social Dogmatism*, New York: Collier Books, 1961.

Moore, Jr., Barrington, *Social Origins of Dictatorship and Democracy*, Boston: Beacon Press, 1966.

———, *Injustice: The Social Bases of Obedience and Revolt*, New York: M.E. Sharpe, 1978.

Mouffe, Chantal (ed.), *Gramsci and Marxist Theory*, London: Routledge & Kegan Paul, 1978.

Mukherjee, Arun, *Crime and Public Disorder in Colonial Bengal 1861–1912*, Calcutta: K.P. Bagchi & Company, 1995.

Mukherjee, Kalyan and Rajendra Singh Yadav, *Bhojpur: Naxalism in the Plains of Bihar*, Delhi: Radhakrishna Prakashan, 1980.

Mukherjee, R., *Awadh in Revolt, 1857-1858: A Study of Popular Resistance*, Delhi: Oxford University Press, 1984.

Mukherjee, S.N., *William Jones: A Study in the Eighteenth Century Attitudes to India*, Cambridge: Cambridge University Press, 1968.

Mukherji, Saradindu, *Peasant Politics and the British Government 1930–40*, Delhi: Anamika Prakashan, 1993.

Mukṭa, Parita, *Upholding the Common Life: The Community of Mira Bai*, Delhi: Oxford University Press, 1994.

Murray, Colin, *Families Divided: The Impact of Migrant Labour in Lesotho*, England: Cambridge, 1981.

Nakamura, Hajime, *A History of Early Vedanta Philosophy*, Part I, Delhi: Motilal Banarsidass, 1983.

Nanda, B.R., *Gokhale, Indian Moderates and the British Raj*, Delhi, 1977.

———, *Gandhi and Religion*, New Delhi: Gandhi Smriti Darshan Samiti, 1990.

Nandy, Ashis, *The Intimate Enemy: Loss and Recovery of Self under Colonialism*, Delhi: Oxford University Press, 1983.

———, 'Shamans, Savages and the Wilderness: On the Audibility of Dissent and the Future of Civilizations', *Alternatives*, vol. XIV, 1989.

———, *At the Edge of Psychology*, Delhi: Oxford University Press, 1990.

Nathan, Dev, 'Agricultural Labour and Poor Peasant Movement in Bihar: Nature of Resistance and Problems of Strategy', *Occasional Papers*, XIX, Delhi: NMML, 1990.

Natrajan, L., *Peasant Uprisings in India (1850–1990)*, Bombay: People's Publishing House, 1953.

Norman, Edward, *Christianity and the World Order*, New York: Oxford University Press, 1979.

O'Flaherty, Wendy D., *Asceticism and Eroticism in the Myth of Shiva*, London, 1973.

O'Hanlon, Rosalind, 'Recovering the Subject: Subaltern Studies and Histories of Resistance in Colonial South Asia', *Modern Asia Studies*, vol. 22, 1988.

Ojha, P.N. (ed.), *History of the Indian National Congress in Bihar*, Patna: K.P. Jayaswal Research Institute, 1985.

Oman, John Campbell, *Cults, Customs and Superstitions of India*, Delhi: Vishal Publishers, 1972.

Palmer, Bryan D., *Dissent into Discourse: The Reification of Language and the Writing of Social History*, Philadelphia: Temple University Press, 1990.

Pandey, B.N., *The Indian Nationalist Movement, 1885-1947, Selected Documents*, Delhi: Macmillan, 1979.

Pandey, Gyanendra, *The Ascendancy of the Congress in Uttar Pradesh, 1926–1934*, Delhi: Oxford University Press, 1978.

——— (ed.), *The Indian Nation in 1942*, Calcutta: K.P. Bagchi & Company, 1988.

———, 'The Prose of Otherness', in David Arnold and David Hardiman (eds.), *Subaltern Studies VIII*, Delhi: Oxford University Press, 1994.

Pandey, Gyanendra and Partha Chatterjee (eds.), *Subaltern Studies VII*, Delhi: Oxford University Press, 1992.

Panigrahi, D.N. (ed.), *Economy, Society and Politics in Modern India*, Delhi, 1985.

Panikkar, K.N., *The Foundation of New India*, London: Allen & Unwin, 1963.

———(ed.), *National and Left Movements in India*, Delhi, 1980.

———, *Against Lord and State: Religion and Peasant Uprisings in Malabar 1836–1921*, Delhi: Oxford University Press, 1992.

Pantham, Thomas, 'Gandhi, Nehru, and Modernity', in Upendra Baxi and Bhikhu Parekh (eds.), *Crisis and Change in Contemporary India*, Delhi: Sage, 1995.

Parashar, Aloka, ' "The Village Given to Us": Intellectual Constructions of the Village Community in Historical Writing', in Alok Bhalla and Peter J. Bumke (eds.), *Images of Rural India in the Twentieth Century*, Delhi: Sterling Publishers, 1992.

Parekh, Bhikhu, *Colonialism, Tradition and Reform: An Analysis of Gandhi's Political Discourse*, Delhi: Sage, 1989.

———, *Gandhi's Political Philosophy*, London, 1989.

Parker, Andrew et al. (eds.), *Nationalisms and Sexualities*, New York and London: Routledge, 1992.

Paswan, Suresh, 'Patrakarita Aeom Aprakashit Chitthiyan' [Hindi, 'Journalism and Unpublished Letters'], in Vijay Chandra Prasad Chaudhary et al., *Swami Sahajanand Saraswati: Onkar Se Hunkar Tak* [Hindi 'From

Religious Contemplation to Militant Political Elan'], Patna: Rahul Press, 1990.

Patel, Sujata, 'Construction and Reconstruction of Woman in Gandhi', *Economic and Political Weekly*, 20 February 1988.

Peterson, Warren and Noel P. Gist, 'Rumor and Public Opinion', *American Journal of Sociology*, LVII, September 1951.

Phule, Jotirao, *Slavery: Collected Works of Mahatma Jotirao Phule,* vol. I, tr. P.G. Patil, Bombay: Education Department, Government of Maharashtra, 1991.

Pinch, William R., *Peasants and Monks in British India,* Delhi: Oxford University Press, 1996.

Pitkin, Hanna F., *The Concept of Representation*, Berkeley: Los Angeles, 1967.

Poitevin, Guy and Hema Rairka, *Indian Peasant Women Speak Up*, tr. Michel Leray, Bombay: The Orient Longman, 1993.

Popkin, Samuel L., *The Rational Peasant: The Political Economy of Rural Society in Vietnam*, Los Angeles: University of California Press, 1979.

Post, Ken, 'The Alliance of Peasants and Workers: Some Problems Concerning the Articulation of Classes', in Robin Cohen et al. (eds.), *Pesants and Proletarians: The Struggles of Third World Workers*, New York: Monthly Review Press, 1979.

Pouchepadass, J., 'Local Leaders and the Intelligentsia in the Champaran Satyagraha (1917): A Study in Peasant Mobilization', *Contributions to Indian Sociology* (ns), vol. 8, 1974.

Prabhu, R.K. and U.R. Rao, *The Mind of Mahatma Gandhi*, Oxford: Oxford University Press, 1946.

Prakash, Gyan, *Bonded Histories: Genealogies of Labour Servitude in Colonial India,* Cambridge: Cambridge University Press, 1990.

———, 'Writing Post-Orientalist Histories of the Third World', *Comparative Studies in Society and History*, vol. 34, 1992.

———, 'Subaltern Studies as Postcolonial Criticism', *The American Historical Review*, vol. 99, no. 5, 1994.

———*After Colonialism: Imperial Histories and Postcolonial Displacements*, Princeton: Princeton University Press, 1995.

Prasad, J., 'The Psychology of Rumour: A Study Relating to the Great Indian Earthquake of 1934', *British Journal of Psychology*, vol. XXVI, July 1935.

Prasad, P.H. and G.B. Rodgers, *Caste, Class and Landholding in Bihar,* The Hague: ILO, 1983.

Pratt, Mary Louise, *Imperial Eyes: Travel Writing and Transculturation*, London and New York: Routledge, 1992.

Propp, V., *Morphology of the Folktale*, tr. Laurence Scott, Austin: University of Texas Press, 1968.

Pyle, David J., *The Economics of Crime and Law Enforcement*, London: Macmillan, 1983.

Quigely, D., *The Interpretation of Caste*, Oxford: Clarendon Press, 1993.

Randall, Adrian, *Before the Luddites: Custom, Community, and Machinery in the English Woollen Industry, 1776–1809*, Cambridge: Cambridge University Press, 1991.

Ranga, N.G., *Revolutionary Peasants*, New Delhi: Amrit Book Company, 1949.

Ranger, T.O., *Peasant Consciousness and Guerrilla War in Zimbabwe*, Berkeley: University of California Press, 1985.

———, 'Religious Movements and Politics in Sub-Saharan Africa', *African Studies Review*, vol. 29, no. 2, 1986.

———, 'Power, Religion and Community: The Matobo Case', in Partha Chatterjee and Gyan Pandey (eds.), *Subaltern Studies VII*, Delhi: Oxford University Press, 1992.

Rasul, M.A., *A History of the All India Kisan Sabha*, Calcutta: National Book Agency, 1974.

Ray, Rabindra, *Naxalites and Their Ideology*, Delhi: Oxford University Press, 1989.

Risley, H.H., *Tribes and Castes of Bengal: Ethnographic Glossary*, Calcutta, 1891.

———, *The Peoples of India*, London: W. Thacker, 1908.

Robb, Peter (ed.), *The Concept of Race in South Asia*, Delhi: Oxford University Press, 1995.

Rose, R.B., 'Eighteenth Century Price Riots and Public Policy in England', *International Review of Social History*, vol. VI, 1961.

Roseberry, William, 'Peasants, Proletarians, and Politics in Venezuela', in Robert P. Weller and Scott E. Guggenheim (eds.), *Power and Protest in Countryside*, Durham: Duke University Press, 1989.

Rothermund, Dietmar, 'A Survey of Rural Migration and Land Reclamation in India, 1885', *Journal of Peasant Studies*, vol. 4, no. 3, 1977.

———, *Government, Landlord, and Peasant in India, 1865–1935*, Wiesbaden: Franz Steiner Verlag GMBH, 1978.

Rothermund, Indira, *The Philosophy of Restraint*, Bombay: Popular Prakashan, 1963.

Roy, M.N., 'Spiritual Communism: A Criticism', in G. Adhikari (ed.), *Documents of the History of the Communist Party of India*, vol. II, *1923–1925*, Delhi: People's Publishing House, 1974.

Rudé, George, *The Crowd in the French Revolution*, London: Oxford University Press, 1959.

———, *Paris and London in the Eighteenth Century: Studies in Popular Protest*, London: Collins, 1970.

Rudolph, S.H. and L. Rudolph, *The Modernity of Tradition*, Chicago: Chicago University Press, 1967.

———, *Gandhi: The Traditional Roots of Charisma*, Delhi: Orient Longman, 1987.

Sabean, D. 'Communal Basis of Peasant Uprisings', *Comparative Politics*, vol. 8, April 1976.

Saha, Panchanan, *Emigration of Indian Labour (1834–1900)*, Delhi: People's Publishing House, 1970.

Sahi, Jyoti, *The Child and the Serpent: Reflections on the Popular Indian Symbols*, London: Routledge & Kegan Paul, 1980.

Said, Edward W., *Orientalism*, New York: Pantheon Books, 1978.

———, *The World, The Text, and The Critic*, Cambridge/Mass.: Harvard University Press, 1983.

———, *Culture and Imperialism*, New York: Alfred A. Knopf, 1993.

Samuel, Raphael, 'British Marxist Historians, 1880-1980: Part One', *New Left Review, 120*, 1980.

———, *Patriotism: The Making and Unmaking of the British National Identity*, London, 1989.

———, 'Reading the Signs', *History Workshop Journal*, vol. 31, Autmn 1991.

Sangari, Kumkum and Sudesh Vaid (eds.), *Recasting Women: Essays in Indian Colonial History*, New Jersey: Rutgers University Press, 1990.

Sankrityayan, Rahul, *Meri Jivan Yatra* [Hindi, 'My Life Journey'], Allahabad: Kitab Mahal, 1950.

———, *Hindi Sahitya Ka Brihat Itihas*, XVI [Hindi, 'A Comprehensive History of Hindi Literature'], Kashi: Nagari Pracharini Sabha, Samvat 2017 (AD 1960).

———, *Naye Bharat Ke Naye Neta* [Hindi, 'The New Leaders of the New India'], vol. I, Allahabad, 1973.

Santiago-Valles, Kelvin, 'Trying to Pin Myself in History: Race, Sex and Colonialism', *Border/lines*, vols. 29–30, December 1993.

———, *'Subject People' and Colonial Discourse: Economic Transformation and Social Disorder in Puertorico, 1898–1947*, Albany: State University of New York Press, 1994.

Saraswati, Swami Sahajanand, *Jhootha Bhay aur Mithya Abhiman* [Hindi, 'Unreal Fear and Imaginary Pride'], Kashi, 1928.

———, *Brahman Samaj ki Sthiti* [Hindi, 'The Condition of Brahman Society'], Banaras: Hitchintak Press, 1928.

———, *The Other Side of the Shield*, Bombay: Indulal Yagnik, 1938.

———, *Rent Reduction in Bihar: How It Works*, Patna: Sitaram Ashram, 1939.

———, *Kisan Kaise Ladate Hain* [Hindi, 'How do Kisans Fight'], Patna: Shramjivi Pustakmala, 1940.

———, *Kisan Sabha ke Sansmaran* [Hindi, 'Reminiscences of the Kisan Sabha'], Allahabad: New Literature, 1947.

———, *Kisanon ke Dave aur Karyakarm ka Kharita* [Hindi, 'Challenges of Kisans and the Record of their Activities'], Patna, 1949.

———, *Mera Jeevan Sangharsh* [Hindi, 'My Life Struggle'], Patna: Sitaram Ashram, 1952.

———, *Kisan Kya Karen* [Hindi, 'What Should the Kisans Do?'], Patna, 1952.

———, *Brahmarshi Vansh Vistar* [Hindi, 'The Expansion of the Brahman Family'], Ghajipur, 1988 [1924].

———, *Gita Hridaya* [Hindi, 'The Heart of Gita], Buxar: Shri Swami Sahajanand Saraswati Smarak Nyas, 1988 [1948].

———, *Gaya Ke Kisanon Ki Karun Kahani* [Hindi, 'A Story of the Miserable Plight of the Kisans of Gaya'], Patna, n.d.

———, *Maharudra ka Mahatandava* [Hindi, 'Maharudra's Great Dance of Destruction'], Patna: Sitaram Ashram, Bihta, n.d.

———, *Kisanon ke Phansane ki Taiyariyan* [Hindi, 'Attempts to Trap Kisans'], Patna: Sitaram Ashram, Bihta, n.d.

Sarkar, Sumit, *'Popular' Movements and 'Middle Class' Leadership: Perspectives and Problems of a 'History from Below'*, S.G. Deuskar Lectures on Indian History, 1982, Calcutta, 1983.

———, *Modern India 1885–1947*, Delhi: Macmillan, 1983.

———, 'The Conditions and Nature of Subaltern Militancy: Bengal from Swadeshi to Non-Cooperation, *c.* 1905-22', in Ranajit Guha (ed.), *Subaltern Studies III*, Delhi: Oxford University Press, 1984.

———, 'Popular Culture, Community, Power: Three Studies of Modern Indian Social History', *Studies in History*, vol. 8, no. 2, 1992.

———, *Writing Social History*, Delhi: Oxford University Press, 1997.

Sarkar, Tanika, 'Politics and Women in Bengal—the Conditions and Meaning of Participation', *Indian Economic and Social History Review*, vol. XXI, January–March 1984.

———, 'Nationalist Iconography: Image of Women in 19th Century Bengali Literature', *Economic and Political Weekly*, 21 November 1987.

Saroja, G.V., *Tilak and Shankara on the Gita*, Delhi: Sterling Publishers, 1985.

Satre, Jean-Paul, *Search for a Method*, tr. Hazel E. Barnes, New York: Vintage Books, 1968.

Satyarthi, Devendra, *Meet My People: Indian Folk Poetry*, Delhi: Navyug Publishers, 1987 [1946].

Saul, John S. and Roger Woods, 'African Peasantries', in Giovanni Arrighi and John S. Saul, *Essays on the Political Economy of Africa*, New York: Monthly Review Press, 1973.

Schwab, Raymond, *The Oriental Renaissance: Europe's Rediscovery of India and the East, 1680–1880*, tr. Gene Patterson-Black and Victor Reinking, New York: Columbia University Press, 1978.

Scott, J., 'Exploitation in Rural Class Relations: A Victim's Perspective', *Comparative Politics*, vol. 714, 1976.

———, *The Moral Economy of the Peasant: Rebellion and Subsistence in Southeast Asia*, New Haven: Yale University Press, 1976.

———, 'Hegemony and the Peasantry', *Politics and Society*, vol. 7, no. 3, 1977.

———, 'Peasant Revolution: A Dismal Science', *Comparative Politics*, vol. 9, no. 2, 1977.

———, *Weapons of the Weak: Everyday Forms of Peasant Resistance*, New Haven: Yale University Press, 1985.

Scott, J. et al. (eds.), *Everyday Forms of Resistance in South East Asia*, London: Frank Cass, 1986.

———, *Domination and the Art of Resistance: Hidden Transcripts*, New Haven: Yale University Press, 1990.

Searle, C.E., 'Custom, Class Conflict and Agrarian Capitalism: The Cumbrian Customary Economy in the Eighteenth Century', *Past and Present*, vol. 110, 1986.

Selden, Mark, *The Political Economy of Chinese Socialism*, Armonk: East Gate 1993.

Seleti, Yonal, 'Finance Capital and the Coffee Industry of Angola, 1865–1895', *Transafrican Journal of History*, vol. 16, 1987.

Sen, Samita, *Women and Labour in Late Colonial India: The Bengal Jute Industry*, Cambridge: Cambridge University Press, 1999.

Sen, Sunil, *Peasant Movements in India: Mid-nineteenth and Twentieth Centuries*, Calcutta: K.P. Bagchi & Company, 1982.

Shah, Ghanshyam, 'Traditional Society and Political Mobilization: The Experience of Bardoli Satyagraha 1920-28', *Contributions to Indian Sociology* (ns), no. 8, 1974.

——— (ed.), *Caste Reservation and Caste Movements*, Delhi: Ajanta, 1985.

Shanin, T., *Peasants and Peasant Societies*, Harmondsworth: Penguin, 1971.

——— (ed.), *Late Marx and the Russian Road: Marx and the 'peripheries of capitalism'*, New York: Monthly Review Press, 1983.

Sharma, K.K., *Agrarian Movements and Congress Politics in Bihar*, Delhi: Anamika Prakashan, 1989.

Sharma, Triveni 'Sudhakar' (ed.), *Swami Sahajanand Smriti Granth* [Hindi, 'Swami Sahajanand Memorial Volume'], Patna, 1982.

Sharma, Ursula and Mary Searle-Chatterjee (eds.), *Contextualising Caste: Post-Dumontian Approaches*, Oxford: Blackwell Publishers, 1994.

Sharpe, Jenny, 'The Violence of Light in the Land of Desire; or, How William Jones Discovered India', *Boundary 2*, vol. 2, no. 1, 1993.

———, *Allegories of Empire: The Figure of Woman in the Colonial Text*, Minneapolis and London: University of Minnesota Press, 1993.

Sherover-Marcuse, Erica, *Emancipation and Consciousness*, Oxford: Basil Blackwell, 1986.

Singer, M. and B.S. Cohn (eds.), *Structure and Change in Indian Society*, Chicago: Aldine, 1968.

Singer, Wendy, *Creating Histories: Oral Narratives and the Politics of History-Making*, Delhi: Oxford University Press, 1997.

Singh, Awadheshwar Prasad, *Bihar Prantiya Kisan Sabha Ki Report* [Hindi, 'Report of the Bihar Provincial Kisan Sabha'], November 1929 through 1935, Patna, 1935.

Singh, Karan, *Prophet of Indian Nationalism: A Study of the Political Thought of Sri Aurobindo Ghosh, 1893–1910*, London: George Allen & Unwin Ltd., 1963.

Singh, Shri Durgashankar Prasad, *Bhojpuri ke Kavi aur Kavya* [Hindi, 'The Bhojpuri Poets and Poetry'], Patna: Bihar Rashtrabhasha Parishad, 1958.

Sinha, Arun, 'The Awakening in Bhojpur', *Frontier*, January 1978.

Sinha, Mrinalini, *Colonial Masculinity: The Manly Englishman and the Effeminate Bengal in the late 19th Century*, Manchester, 1995.

Sinha, Ram Narayan, *Bihar Tenantry (1783–1833)*, Delhi: People's Publishing House, 1986.

Sitaramayya, P., *History of the Indian National Congress*, 2 vols., Bombay: Padma Publications, 1946–7.

Skaria, Ajay, 'Writing, Orality and Power in the Dangs, Western India, 1800s–1920s', in Shahid Amin and Dipesh Chakrabarty (eds.), *Subaltern Studies IX*, Delhi: Oxford University Press, 1996.

Skocpol, Theda, 'What Makes Peasants Revolutionary', in Weller and Guggenheim (eds.), *Power and Protests in the Countryside*, Durham: Duke University Press, 1989.

Smart, Ninan and Shivesh Thakur (eds.), *Ethical and Political Dilemmas of Modern India*, New York: St. Martin Press, 1993.

Smith, Joan et al. (eds.), *Racism, Sexism, and the World System*, New York: Greenwood Press, 1988.

Sommerville, Augustus, *Crime and Religious Beliefs in India*, Calcutta: Thacker, Spink and Company, 1929 [1966].

Spivak, Gayatri Chakrabarty, 'Subaltern Studies: Deconstructing Historiography', in R. Guha and G. Spivak (eds.), *Selected Subaltern Studies*, New York: Oxford University Press, 1988.

———, 'Who Claims Alterity?', in B. Kruger and P. Mariani (eds.), *Remaking History*, Seattle: Bay Press, 1989.

Spodek, Howard, 'On the Origins of Gandhi's Political Methodology: The Heritage of Kathiawar', *Journal of Asian Studies*, vol. 30, 1971.

Spratt, P., *Hindu Culture and Personality*, Bombay: Manaktalas, 1966.

Sprinker, Michael (ed.), *Edward Said: A Critical Reader*, Oxford: Blackwell, 1992.

Srinivas, M.N., *Caste in Modern India*, Bombay: Asia Publishing House, 1962.

———, *Social Change in Modern India*, California, 1966.

Standing, Guy, 'Migration and Modes of Exploitation: Social Origins of Immobility and Mobility', *Journal of Peasant Studies*, vol. 8, no. 4, 1981.

Stepan, Nancy, *The Idea of Race in Science: Great Britain 1800–1960*, London: Macmillan, 1982.

Stevenson, Robert W., 'Tilak and the Bhagavadgita's Doctrine of Karmyoga', in Robert Minor (ed.), *Modern Indian Interpreters of the Bhagavadgita*, Albany: SUNY Press, 1986.

Stokes, Eric, *The English Utilitarians and India*, Oxford: Oxford University Press, 1959.

———, *The Peasant and the Raj: Studies in Agrarian Society and Peasant Rebellion in Colonial India*, Cambridge: Cambridge University Press, 1978.

Szasz, Thomas, *The Second Sin*, London: Routledge & Kegan Paul, 1974.

Talmon, J.R., *Political Messianism: The Romantic Phase*, New York: Frederick A. Praeger, 1960.

———, *Romanticism and Revolt: Europe 1815–1848*, Harcourt: Brace & World Inc., 1967.

Tambiah, Stanley J., *World Conqueror and World Renouncer*, Cambridge: Cambridge University Press, 1977.

———, 'The Renouncer: His Individuality and His Community', *Contributions to Indian Sociology*, vol. 15, 1981.

Tarachand, *History of the Freedom Movement in India*, 4 vols., Delhi, 1961–72.

Tendulkar, D.G., *Mahatma: The Life of Mohandas Karamchand Gandhi*, vols. I–VIII, Bombay, 1951-4.

Tendulkar, D.G. and V.K. Jhaveri (eds.), *Mahatma, 1951–54*, vols. I-VIII, Bombay, 1951–4.

Thapar, Romila, 'Interpretations of Ancient Indian History', *History and Theory* 7, no. 3, 1968.

———, 'Renunciation: The Making of a Counter Culture?', in Romila Thapar, *Ancient Indian Social History: Some Interpretations*, Delhi: Orient Longman, 1978.

———, *Ancient Indian Social History: Some Interpretations*, Delhi: Orient Longman, 1978.

———,The Householder and the Renouncer in the Brahmanical and Buddhist Traditions', *Contributions to Indian Sociology*, vol. 15, nos. 1–2, 1981.

———, 'Syndicated Moksha?', *Seminar*, 313, 1985.

Thaxton, Ralph, 'Mao Zedong, Red Misérables, and the Moral Economy of Peasant Rebellion in Modern China', in Weller and Guggenheim (eds.), *Power and Protest in the Countryside*, Durham: Duke University Press, 1989.

Thomas, P.M., *20th Century Interpretations of Bhagavadagita: Tilak, Gandhi and Aurobindo*, Delhi: ISPCK, 1987.

Thompson, E.P., *The Making of the English Working Class*, Harmondsworth: Penguin, 1966 [1963].

———, 'The Moral Economy of the Crowd in the Eighteenth Century', *Past and Present*, 50, 1971.

———, *Whigs and Hunters: The Origin of the Black Act*, London: Allen Lane, 1975.

Thompson, E.P., et al. (eds.), *Albion's Fatal Tree: Crime and Society in Eighteenth-Century England*, London: Allen Lane, 1975a.

———, 'Folklore, Anthropology and Social History', *Indian Historical Review*, vol. III, 2, 1977.

———, 'Eighteenth Century English Society: Class Struggle without Class?', *Social History*, vol. 3, no. 2, 1978.

———, 'Patricians and Plebs', in E.P. Thompson (ed.), *Customs in Commons*, New York: The New Press, 1991.

———, *Customs in Common*, New York: The New Press, 1991.

Tilak, Bal Gangadhar, *Srimaḍ Bhagavadgita Rahasya or Karm-Yoga Sastra* [Hindi, 'The Mystery of Gita or The Book of Karmyoga'] tr. B.S. Sukthankar, 2 vols., Poona: Tilak Bros., 1935.

Tilly, Charles, 'Food Supply and Public Order in Modern Europe', in C. Tilly (ed.), *The Formation of National States in Europe*, Princeton: Princeton University Press, 1975.

Tilly, Charles. (ed.), *The Formation of National States in Europe*, Princeton: Princeton University Press, 1975.

Tiwary, Hiralal, *Ganga Ghati Ke Geet* [Hindi, 'Songs of the Ganges Valley'], Varanasi: Vishwavidyalaya Prakashan, 1980.

Torres, Sergio and John Eagelson, *Theology in the Americas*, New York: Maryknoll, 1976.

Tucker, Robert C., *Philosophy and Myth in Karl Marx*, Cambridge: Cambridge University Press, 1972.

Turner, Denys, *Marxism and Christianity*, Oxford: Basil Blackwell, 1983.

Turner, Victor, *Dramas, Fields, and Metaphors*, Ithaca: Cornell University Press, 1974.

———, *The Anthropology of Performance*, New York: PAJ Publications, 1986.

Uberoi, Patricia, 'Feminine Identity and National Ethos in Indian Calendar Art', *Economic And Political Weekly*, vol. XXV, no. 17, 1990.

Upadhyay, Yamuna Prasad, *Amar Shahid Kavi Kailash* [Hindi, 'The Immortal Martyr Poet Kailash'], Arrah: Sansar Press, n.d.

Vachek, Josef, 'Some Remarks on Writing and Phonetic Transcription', in Eric P. Hamp et al., *Readings in Linguistics II*, Chicago, 1966.

Vansina, Jan, *Oral Tradition: A Study in Historical Methodology*, London, 1961.

Vatuk, Ved Prakash, *Studies in Indian Folk Traditions*, Delhi: Manohar, 1979.

Viswanathan, Gauri, *The Masks of Conquest: Literary Study and British Rule in India*, New York: Columbia University Press, 1989.

Viswanathan, Gauri, 'Raymond Williams and British Colonialism', *The Yale Journal of Criticism*, vol. 4, no. 2, 1991.

Vivekanand, Swami, *The Complete Works of Vivekanand*, vol. III, Mayavati Memorial Edition, Calcutta: Advaita Ashram, 1964.

Vopa, J. La, 'Conceiving a Public: Ideas and Society in Eighteenth Century Europe', *Journal of Modern History*, vol. 64, March 1992.

Wallerstein, Immanuel, 'The Ideological Tensions of Capitalism: Universalism Versus Racism and Sexism', in Joan Smith et al. (eds.), *Racism, Sexism, and the World System*, New York: Greenwood Press, 1988.

———, *The Modern World System*, vol. III, New York: Academic Press, 1989.

———, 'The End of What Modernity?' (Paper presented to President's Forum, *Conference on The End of Modernity*), Bucknell University, 30 September 1993.

Weller, Robert P. and Scott E. Guggenheim (eds.), *Power and Protest in the Country-side*, Durham: Duke University Press, 1989.

Wessell, Jr., Leonard P., *Prometheus Bound: The Mythic Structure of Karl Marx's Scientific Thinking*, Baton Rouge: Louisiana State University Press, 1984.

Whipple, Guy Montrose, 'The Observer as Reporter: A Survey of the Psychology of Testimony', *Psychology Bulletin*, vol. VI, May 1909.

Wiener, Martin J., *Reconstructing the Criminal: Culture, Law, and Policy in England 1830–1914*, Cambridge: Cambridge University Press, 1990.

Williams, Dale Edward, 'Morals, Markets and the English Crowd in 1766', *Past and Present*, no. 104, August 1984.

———, 'Were "Hunger" Rioters Really Hungry?: Some Demographic Evidence', *Past and Present*, no. 71, May 1975.

Williams, Raymond, *The Country and the City*, London: Chatto and Windus, 1973.

Wilson, H.H., *Religious Sects of the Hindus*, Calcutta: Sushil Gupta (India) Pvt. Ltd., 1958.

Wilson, Minden, *History of Behar*, Calcutta: The Calcutta General Printing Press, 1908.

Wolf, Eric, *Peasant Wars in the Twentieth Century*, New York: Harper, 1969.

———, *Europe and the People Without History*, California: University of California Press, 1990 [1982].

Wolfgang, M.E., 'Cesare Lombroso 1835-1909', in H. Mannheim (ed.), *Pioneers in Criminology*, London: Stevens, 1960.

Yadav, D.S., *Ahir Itihas Ki Jhalak* [Hindi, 'A Glimpse of the History of Ahirs'], Lucknow, 1915.

Yang, Anand A. (ed.), *Crime and Criminality in British India*, Tucson: University of Arizona Press, 1985.

———, *The Limited Raj: Agrarian Relations in Colonial India, Saran District, 1793–1920*, Delhi: Oxford University Press, 1989.

Yuval-Davis, Nira and Floya Anthias (eds.), *Woman-Nation-State*, London: Macmillan, 1989.

Zagorin, Perez, *Rebels and Rulers*, vol. I, Cambridge: Cambridge University Press, 1982.

Zimmer, H., *Philosophies of India*, Delhi: Motilal Banarsidass, 1990 [1969].

Index